Kai Ambos

National Socialist Criminal Law

Continuity and Radicalization

Preface by R.A. Duff

Nomos

HART
PUBLISHING

Translation from German by Margaret Hiley
Revision and update by the author

The Deutsche Nationalbibliothek lists this publication in the Deutsche Nationalbibliografie; detailed bibliographic data are available on the Internet at http://dnb.d-nb.de

ISBN: HB (Nomos) 978-3-8487-5808-1
ePDF (Nomos) 978-3-8452-9925-9

British Library Cataloguing-in-Publication Data
A catalogue record for this book is available from the British Library.

ISBN: HB (Hart) 978-1-5099-3678-6

Library of Congress Cataloging-in-Publication Data
Ambos, Kai
National Socialist Criminal Law
Continuity and Radicalization
Preface by R.A. Duff
Kai Ambos
205 pp.
Includes bibliographic references and index.
ISBN 978-1-5099-3678-6 (hardcover Hart)

1st Edition 2019

For Analu, Patrick and Lara

"Does such a system deserve the name of law? Yes, if law is merely the will of the sovereign; definitely not, if law, unlike the sovereign's command must be rational either in form or in content. The National Socialist legal system is nothing but a technique of mass manipulation by terror. Criminal courts, together with the Gestapo, the public prosecutor, and the executioners, are now primarily practitioners of violence."

(Franz Neumann, *Behemoth*, 1942, p 458)

"But precisely because the Third Reich destroyed a tradition with which German identity was so profoundly connected, the Germans… need to think back before Auschwitz and forward beyond Auschwitz… In any case, Jewishness forms an inalienable part of German identity, and those born after [the Holocaust] should see it as their duty not only to lastingly commemorate the important history of Jewishness, but also to scatter the fruitful seed of this commemoration, sowing it in Germany's and Europe's future."

(Dieter Borchmeyer, *Was ist Deutsch?*, 2017, p 22
[translation from German])

"How arrogant to believe we could get away so easily! As if there were any way or any time that anything could ever be normal once more. … *Nothing will ever be alright again.*"

(Max Czollek, *Desintegriert Euch* ["Disintegrate Yourselves"], 2018, p 182 [italics in original, translation from German]).

Preface

Mention 'National Socialist criminal law' to many people, at least in the common law world, and they will suppose it to have been simply an aberration: if it should be counted as 'law' at all (given that it was part of the *Unrechtsstaat* of Nazi Germany), it must be seen as marking a radical hiatus in the history of German criminal law, utterly disconnected both from what had gone before and from what was then reconstructed after 1945. Mention 'National Socialist criminal law theory', and the reaction is likely to be the same: no doubt Nazi propagandists offered 'theories' of criminal law, as part of their efforts to rationalise their regime; but such theories could have no real connection with the doctrines that informed and structured German criminal law before and after the Nazi era. In this fascinating book Kai Ambos shows just how mistaken such reactions would be.

Ambos meticulously traces the deep continuities between National Socialist criminal law doctrine and pre-1933 criminal law scholarship, as well as the traces that it left in post-1945 doctrine (in Germany, but also in Latin America). He does this by paying careful attention to the writings of doctrinal theorists of the period, to their relationships and disagreements with each other, and to the ways in which they drew on earlier doctrines and philosophical ideas, whilst also more or less profoundly modifying those doctrines and ideas in the service of the Nazi ideology. He presents these authors in their own words, and thus enables us to see for ourselves the ways in which they developed doctrines that would sustain a National Socialist criminal law.

The book offers us an illuminating history of this dark period of German criminal law doctrine and theory, and revealing insights into the doctrinal theorists who helped to form it (as well as those who resisted it); but it also shows us revealingly how, as Ambos puts it in his Foreword, 'National Socialist criminal law neither came out of nowhere nor disappeared completely after 1945'. If we reflect on the historical character of the institutions of criminal law, and the historically situated character of criminal law doctrine and theory, this should not surprise us: but given prevalent conceptions of the Nazi era, it might surprise many of us; this book, apart from its intrinsic historical interest, provides an invaluable corrective.

R A Duff, July 2019

Foreword

The present study came about as a result of reading the famous Argentinian criminal law scholar Eugenio Raúl Zaffaroni's recent monograph on National Socialist criminal law doctrine ("Doctrina Penal Nazi", 2017). While the initial aim was to produce only a brief review, the in-depth examination of the sources cited by Zaffaroni and consultation of further primary and secondary sources have resulted in an independent treatise of its own. In line with theories of National Socialism as a continuation and radicalisation of existing trends, it interprets Nazi criminal law as a racist (anti-Semitic), nationalist ("Germanic"), and totalitarian construct that continues and develops further the authoritarian and anti-liberal tendencies of German criminal law of the *fin-de-siècle* and the Weimar Republic. This is borne out by a systematic analysis of writings by relevant authors that focuses first and foremost on the texts, which speak for themselves, and is less concerned with morally judging the scholars who produced them. Readers will also learn about the reception of German (National Socialist) criminal law in Latin America.

A brief word on the aforementioned continuity: it existed not only between the Nazi period and the eras preceding it, but also between National Socialism and the period that followed (the Bonn and even the Berlin Republic). In short, National Socialist criminal law neither came out of nowhere nor disappeared completely after 1945. Current identitarian attempts by the so-called *Neue Rechte* ("New Right") to reconstruct the Germanic myth represent yet another continuation that links seamlessly to National Socialist ideology. In today's digital age, the New Right's populist style of politics is seeking to replace argumentative discourse by "supposedly direct and immediate agreement in a virtual ethnic community" (Stollberg-Rilinger, Interview, faz.net, updated 2 September 2018). This discourse is disturbingly reminiscent of Nazi language and its racist undertones (Detering, 2019).

There are many colleagues I would like to thank for their critical comments, which helped to develop this study. Thomas Vormbaum and Fritz Loos read the manuscript in its entirety. Friederike Wapler provided me with valuable suggestions for the fourth chapter (NS criminal law and Neo-Kantianism), as did Gunnar Duttge, Katrin Gierhake, Luis Greco, Katrin Höffler, Tatjana Hörnle, Günther Jakobs, Urs Kindhäuser, Uwe Murmann and Dietmar von der Pfordten. Paulo de Sousa Mendes, Leandro Dias, Michael Kubiciel, Javier Llobet, Eva Schumann and Fernando Velásquez commented on other aspects. Florian Jessberger and Moritz Vormbaum kindly provided me with their forthcoming contributions on H. Henkel, and Urs Kindhäuser let me have a copy of his forthcoming essay on “Günther Jakobs and Hans Welzel”. Furthermore, I would like to thank my student assistants Marieke Buchholz, Matthias Friese, Leon Augustin Hill, Roman Jusen, Alina Sviridenko, Dara-Lisa Szielinski and Tjorven Vogt for their support in researching this project (Tjorven's help was indispensable to create the list of figures). My gratitude also goes to my doctoral student Yingxin He for comments on the Chinese understanding of the rule of law.

This English version would not have been possible without the help of Dr Margaret Hiley, who produced a translation from the German original in close collaboration with myself. I also want to thank Antony Duff, who not only took it upon himself to write a preface, but also read the translation carefully, suggesting improvements. Last but not least, the publisher, especially Prof. Rux and Mr. Schwarzenberger, have been extremely helpful and flexible. This research is a work in progress, and therefore not only updates but also substantive additions have been made to this English version.

Kai Ambos, Göttingen, August 2019

Table of Contents

List of figures

List of Abbreviations

ADPCP:	*Anuario de Derecho Penal y Ciencias Penales*
ARSP:	*Archiv für Rechts- und Sozialphilosophie / Archives for Philosophy of Law and Social Philosophy*
BGBl:	*Bundesgesetzblatt* (Federal Law Gazette)
BGH	Bundesgerichtshof (Federal Supreme Court)
BGHSt	BGH in Strafsachen (Official collection of BGH decisions in criminal matters)
BMJ:	Bundesministerium der Justiz (Federal Ministry of Justice)
BVerfG:	Bundesverfassungsgericht (Federal Constitutional Court)
cf:	conferatur ("compare")
cit:	cited
col:	column(s)
DJ:	*Deutsche Justiz* (1933–1945; ed. Reichsminister der Justiz; "amtliches Organ der deutschen Rechtspflege und Rechtspolitik" ["official organ of German administration of the law and legal policy"]; predecessor in title: *Zeitschrift Preußische Justiz*)
DJZ:	*Deutsche Juristenzeitung* (under National Socialist control after 1933; ed. Carl Schmitt [from 1934 onwards]; prior to this, the journal had been published since 1896 by Otto Liebmann, who suffered Nazi persecution as a Jew; discontinued in 1936 and replaced by the *ZAkDR*)
DPC:	*Derecho Penal y Criminología* (Bogotá, Colombia: Universidad Externado)
DR:	*Deutsches Recht* (1931–1945, "Zentralorgan des National-Sozialistischen Rechtswahrerbundes" ["central organ of the National Socialist Association of Legal Professionals", merged with *JW* in 1939)
DRWis:	*Deutsche Rechtswissenschaft* (founded in 1936 to support the "renewal of the law" / disseminate the ideas of the Kiel School)
DStR:	*Deutsches Strafrecht. Strafrecht. Strafrechtspolitik. Strafprozess* (a supplement to *DJ*) (1934–1944, ed. Roland Freisler, published under its former title of "Goltdammer's Archiv für Strafrecht" from 1953 onwards)
ed:	edited by / editor / edition
eds:	editors
eg:	exempli gratia ("for example")
et al:	et alia ("and others")
FG:	*Festgabe*
fn:	footnote

FS:	*Festschrift*
GDR:	German Democratic Republic
GerS:	*(Der) Gerichtssaal*
GLJ:	*German Law Journal*
HRG:	*Handwörterbuch zur deutschen Rechtsgeschichte*
ibid:	ibidem ("in the same place")
id:	idem ("the same")
JCL&Crim:	*Journal of Criminal Law and Criminology*
JJZG:	*Jahrbuch der juristischen Zeitgeschichte*
JoJZG:	*Journal der juristischen Zeitgeschichte*
JW:	Juristische Wochenschrift ("Organ des Deutschen Anwaltsvereins" ["organ of the German Lawyers' Association"] until 1939, then merged with *DR*; influenced by NS concepts of the law during the NS period; only became a more practice-oriented and the most important legal journal when refounded as *NJW* in 1947)
JJZ:	*Jahrbuch für Juristische Zeitgeschichte*
JZ:	*JuristenZeitung* (since 1951, succeeding *SJZ*)
KJ:	*Kritische Justiz*
KritV:	*Die Kritische Vierteljahresschrift für Gesetzgebung und Rechtswissenschaft*
LH:	Libro Homenaje (Festschrift)
LTO:	*Legal Tribune Online*
MDR:	*Monatsschrift für Deutsches Recht* (since 1947)
MIH:	*Modern International History*
mn:	margin number
MS:	manuscript
MSchKrim:	*Monatsschrift für Kriminologie und Strafrechtsreform*
MSchKrimBio:	*Monatsschrift für Kriminalbiologie und Strafrechtsreform*
MSchKrimPsych:	*Monatsschrift für Kriminalpsychologie und Strafrechtsreform* (published under this name from its foundation until 1936, then *MSchKrimBio*, now *MSchKrim*)
MüKoStGB:	*Münchener Kommentar zum Strafgesetzbuch*
NDP:	*Nueva Doctrina Penal*
NFP:	*Nuevo Foro Penal* (Medellín, Colombia: Temis, Universidad Eafit)
NJW:	*Neue Juristische Wochenschrift*
NK:	*Nomos Kommentar*
NS:	National Socialism / National Socialist
NSDAP:	Nationalsozialistische Deutsche Arbeiterpartei (National Socialist German Workers' Party)
OGH:	Oberster Gerichtshof (Supreme Court)
OJLS:	*Oxford Journal of Legal Studies*
pos.	position (e-book)

Prussian Memorandum:	Memorandum of the Prussian Justice Minister on NS criminal law (Preußischer Justizminister, 1933).
RDP:	*Revista de Derecho Penal* (Buenos Aires, Argentina: Ediar)
RDPC:	*Revista de Derecho Penal y Criminología* (Madrid, Spain: UNED and Buenos Aires, Argentina: La Ley)
REP:	*Revista de Estudios Penales* (Valladolid, Spain: Universidad de Valladolid)
RG:	Reichsgericht (Supreme Court of the Reich)
RGBl:	*Reichsgesetzblatt* (Reich Law Gazette)
RJ:	*Rechtshistorisches Journal*
RStGB:	Reichsstrafgesetzbuch (Reich Criminal Code)
RW:	*Rechtswissenschaft*
SchwZStW:	*Schweizerische Zeitschrift für Strafrecht*
StGB:	Strafgesetzbuch (Criminal Code)
SJZ:	*Süddeutsche Juristenzeitung* (1946–1950, precursor to *JZ*)
TWC:	Trial of War Criminals before the Nuernberg Military Tribunals under Control Council Law No. 10, 15 volumes, Washington D.C. 1946 ff.
UCLA J. Int'l L & For. Aff.:	*University California at Los Angeles Journal of International Law and Foreign Affairs*
ZakdR:	*Zeitschrift der Akademie für deutsches Recht* (journal of the "Academy of German Law", an institution subject to the NS Reich Ministry of Justice and Ministry of the Interior)
ZDRW	*Zeitschrift für Didaktik der Rechtswissenschaft*
ZIS:	*Zeitschrift für Internationale Strafrechtsdogmatik*
ZJJ:	*Zeitschrift für Jugendkriminalrecht und Jugendhilfe*
ZKph:	*Zeitschrift für deutsche Kulturphilosophie*
ZRG-GA:	*Zeitschrift der Savigny Stiftung für Rechtsgeschichte. Germanistische Abteilung*
ZStW:	*Zeitschrift für die gesamte Strafrechtswissenschaft*

Chapter I. Preliminary Remarks

1. *Zaffaroni's "Doctrina Penal Nazi"*

As already mentioned in the Foreword, the present text is based on my critical review of the Argentinian criminal law scholar Eugenio Raúl Zaffaroni's most recent book on National Socialist criminal law doctrine.

> Zaffaroni's book is made up of nine chapters. The first three are dedicated to the fundamental principles of National Socialist ideology and the institutional framework of the NS state; chapters four to eight deal with the orientation of NS criminal policy and criminal law doctrine in the narrower sense, concentrating particularly on the so-called Kiel School with its protagonists Dahm and Schaffstein; and the ninth and final chapter recapitulates the book's observations and provides valuable insights concerning the continuity of NS criminal law ideology. The study is preceded by a prologue written by the Spanish criminal law scholar Francisco Muñoz Conde, whose own work on Edmund Mezger caused a certain sensation, particularly in Spanish-language circles.[1] Despite numerous inaccuracies[2] and orthographical errors,[3] Zaffaroni has produced an impressive study[4] that will certainly shape the debate on this subject in the Spanish and Portuguese world for many years to come. It draws on his earlier work on the topic as the editor of a series on "forgotten criminal law" ("penalismo olvidado").[5]

---

1 Muñoz Conde (2003).

2 Unfortunately, in numerous instances the primary sources are missing, which is particularly problematic where Zaffaroni accuses the authors he refers to of moral misconduct, *cf* eg Zaffaroni (2017), p 104, 107, 116–17, 141, 151, 207 and 287. Further inaccuracies will be pointed out over the course of this study.

3 The text contains numerous misspellings, especially of German names and terms, *cf* Zaffaroni (2017), p 22, 64, 65, 79, 105, 107, 111–12 and 204; on Germans terms and names id, p 28, 59, 93, 98, 109, 149 and 202. The incorrect spelling of Schaffstein's name in the cover blurb ("Shaffstein") is particularly embarrassing.

4 Guzmán Dalbora, *RDPC* VII (2017), 230 is somewhat too effusive in his claim that the study contains "a fully complete ("completísima") reconstruction" of 1930s and 1940s German criminal law scholarship. The imprecise citations referred to in fn 2 already suggest that this is not the case, as does Zaffaroni's only selective reception of the German debate, which will be mentioned several times over the course of the present study.

5 Zaffaroni, ed (2009a), (2009b), (2011) and (2017). Each volume contains an introduction by Zaffaroni, on which the study under discussion here is in part based and which are

Readers, especially from Germany and similar criminal law systems, will be particularly interested in Zaffaroni's book—not only because of its theme,[6] but also because of German criminal law science's huge significance in Latin America, the National Socialist networks that continued to exist there for a long time (especially in Argentina),[7] and not least the author's major importance within the Spanish- and Portuguese-speaking world.

Eugenio Raúl Zaffaroni was born on 7 January 1940 in Buenos Aires and studied under Luis Jiménez de Asúa (1889–1970), whom many consider the founder of criminal law doctrine in the Spanish (and Portuguese) speaking jurisdictions.[8] Zaffaroni has authored a highly significant oeuvre, including his seminal five-volume "Tratado de Derecho Penal" (Buenos Aires 1980–83) as well as numerous monographs and essays. The recipient of more than 30 honorary doctorates, he has been a guest lecturer and visiting professor at too many institutions to count. Zaffaroni has also enjoyed an impressive career as a judge: 1969–1990 as a provincial and federal judge[9] (with an interval of two years as "Procurador General de Justicia de la Provincia de San Luis"), 2003–2014 as a judge at the Argentinian Supreme Court ("Corte Suprema de Justicia de la Nación"), and since 2016 as a judge at the Inter-American Court of Human Rights. Retirement is far from his mind, however, as this study and the simultaneously published "Derecho penal humano"[10] (a counter-project, as it were) go to show. Zaffaroni also held a judge's office during the Argentinian military dictatorship (1976–1983), namely as a sentencing judge in Buenos Aires ("Juez Nacional en lo Criminal de Sentencia de la Capital Federal"), after

---

quoted at various points below. This series contains not only NS texts, but also a volume on the Utrecht school of criminal law, for example (Zaffaroni, ed., 2016).

6 It takes its place among a number of other studies on NS criminal law (both monographs and articles) by Latin American scholars, as we will see below (ch VII, especially 2.). At this point it is worth mentioning what is perhaps the most important of the monographs by Llobet (2018), which provides a detailed account of the foundations of the NS legal system, criminal law and criminal procedural law as well as a separate enquiry into Hans Welzel's role.

7 Thereto recently in a documentary, novelistic account Guez (2018), p 30, 36, 45 and *passim* (e-book).

8 On Jiménez de Asúa and his works—in particular his ten-volume analysis of the comprehensive study of criminal law (Jiménez de Asúa, 1946–52) and his seven-volume "Tratado de Derecho penal" (1957–1970)—Oneca, *ADPCP* 23 (1970), 547 ff.

9 Argentina's justice system has a federal structure that includes a federal level as well as 23 provinces and the autonomous city of Buenos Aires.

10 Zaffaroni (2017a).

serving as one of the three federal judges of the autonomous city of Buenos Aires under Isabel Perón's government when only 36 years of age (1975–1976)—a fact that seems particularly piquant against the background of the study discussed here.[11] Allegations have recently been made against him in this context.[12]

2. *My approach*

In line with theories of NS law as not only a continuation but a *radicalisation*[13] of existing trends, the present study interprets Nazi criminal law as a racist (anti-Semitic), nationalist ("Germanic"), and totalitarian construct that continues and develops further the authoritarian and anti-liberal tendencies of German criminal law of the *fin-de-siècle* and the Weimar Republic.[14] As part of this radicalisation, the social element was completely replaced by published in German in 1974 a thoroughly authoritarian and nationalistic renewal of criminal law on the basis of a mystically inflated con-

11 These biographical data are available on Wikipedia among other sources and have been confirmed and supplemented by Argentinian colleagues.

12 For example, Graciela Fernández Mejide, a former member of the renowned National Commission on the Disappearance of Persons (Comisión Nacional sobre la Desaparición de Personas, CONADEP), reprimanded Zaffaroni for his failure to accept a *habeas corpus* for her son in 1976 (during the military dictatorship) (*La Nacion*, 15 February 2018, https://www.lanacion.com.ar/2109256-meijide-revelo-que-le-nego-un-habeas-corpus-por-su-hijo?utm_source=FB&utm_medium=Cali&utm_campaign=2109256, last accessed: 22 October 2018).

13 On the concept, *cf* Vormbaum, in Grundmann et al (2010), p 523, 534 ff; Vormbaum (2015), p 153, 181, 184, 188, 204, 212, 268, 272 (an English translation of a previous edition of Vormbaum's book is available: Vormbaum [2014]).

14 For a fundamental account, see Marxen (1975) (for individual references *cf* fn 29 below); also Rüping, in: Dreier/Sellert (1989), p 180, 192 (the NS state was "not created artificially out of nothing" ["nicht voraussetzungslos und künstlich geschaffen"]); Wolf, *JuS* 1996, 195 ("historically prepared", "taken to the extreme with brutal consistency" ["historisch vorbereitet", "mit brutaler Konsequenz auf die Spitze getrieben"]); Hartl (2000), p 336 ("numerous precursors" ["zahlreiche Vorläufer"]), 377 "long before the NS epoch" ["lange vor der NS-Epoche"]); Cattaneo (2001), p 223 (according to whom the "authoritarian positivist theory of crime prepared the ground for the totalitarian National Socialist doctrine" ["autoritäre positivistische Straftheorie den Weg zur totalitären nationalsozialistischen Lehre bereitet hat"]); Vogel (2004), p 8 ff, 18, 20 (including further references in fn 29); Hoyer, *GS Eckert* (2008), p 359 (a culmination of lines of development that existed "long before 1933" ["lange vor 1933"]); Rüping/Jerouschek (2011), p 107 ("backward-reaching continuities" ["zurückreichende Kontinuitäten"]); Zaffaroni (2017), p 129 ff; in reference to the victim's self-responsibility (autonomy) Murmann (2005), p 126.

cept of race and nationhood[15]—as noted as early as 1933 by Gustav Radbruch, one of Nazi criminal law's fiercest critics.[16]

Figure 1: The infamous Memorandum of the Prussian Ministry of Justice on NS Criminal Law ("Prussian Memorandum", Preußischer Justizminister, 1933)

Figure 2: Gemmingen's book on criminal law in accordance with Hitler's ideas (not authorized by Hitler), 1933

15 This concept of the nation or *Volk* (people) and the characteristics building on or arising from it, as described in the following (also *cf* the next fn), can be used to delineate the rough outlines of the National Socialist criminal law programme—*contra* Werle (1989), p 45 ff (48, 52)—especially as its essential features are already present in the Prussian Memorandum (Preußischer Justizminister, 1933) and the NS guiding principles (Frank, 1935). Also *cf* Gemmingen (1933), p 25 f, who develops some "guidelines" despite the lack of a formal programme (the idea of the *Volksgemeinschaft*, punishment as retribution, loosening and ethicisation). Besides the Prussian Memorandum and Gemmingen, von Hentig, *MSchrKrimPsych* 24 (1933), 633–4 refers to Nicolai (1932), thereto chapter II 1. below including fn 103 ff and main text. From a contemporary perspective see *Rückert*, KritV 94 (2001), 242 ff, 260 (identifying primacy of policy and unequal treatment of non-Aryans as "minimal" characteristics); for a succinct summary also Hoyer, *GS Eckert* (2008), p 358; see also Gúzman D., in Zaffaroni (2017), p 91 (pointing out that NS criminal law theory was neither well developed nor complete ["no…bien elaborado ni completo"]).

Indeed, it is striking how widespread critical accounts of NS (criminal) law already were in the 1930s and 1940s, although written mostly by exiled or foreign authors. Most importantly, in his study on the "Criminal Law in National-Socialist Germany", originally published in English in 1939/40 and retranslated and published in German in a collection of essays in 1976, Otto Kirchheimer identified several characteristics of NS criminal law[17] which informed the research for years to come.[18] Ernst Fraenkel, in his famous "The Dual State" ("Der Doppelstaat"), originally published in English in 1941 and then retranslated and published in German in 1974, shows how the NS "Prerogative State" ("Maßnahmenstaat") displaces and overrules the "Normative State" (Normenstaat"), including and especially in the area of criminal justice.[19] I note in passing that such a dualist approach is difficult to reconcile with the overall primacy of policy (policy reservation) in the NS state[20] as one of its most important characteristics (more on this in a moment). Last but not least, Franz Neumann, in his "Behemoth", also first published in English in 1942 and retranslated/published in German in 1984, analyses the Nazi "terror" law, including criminal law, and praises Kirchheimer's account as the best.[21] Interestingly, in the preface to the second English edition of 1944, Neumann argues that, contrary to Fraenkel's dualist thesis, "the still existing dualism of State and Party" will soon disappear and thus the "remnants of the rational and administrative state" will be replaced by an "amorphous, shapeless Movement, thus transforming the little that remains of the

16 Radbruch (1933/1957), p 63 (71) ("When we look more closely, these reforms leave only the authoritarian element, while the social element disappears completely" ["Wenn man genauer zusieht, bleibt bei diesen Reformen freilich nur das autoritäre Element übrig, während der soziale Einschlag völlig verschwindet"]), subsequently identifying six characteristics of NS criminal law, p 72 ff. — Erik Wolf (who will be discussed in detail in ch VI) likewise claims already to have recognised the predominance of the national-authoritarian over the social element in 1933, *cf* letter to Karl Barth of 15 October 1945 and 11 November 1968, published by Hollerbach, in: *Heidegger-Jahrbuch* 4 (2009), p 288; on this letter in closer detail, see ch VI 2. including fn 767 below.

17 Kirchheimer, in *Studies in Philosophy and Social Science* VIII (1939/40), 444 ff; id, in id (1976), p 186 ff (referring, *inter alia*, to the criminal law of the will, the ethicisation, the theory of agency, the "healthy sentiment of the people", the concept of "material wrongdoing" and the harsh punishments, including the death penalty); for further considerations on criminal law see also id., *KJ* 9 (1976), 41 ff.
'Staatsgefüge etc.', in id (1976), p 155 ff.

18 Cf Rückert, *KritV* 94 (2001), 240–1 with further references.

19 Fraenkel (1941), p 31–3, 41–3, 49–53; id. (1974), p 59–62, 70–2, 79–83.

20 Therefore critical of Fraenkel Rüthers, *JZ* 2015, 799.

21 Neumann (1942), p 440–458 (452 ff, referring to Kirchheimer in fn 88); id. (1984), p 509–30 (524 ff, referring to Kirchheimer in fn 100).

> state into more or less organised anarchy".[22] From a more doctrinal perspective, the abovementioned Spanish-Argentinian scholar Jiménez de Asúa sharply criticised NS criminal law as early as 1933, referring in particular to the infamous Prussian Memorandum.[23] French scholar Henri Donnedieu de Vabres (who later served as a judge at the Nuremberg IMT) lists three characteristics of NS criminal law in 1938[24] which are then taken up by Jiménez de Asúa, who adds the unified concept of crime as a fourth one.[25]

The continuity theory is widely shared among the select group of (German) criminal law scholars who have taken it upon themselves to research NS criminal law from a largely doctrinal perspective.[26] Klaus Marxen, for example, identifies a "continuation and intensification of existing approaches"[27] by anti-liberal criminal law scholars of the 1930s, who served as the "stirrup holders"[28] of National Socialism. Marxen's view is borne

22 Neumann (1944), p xii.

23 Jiménez de Asúa (1933), p 374, 377 ff (381) ("maximas exageraciones", "tendencia autoritaria" [377], the "inept cruelty" ["torpe crueldad"], "primitiva" [381], which will lead to the death of the "técnica penal alemana" [382]). Of course, at an earlier point in time (1920 and 1922) he himself had put the case for a criminal law oriented upon the danger posed by the perpetrator, advocating coercive measures for a so-called pre-delictual "dangerous state" (*estado peligroso*) (thereto in greater detail Mercurio, 2013, 350 ff).

24 Donnedieu de Vabres (1938), p 71 ff, 92 (*Willensstrafrecht* [the criminal law of the will], racial criminal law and orientation towards *"gesundes Volksempfinden"* [the "healthy sentiment of the people"]).

25 Jiménez de Asúa (1947), vol VII, p 63–186, 141–2. In this impressive study, Jiménez de Asúa presents the "authoritarian criminal law of the Third Reich" (p 74) as contrasting with the liberal, enlightened criminal law of the *fin-de-siècle* and the Weimar Republic (p 65 ff), compares it to the authoritarian criminal law of Russia and Italy (p 67 ff), and mentions the most important NS criminal law theorists (p 76 ff)—many of whom are only "penalistas improvisados" (p 79)—as well as the most significant themes in the criminal law doctrine (p 95 ff), reform plans and laws (p 108 ff, 116 ff, 124 ff) of the "new order" (p 95). Finally, he summarises the foreign criticism on NS criminal law, which was already surprisingly widespread in the 1930s and 1940s (p 142 ff); on this criticism, also *cf* Blasco y Fernández de Moreda, *Criminalia* (Mexico) IX (4/1943), 235, 247 ff (for more detail on this author, *cf* Zaffaroni, in Zaffaroni, 2011, p 29 ff); by contrast, a predominantly descriptive account (albeit with approving undertones) is given by Cavaleiro de Ferreira (1938), p 72 ff (discussing crimes against the state in the Special Part as well as the admission of analogy, the subjectivising criminal law of the will and the Habitual Offender Act; on his close links with NS jurists, while emphasising his belief in the rule of law, Sousa Mendes [2013], p 36–7 and id, in Sousa Mendes [2018], p 21 ff).

26 See the references in fn 13 and 14 above.

27 Marxen (1975), p 247.

28 The term was used by Sontheimer (1962), p 376 (on the "stirrup-holding role" of the conservative, anti-democratic right wing for National Socialism).

out by the classical and modern schools of criminal law theory[29] (*cf* eg Binding's authoritarian concepts of the state and criminal law[30] and von Liszt's typology of perpetrators[31]), as well as by legislation;[32] from this perspective, as will be seen in chapter III, the so-called *Schulenstreit* or "Dispute of the Schools" proves less controversial than is generally assumed. Joachim Vogel sees Nazi criminal law as embedded in five developmental trends in criminal law in the 20th century (expansion, materialisation, ethicisation, subjectivisation, social functionalisation). These trends were radicalised by the National Socialists between 1933 and 1945 and continue to affect criminal law in our own day and age.[33]

In light of this scholarship, NS criminal law can be characterised as a politicised and radical continuation of the neoclassical and "finalist" theories of crime,[34] as the two main academic schools represented by "the Marburg scholars" (Schwinge and Zimmerl) and "the Kiel scholars" (Dahm and Schaffstein) were both committed to (criminal) law scholarship's[35] **political task** of implementing the nationalist, racist and total NS state

29 For a summary, *cf* Marxen (1975), p 247 ff, 270–1, 272, 275; on the so-called *Neuklassiker* or neoclassicists (including Nagler, Sauer) and their orientation towards the authoritarian state and traditional nationalism ibid, p 121, 128 ff, 131, 158; on the "younger criminalists" ("jüngeren Kriminalisten") and the "conservative revolution" ("konservativen Revolution") ibid, p 153 ff; on the anti-liberalism of the modern school ibid, p 159 ff.

30 See ch III including fn 262 below.

31 Thereto recently Vormbaum, in: Jeßberger/Kotzur/Repgen (2019), p 409-10; for more detail, see ch III including fn 270 ff below.

32 Thereto eg Schreiber, in: Dreier/Sellert (1989), p 151, 166 ff (focusing upon individual NS legislation—more than 50 laws and decrees—and making a distinction between specifically National Socialist, terrorist laws and legislation that "drew on the criminal policy of the Weimar period or on Austrian models" ["auf kriminalpolitische Vorstellungen der Weimarer Zeit bzw. auf österreichische Vorbilder zurückgriffen", 167]); Werle (1989), p 57 ff provides a detailed account of substantive criminal legislation; Hoefer, *JCL&Crim* 35 (1945), 386 ff gives a brief summary.

33 Vogel (2004), p 14 ff, 43 ff including further references.

34 *Cf* Marxen, in: Rottleuthner (1983), p 55, 57 ff (continuity in reference to National Socialism [57], political orientation of Schwinge/Zimmerl (1937) and Dahm/Schaffstein (1933) [58], who were both equally oriented towards the NS state's national project [62 f]); Marxen, in: Reifner, (1984), p 77, 82 ff; Marxen, *KritV* 73 (1990), 287 ff (eg *Willenstrafrecht* as the "culmination" ["Höhepunkt", 294]). – For an English account of Welzel's finalist theory, which was based on a particular (ontological, will-based) understanding of the human act, in contrast to the dualist (objective/actus reus vs. subjective/mens rea) approach of the (neo)classical theories see Ambos, *Cardozo Law Review* 28 (2007), 2649–50.

35 For a fundamental account, see Schaffstein (1934), p 6 ff ("political criminal law science" as expressing the "primacy of the political" as the "shared fundamental principle that constitutes the precondition of all scholarly insight and precisely thereby guarantees its unity" ["politische Strafrechtswissenschaft", "Primat des Politischen", "gemeinsamen Grundprinzip, das die Voraussetzung alles wissenschaftlichen Erkennens darstellt und eben dadurch seine Einheit verbürgt", 6]; as a science that, while not subservient, is nev-

through the means of criminal law[36] (although the classical "judicial" criminal law was classified as part of police crime fighting and was largely subordinate to it in organisational and institutional terms).[37] This political

ertheless focused upon the "idea of the state", namely the totalitarian NS state and its "national way of life" ["Idee des Staates", "völkische Lebensordnung", 15], as only once this had been realised could the "political...become a distinct principle of the conceptualisation of criminal law, since when it has become identical with National Socialism through National Socialism's claim to totality" ["Politische…zum bestimmten Prinzip der strafrechtlichen Begriffsbildung werden, seitdem es im neuen Staat durch den Totalitätsanspruch des Nationalsozialismus mit dem Nationalsozialistischen identisch geworden ist", 23], which is why its sole focus now is "the recognition and implementation of the 'right' National Socialism" ["um die Erkenntnis und Durchsetzung des 'richtigen' Nationalsozialismus", 23 f]; also Schaffstein, *ZStW* 56 (1937), 104, where the call for a "completely different way of thinking" adapted to the "new Reich" is also understood in the sense of "a political demand" ["neuen Reich", "völlig anderen Denkweise", "einer politischen Forderung"]. Schwinge/Zimmerl (1937) recognise the "grand ideas" ("großen Gedanken", p 13) and the "primacy of political leadership" ("Primat der politischen Führung", p 75) as well as the interpretative requirements arising from the "idea of the new state" ("Idee des neuen Staates", p 76); for more detail on these two authors, see ch IV 2. below. Also *cf* Welzel (1935), p 57–8 ("'political' task" as "exploring the concrete values of the historical situation", as a "decision for or against the life'style' of the concrete historical epoch", which is shaped by "the current fate of the *völkisch* and state community" ["'politische' Aufgabe", "Ergründung der konkreten Werte der historischen Situation", "Entscheidung für oder gegen den Lebens-'Stil' der konkreten historischen Epoche", "das gegenwärtige Schicksal der völkisch-staatlichen Gemeinschaft"]), 75–6 ("'political' task" as orienting "legal valuations" towards the "reality" of the "*völkisch* and state community" "in its concrete historical situation, in its respective present fate, with which it needs to engage as a matter of life and death" ["'politische' Aufgabe", "rechtlichen Wertungen", "Wirklichkeit", "völkisch-staatlichen Gemeinschaft", "in ihrer konkreten historischen Situation, in ihrem jeweils gegenwärtigen Schicksal, mit dem es sich auf Leben und Tod auseinandersetzen muß"]) and Henkel, in Krieck/Staufing (1933), p 19 ff (19-20, 22-3: rejection of a "neutral" (legal) science "without preconditions" ["wertfreien", "voraussetzungslosen"], instead relating it to the nation and ethnicity and recognising its "character as aware of and bound to the nation" ["nationalbewußten und nationalgebundenen Charakter"]). *Cf* as a secondary source Marxen (1975), p 55, 169 ff; Marxen, in: Rottleuthner (1983), p 58–9 ("political dogmatism of the Kiel School" ["Politikdogmatik der Kieler Schule"] and "primacy of political leadership" ["Primat der politischen Führung"] in Schwinge/Zimmerl); Stefanopolou, *JoJZG* 2010, 112 (on Schaffstein). Aptly characterising the linking of law and politics as a totalitarian trait Gúzman D., in Zaffaroni (2017), p 89.

36 *Cf* on national-racial legal thinking eg Alexy, in: Säcker (1992), p 219-20; also Murmann (2005), p 127 ("legal science's contest to implement the called-for racial-national renewal of the law as a legal-political aim of National Socialism in the best way possible" ["Wettbewerb der Rechtswissenschaft zur bestmöglichen Durchführung der geforderten rassisch-völkischen Rechtserneuerung als rechtspolitisches Ziel des Nationalsozialismus"]).

37 As proven convincingly by Werle (1989), p 730 ff and *passim*; briefly also Stolleis (2016), p 30 ff. Hoefer, *JCL&Crim* 35 (1945), 390 already assumed a "duplicity of legal and illegal action", seeing the Gestapo as responsible for the latter. Dahm, *DRWis* 1938, 148 gives a differentiated account of the state of the debate at that time concerning the relation between the criminal police and the prosecution (rejecting the integration of one authority into the other, which would make the integrated authority subordinate, due to the fundamentally different nature of the police and the prosecution [150 ff], although

or politicised approach to legal scholarship entails, on the one hand, the law's and legal doctrine's subordination to the dominant criminal policy of the NS leadership in the sense of an all-encompassing "policy reservation" ("*Politikvorbehalt*"); the law turned into "an annex of NS policy"[38] and the Nazis quickly recognised the "eminent political function" of criminal law.[39] In practical terms this meant that old law was either (explicitly) replaced ("renewal of the law" ["Rechtserneuerung"]) or it was re-interpreted/adjusted in line with the new NS *Weltanschauung*.[40] On the other hand, the inherent aspiration towards a total or totalitarian criminal law (including a "Führer state" and "Führer principle")[41] excludes any assumption of a duality of law and ideology[42] in the sense of the Two Worlds Theory.[43] Accordingly, the purpose, the finality (final end) of the Nazi state determined *all* of National Socialist criminal law scholarship, and this scholarship was thus "shaped by a finalist stance".[44] This terminological affinity to Welzel's *finale Handlungslehre* (finalist theory of action) is no coincidence.[45]

---

he considers making fighting crime a police matter for reasons of "expediency" ["Zweckmäßigkeit", 154] understandable; instead, he argues in favour of distinguishing more clearly between the two, with only the police responsible for crime —although he is against an independent "criminal police investigation process" ["kriminalpolizeiliches Aufklärungsverfahren", 161]— and the prosecution responsible for bringing charges and pursuing the matter in court [161 ff], and a freer development of police investigation with less control by the prosecution [166-7], but without the police extending their repressive powers beyond preventive activities [168-9]).

38 Cf Rückert, *JZ* 2015, 797, 799–800, 802; id, in id (2018b), p 361 ("ein Annex der NS-Politik"); id, *ZDRW* 2019, 32, 44 ff; previously id, *KritV* 94 (2001), 223 ff, 242 ff ("policy precedence" ["Politikvorrang"], "primacy of policy" ["Primat der Politik"]).

39 Stolleis (2016), p 29 ("eminent politische Funktion").

40 On this "dual strategy" ("Doppelstrategie") see Rüthers, *JZ* 2015, 802.

41 Thereto in greater detail ch II 1. and 2.

42 Also see Hartl (2000), p 39, who rightly emphasises that NS criminal law "can only be explained against the backdrop of National Socialist ideology" ("nur vor dem Hintergrund der nationalsozialistischen Ideologie erklärbar") (which he describes as a diffuse "conglomerate" ["Konglomerat"] of various nationalist, traditional German, anti-Marxist and authoritarian ideas [p 40]).

43 *Cf* Werle (1989), p 30 ff. including further references, especially on Buchheim and Jäger.

44 Marxen, in: Rottleuthner (1983), p 63 ("von einer finalistischen Grundhaltung geprägt").

45 *Cf* Matus, *ZIS* 9 (2014), 622 (623, 625), who, like Marxen, sees a continuity particularly in regard to teleological theory and a basic agreement with the Kiel School; Frommel, *JZ* 2016, 920 including fn 43 (close relation between teleological theory and NS *Willensstrafrecht*). We will return to this issue (ch VII 2. including fn 798 ff and main text below).

Politische
Strafrechtswissenschaft

Von

Dr. Friedrich Schaffstein

Professor der Rechte in Leipzig

1934

Hanseatische Verlagsanstalt Hamburg

Figure 3: Schaffstein's fundamental text on a "Political Criminal Law Science" based on his inaugural lecture at Leipzig University, 1934

From a temporal perspective, both the radicalisation theory and the continuity theory are based upon a perspective that is back- and forward-looking at the same time. National Socialist criminal law *neither came out of nowhere nor disappeared completely after 1945*. In historical terms, NS criminal law was not just an episode but part of an epoch of authoritarian criminal law;[46] this authoritarianism was, of course, not limited to criminal law.[47] As will be seen throughout the following text, authoritarian crimi-

46 *Cf* Rückert, *KritV* 94 (2001), 227 ff, who distinguishes basically between two historical models (dictatorship as an episode with liberal [rechtsstaatliches] criminal law as an epoch or, in turn, the latter as an episode and the dictatorship as part of an epoch).

47 *Cf* Rückert, in Rückert/Willoweit (1995), p 4–5; Klippel, in Rückert/Willoweit (1995), p 31, 53–4.

nal law had its roots in the writings of criminal law theorists of the 19th century and in concepts of German idealist thinking and thus originated well before the Weimar Republic.[48] After 1945, there was a continuity[49] in terms of both staff[50] and content,[51] including and indeed particularly in

48 A good example in this regard is Savigny's *Volksgeist* ("spirit of the people") which was invoked by a series of Nazi writers (eg Dahm/Schaffstein, 1933, p 5; for further references see Rückert, *ZRG-GA* 103 [1986], 200 ff; from an external perspective Friedmann [1967], p 213) and can be seen, at least in conceptual terms, as the basis of the *gesundes Volksempfinden* ("healthy sentiment of the people"); for a nuanced analysis see insofar Rückert, op. cit., 238 ff, demonstrating that, while there are methodological and conceptual parallels ("Denkfigur"), the original concept underwent a "change of function" ("Funktionswandel") and decisively political abuse by the National Socialists with a view to the expansion of criminal law, while Savigny used it in a more restrictive sense, for example upholding the *nulla poena* principle.

49 Summarised by Wolf, *JuS* 1996, 189 ff; Rüthers, *JZ* 2017, 457 ff.; regarding public law Stolleis (2016), p 144 ff.

50 Maus, in: Dreier/Sellert (1989), p 80, 81 f; Wolf, *JuS* 1996, 189; Gross (2010), position 395 including fn 43; Rüping/Jerouschek (2011), p 110; Görtemaker/Safferling (2016), p 86 ff; Rüthers (2017), p 16 ff; Frei et al. (2019), pos. 326 (West-Germany), 686 (GDR); in reference to Schleswig-Holstein Vormbaum, *GA* 1995, 147–8 (reviewing Godau-Schüttke); with a special focus on Hessen Falk (2017), p 1, 4; on the paradigmatic public law scholar Theodor Maunz (who quickly moved from his Freiburg chair, obtained in 1937, to Munich in 1952, always—anonymously—supporting the Nazis, including by writing for the *Deutsche National-Zeitung*) Stolleis (2016), p 306 ff.

51 For a fundamental account, see Marxen (1975), p 254 ff (uncritical continuation instead of a fresh start, disregarding the anti-liberal NS heritage and depoliticising NS criminal law, covering up connections and links, with improper omission [commission by omission] as an exemplary case); Marxen, *KritV* 73 (1990), 287 ff (in reference to the prohibition of analogy and *Willensstrafrecht*); Wolf, *JuS* 1996, 189 ff (criminal laws [190, 191 ff] and NS doctrine [191] continued to be valid or were taken over, eg agent-oriented subjectivisation, finalism, and a focus on the *Handlungsunwert*, ie the wrongfulness of act as opposed to the wrongfulness of the result [193 f], making a return to the liberal foundations of the 1871 Criminal Code necessary [195]); Hartl (2000), p 334 ff, 380–1 (continuity in regard to "the ideology of the criminal law of the will" and "subjectivist precursors" ["willenstrafrechtlichem Gedankengut", "subjektivistischen Vorläufern", 337]; the will-based criminal law's subjectivisation and anticipatory liability are developed further into a guilt-focused criminal law that emphasises degrees of responsibility, albeit no "blanket equation" with the criminal law of the will ["pauschale Gleichsetzung", 337 ff, 375]; remnants in the General Part [doctrine on participation, attempt, 342 ff] and Special Part [eg punishability of preparation to commit an offence, 365 ff]); Hoyer, *GS Eckert* (2008), p 360 ff (infringement of duties rather than of legally protected interests, collective rather than individual legally protected interests, formation of analogies instead of the principle of legality, objectionable attitudes and moral transgressions as reasons for punishment); also *cf* Stefanopolou, *JoJZG* 2010, 116–7 (special offences and degrees of responsibility); Höffler, in: Schumann/Wapler (2017), p 61, 69–70 (in reference to youth criminology); id, FS Kreuzer (2018), p 240 ff (regarding "harmful tendencies" ["schädliche Neigungen"]); briefly Vormbaum, *GA* 1995, 148; Rüping/Jerouschek (2011), p 110–11; Görtemaker/Safferling (2016), p 358; on the NS background of § 323c Harzer (1999), p 57 ff. For a more nuanced view see Alexy, in: Säcker (1992), p 224 f, who sees a "comparatively faint continuity in terms of theory and content" ("relativ

academia.[52] We will return to this several times below, usually in passing, but highlighting the term "continuity" in bold.[53] In any case, one must not overlook that the continuity of content is for the most part not readily apparent since the former Nazi language has been replaced in law and academic discourse,[54] leaving the underlying legal thinking and structural premises largely intact, however.[55]

The said continuity explains not only the widespread "communicative silence"[56] —which made it difficult, if not impossible to do research on the NS legacy[57]—but also the failure to hold numerous jurists to account

---

schwache theoretische und inhaltliche Kontinuität"), but refers insofar only to racial and national thought (and not to the authoritarian and neo-Hegelian legal thought he also identifies); against continuity with regard to the core (racially discriminatory) characteristics of NS criminal law Rückert, *KritV* 94 (2001), 248 ff, 261, 262–3, although he puts too much emphasis on the (Allied) denazification policy (including the abolition of hardcore NS legislation) and admits that this was not supported by mainstream legal discourse and practice; more critical with regard to some public and civil law writers Rückert, in Lehmann/Oexle (2004), p 664 ff. Hartung (1971), p 123 even welcomes this continuity ("progress of fundamental significance…that still exists today" ["Fortschritte von grundlegender Bedeutung…die bis heute Bestand haben"]), referring, *inter alia*, to the "Gewohnheitsverbrechergesetz" (sic!).

52 Usually, academics with NS connections were at most classified as "followers" and temporarily barred from teaching (financial penalties were usually not imposed), so that they were able to return to the universities after a certain time had passed, *cf* eg on Henkel ch II 1. including fn 157 below, and on Dahm/Schaffstein ch V 1. below. Wolf, *JuS* 1996, 189 mentions Mezger, Henkel, Schaffstein and Bruns. On the NS involvement of legal publishers and the ensuing continuity see Rüthers/Schmitt, *JZ* 1988, 369 and recently Amos, *LTO* 7 August 2019.

53 In regard to continuity in terms of content, *cf* eg on *authorisations of analogy* ch II 2. including fn , on *undertaking offences* ch II 3. including fn 249 and on *breaches of trust* ch V 4. including fn 597 ff and main text.

54 The perhaps most suitable and paradigmatic example is the replacement of the infamous "gesundes Volksempfinden" ("healthy sentiment of the people") by the concept of "Verwerflichkeit" ("reprehensibility"); cf eg the coercion offence of § 240 (2) RStGB as amended by the "Criminal Law Harmonisation Decree" ("Strafrechtsangleichungsverordnung") of 29 May 1943 (RGBl I 341) and its current version in the StGB. The failure to rescue provision of § 330c RStGB (RGBl I 1935, 839) also contained the "gesundes Volksempfinden", but it was only amended in 1953 (BGBl I 735).

55 *Cf* Rückert, in id (2018a), p 284–5 (seeing a continuity in terms of "binding oneself methodologically to *substantialist legal thinking*" ["methodische Selbstbindung an ein *substantialistisches Rechtsdenken*"] and with regard to the structural premises ["strukturellen Prämissen"]) (italics in original).

56 *Cf Lübbe* (2007), p 32 ["kommunikatives Beschweigen"]; also Wolf, *JuS* 1996, 189, 195 (no public engagement with and inquiry into the past); Stolleis (2016), p 127 (talking considered as "tactless" ("taktlos")]); recently Frommel, *JZ* 2016, 916, 919; id, *JZ*, 2017, 455 ("cartels of silence" ["Schweigekartelle"]); Rüthers, *JZ* 2017, 458 ("spirals of silence", "dictate of silence" ["Schweigespirale", "Schweigegebot"]).

57 Scholarly investigations into the NS legacy were hardly conducive to one's career, *cf* eg Herbert Jäger's mention of being warned by his teacher Henkel (Jäger, in Horstmann/

for their conduct under National Socialism;[58] a lack of accountability that was sanctioned at the highest level by the Adenauer government's "tabula rasa policy".[59] In terms of moral philosophy, this continuity derives from the fact that National Socialist morals were so strongly anchored in German society that they continued to shape it long after 1945 and ensured the integration of postwar society, including the National Socialists still living in that society.[60] Current identitarian attempts by the so-called *Neue Rechte* ("New Right") to reconstruct the Germanic myth[61] represent yet another continuation that links seamlessly to National Socialist ideology.[62] Of course, neither continuity nor radicalisation in this sense—looking both back (post-Weimar) and forward in time (the Bonn Republic)—mean to imply a continuation of the NS *Unrechtsstaat*, the "state of injustice", which was quite unique in this regard;[63] the liberal, rule-of-law-based orientation of *both* the Weimar and Bonn Republics precludes this, especially

---

Litzinger, 2006, p 49) or Hoyer, *GS Eckert* (2009), p 351 (the "threat" posed by "fouling one's own nest" ["Gefährdungen", "Nestbeschmutzen"] in regard to analyses of legal history, including of the Kiel School, by Jörn Eckert). Before 1965 any attempt at a *Habilitation* —the post-doctoral qualification procedure in the German (and Austrian, Polish, Swiss etc) academic system in order to obtain a professorship—in this area encountered great obstacles (Stolleis, 2016, p 43).

58 Thereto recently Safferling, in: Lüttig/Lehmann (2017), p 19 ff including further references; on the lacking accountability of NS judges Graver, *GLJ* 19 (2018), 845, 848.

59 *Cf* Konrad Adenauer's programmatic statement in the seventh cabinet meeting on 29 June 1949 during a discussion on amnesty: "The times behind us were so confusing that it seems advisable to create a general tabula rasa" ("Wir haben so verwirrende Zeitverhältnisse hinter uns, daß es sich empfiehlt, generell tabula rasa zu machen"), available at http://www.bundesarchiv.de/cocoon/barch/0000/k/k1949k/kap1_3/para2_4.html, last accessed 9 August 2019.

60 *Cf* in greater detail Gross (2010), position 24 ff, 165 (in reference to anti-Semitic discrimination), 2519 ff ("integration was achieved" by "the handing down of National Socialist ideas and thought patterns" ["Integrationsleistung", "Tradierung nationalsozialistischer Ideen und Denkmuster"]); for a fundamental account of the Nazis' social reintegration Frei (1996), p 7 ff; Czollek (2018), p 47 ff including further references.

61 *Cf* Geyer, *FAZ*, 7 June 2018, 13. On Germanic NS legal thought, see ch II 1. including fn 84 and main text below.

62 On continuity via the identitarian movement, see eg Caroline Sommerfeld as one of the icons of the "New Right": "When asked whether somebody non-white can be German, her response is: 'No!' Being German is not purely a question of race. 'But it certainly has a very basic ethnic element. Citizenship alone is not enough.'" ("Auf die Frage, ob jemand, der nicht weiß ist, Deutscher sein könne, antwortet sie: 'Nein!' Deutschsein sei zwar keine reine Rassenfrage. 'Aber es hat auf jeden Fall ganz elementar eine ethnische Komponente. Mit der Staatsbürgerschaft allein ist es nicht getan.'" *Kazim*, 2018). Recently on parallels between the New Right and National Socialism, Czollek (2018), p 13-4, 33.

63 *Cf* in this regard Werle (1989), p 6-7, 27, 733 ff, who assumes that the criminal law of the NS period was "degenerate" ("entartet") (dominated by police crime fighting) and thus rejects a continuity in the (wider) sense of the rule of law ("there is an unmistakeable break in the historical development" ["Bruch in der historischen Entwicklung un-

in the case of the more recent Bonn Republic, which in its transition to the "Berlin Republic" left the "protected space of the postwar period" and has proven its commitment to the rule of law.[64]

In the following, I hope to be able to confirm the theory of continuity and radicalisation (understood in this narrower sense) by systematically analysing texts by relevant authors. I will focus on the texts themselves, rather than on moral judgements of the men who wrote them, as such judgements are only possible *ex ante* and even then only when the person judging is able to place him- or herself in the situation of the relevant time. Some of the early texts, as we will see below, are veritably bubbling with idealism and occasionally even missionary zeal, associated with the hope for a new (better) criminal law for the new (better) German state.[65] Probably more than just the protagonists' youthful age is at play here,[66] but at least this hopeful fervour explains why even some of those who later adopted a critical stance were themselves euphoric at the beginning.[67] The texts speak for themselves, so that readers can make their own judgements without any need for a conclusive classification or definition[68] of "NS ju-

---

verkennbar"], 734). At least he concedes that (alarmingly) certain concepts were adopted (27), although he refrains from giving any conclusive evaluation, including an answer to the question of continuity (733). Critically regarding Werle insofar Rückert, *KritV* 94 (2001), 240 who, however, does not support the continuity thesis fully (see already fn 51 above *in fine*).

64 *Cf* Krüper, in: Duve/Ruppert (2018), p 238 ff ("Schonraum der Nachkriegszeit").

65 Here, we can already point out Gemmingen's remarkable text of 1933, in which he attempts—without being authorised to do so by the Party (p 6)—to develop a National Socialist criminal law in accordance with Hitler's wishes, warning against a "barbarisation of criminal law that is both nonsensical and counterproductive" ("sinn- und zweckwidrigen Barbarisierung des Strafrechts", p 18) and propagates the "overcoming of criminal law" as a "higher...long-term goal" ("Überwindung des Strafrechts", "höheres... Fernziel", p 18 ff).

66 Although this youthfulness is certainly one reason, see eg Riemer *MSchrKrimPsych* 24 (1933), 223 ("It is no coincidence that precisely the younger generation took an interest in...reaching for absolute authority...The nihilism the younger generation considered so contemptible reflects their own lack of orientation" ["Es ist kein Zufall, daß gerade die junge Generation es sich angelegen sein läßt,...nach einer absoluten Autorität zu greifen...Im Nihilismus, der der jungen Generation so nichtswürdig erscheint, spiegelt sich ihre eigene Desorientiertheit"]).

67 Eb. Schmidt is a paradigmatic example, see in this regard ch V 1. including fn 512 towards the end.

68 For attempts at categorisation, see Marxen (1975), p 152 ff; for an attempt at definition, see Schumann, in: *BMJ* (2013), p 70 ff (according to whom at least the defendants of the Nuremberg Judges' Trial and those convicted of perverting the course of justice fall into this category; however, the Allied classification based on Control Council Directive no. 38 of 12 October 1946, which divides perpetrators into the groups of major offenders, offenders, lesser offenders, and followers, is not reliable, which is why reference needs to

rists".[69] However, it is somewhat surprising that only one of the criminal law scholars in question[70] *publicly* distanced himself from his former teachings.[71]

be made to "nazification and denazification processes" regarding the academic environment ["Nazifizierungs- und Entnazifizierungsvorgänge"]).

69 On the difference between a "Nazi jurist"/"juristic Nazi" ("nazista jurista") (such as Freisler) and a "National Socialist jurist" ("jurista nazista") (such as Schaffstein) Batista, in Zaffaroni (2017), p 103.

70 This is Friedrich Schaffstein, although opinions are divided on the quality of his dissociation, *cf* ch V 1. including fn 517 below. Dahm only admitted that he had made "errors and mistakes" ("Irrtümer und Fehler") in a private letter to Eb. Schmidt, see ch V 1. including fn 512 below. Similarly, Erik Wolf dissociated himself privately in the abovementioned letter to Karl Barth, thereto ch VI 2. including fn 767 below.

71 Vogel (2004), p 109, who otherwise refrains from making any judgement, calls this a "serious failure in scholarly ethics" ("schweres wissenschaftsethisches Versagen").

Chapter II. The Foundations of National Socialist Criminal Law

1. *Racism, Volksgemeinschaft, Führer state, Führer principle and exclusion*

In his introductory chapter, Zaffaroni already emphasises the importance of German criminal law doctrine for Latin America, especially in regard to this doctrine's development between 1933 and 1945.[72] This confirms his book's relevance for German readers in particular. He lists a number of reasons for the success of German criminal law doctrine in Latin America, particularly the rational or at least not completely irrational solutions it offers.[73] At the same time, he warns that any adoption needs to be mindful of this doctrine's history—a history that ininterccludes NS criminal law, which provided the "most intricately refined legitimation" of the Nazis' genocide.[74] This criminal law in turn did not arise from thin air, but was the product of a "racist Europe", radicalising and intensifying the racist perspective[75]—a perspective which, one should add, already dominated 19th-century German colonial history in Africa.[76]

Furthermore, the influence of US immigration and race law must not be underestimated. As recently demonstrated by Whitman, the Nazis recognized America's "historic racist mission" and its "leadership" in the "Aryan struggle for world domination",[77] "American white supremacy…provided…some of the working materials for the Nazism of the 1930s".[78] While the Nazis did not copy the American model unmodified[79]—after all, they primarily targeted Jews, not Negroes, and had their own legal tradition and social context which, for example, did not lend itself to racial segrega-

72 Zaffaroni (2017), p 27 ff.

73 Zaffaroni (2017), p 31 ("innegable capacidad de proporcionar soluciones racionales o, por lo menos, con menores niveles de irracionalidad y arbitrariedad").

74 Zaffaroni (2017), p 31 ("legitimación genocida más finamente elaborado de todos los tiempos").

75 Zaffaroni (2017), p 32.

76 *Cf* Grill (2019), p 57, 58, 63, 70, 97, 147 (with references to NS policy and propaganda); on (German) colonial criminal law as a model, Vormbaum (2015), p 140–1.

77 Whitman (2017), p 71; for a learned review see Rückert, *ZRG-GA* 135 (2018), 669.

78 Whitman (2017), p 145.

79 Ibid., p 70 (no "unmodified borrowing").

tion and made some American measures look overly harsh[80]—the American model clearly served as an inspiration and justification for NS discriminatory and racist policies.[81] This, in turn, gives rise to fundamental questions about America's role "in the larger world history of racism" and "the character of American legal culture"[82] that seem particularly pertinent under President Trump. At any rate, given the influence of the "American model", it is somewhat ironic that it was the US government of the time that, as part of the Allied Control Council and as an occupying power, pushed the most to get the hardcore (racially discriminatory) NS legislation abolished.[83]

Against this background, Zaffaroni is right in situating National Socialism within the historical and political continuity of its time, a continuity that he later also sets out to prove in relation to criminal law doctrine specifically. Here, he already accurately sums up the core of National Socialist thinking: the racist idealisation of the German *Volksgemeinschaft* or "community of the people", drawing on a romanticised and biologistic concept of the Germanic Aryans.[84] He then turns to NS **racism** in its specifically juristic form,[85] emphasising the historical continuities that exist in this regard, too. He sees it as continuing a romanticisation of law that

---

80 Ibid., p 131 ("The bottom line is that the Nazis regarded American classification schemes as too harsh, and the American race problem as too different, for any unmodified borrowing to have taken place"); on the "one-drop rule"—which was too harsh for the Nazis—in particular see ibid, p 77, 128, 135 (this "rule"—according to which "one drop of Negro blood" was enough to lead to racial impurity—was "invented" by southern Senator Bilbo invoking Hitler's *Mein Kampf* [p 77]).

81 Ibid, p 16 ("In the early 1930s, Nazi lawyers were engaged in creating a race law founded on anti-miscegenation law and raced-based immigration, naturalization, and second-class citizenship law. They went looking for foreign models, and found them—in the United States of America."), 139 ("It was American immigration, citizenship, and anit-miscegenation law that the Nazis cited over and over again"), 160 ("America had things to teach Germany: ...an admirably uninhibited racist jurisprudence...that did not trouble itself about juristic niceties and that would therefore 'suit us perfectly' [Freisler]...the US....was the country that produced the really 'interesting' [Freisler] innovations...for anybody in the business of planning a 'race state'").

82 Ibid, p 137.

83 For groundbreaking research in this respect see Etzel (1992), especially p 80 ff; Waibel (1996), p 37 ff (on the foundation of the American policy), 166 ff (on denazification); summarising Kroeschell (1992), p 123 ff; Rückert, *KritV* 94 (2001), 245 ff.; Stolleis (2016), p 250 ff.

84 Zaffaroni (2017), p 37. On the recourse to Germanic criminal law, *cf* eg Dahm (1935a), p 6; on the significance of Germanic legal thought in National Socialism in general, Klippel, in Rückert/Willoweit (1995), p 39 ff (particularly on the alleged contrast to individualistic Roman law). Critically on the recourse to Germanic law as an "irresponsible backward step", however, Gemmingen (1933), p 16–7, as its grounding of punishment in disobedience contravenes the principle of culpability.

85 Zaffaroni (2017), p 41 ff.

culminated in the focus on the German *Volksgemeinschaft* and the German Führer, with the addition of a specifically anti-Semitic component.[86] He places NS racism within the context of the neo-colonial European genocides[87] (overlooking the abovementioned US influence[88]), distinguishing it from the English evolutionary racism of Herbert Spencer, however. According to Spencer—to provide more background to Zaffaroni's somewhat deficient explanation[89]—there was a social evolution (in the sense of a development) in which the stronger, white "race" established itself through social Darwinist selection.[90] By contrast, NS racism was an "involutive" racism à la Arthur de Gobineau,[91] according to which—in marked contrast to evolutionary racism—the racially pure society (the Aryan master race) still needed to be created; accordingly, the German *Volksgemeinschaft* first needed to be cleansed of "impure" elements in the sense of a regression or involution.[92]

Roland Freisler,[93] who was also strongly inspired by the American model,[94] understood the **Volksgemeinschaft** *in terms of race and blood* and made this concept the main foundation of NS criminal law. It is worth-

86 Zaffaroni (2017), p 42 ff, 61 ff.

87 Zaffaroni (2017), p 43.

88 Zaffaroni (2017), p 151 only refers to an article in the *ZStW* that commented positively on a law on sterilisation enacted in the US state of Indiana in 1907 ("artículo elogioso"). This article supposedly met with considerable criticism ("reacción sumamente negativa"), forcing Liszt to distance himself. However, Zaffaroni fails to provide a precise source; nor is one to be found in the work he quotes by Wetzell (2000), p 163. A review of *ZStW* 27 (1907) likewise failed to produce any results.

89 Zaffaroni neither quotes Spencer's writings in his text nor references them in his bibliography.

90 *Cf* in particular Spencer (1864), where he adopts the catchphrase of the "survival of the fittest" from Darwin's *On the Origin of Species* and applies it to sociology and ethics, without however making natural selection in a Darwinian sense the foundation of his social theory. Rather, his social Darwinism was influenced by Lamarckism, that is, the French biologist Jean-Baptiste Lamarck's (complex) theory on the inheritability of certain acquired character traits (thereto Spencer [1851] and *The Westmininster Review* 17 [1860]).

91 Gobineau (1853–1855).

92 Zaffaroni (2017), p 45–6, but here, too, his remarks need to be supplemented. Gobineau's influence on NS racism is controversial, *cf* Kale, *MIH* 7 (2010), 33, 59 ff (according to whom Gobineau was "the first to theorize that race was the deciding factor in history and the precursors of Nazism repeated some of his ideas, but his principle arguments were either ignored, deformed, or taken out of context in German racial thought", so that "Gobineau's influence on German racism has been repeatedly overstated").

93 On Freisler's reception abroad, see for example Arnedo, in Zaffaroni (2017), p 9 ff (including an account of Freisler's career and his criminal law theory).

94 This follows particularly from the debates within the Criminal Law Reform Commission headed by Reich Minister of Justice Franz Gürtner (see Gürtner, 1934 and 1935), as documented in the transcript reproduced in Regge and Schubert (1989), p 223 ff (37th

Figure 4: Roland Freisler

while noting in that regard, however, that the *Volksgemeinschaft* has its roots in the concept of "community" ("Gemeinschaft") which has a long

session, 5 June 1934) (unedited version p 277 ff). In this meeting, Gürtner, Freisler and others, when discussing the topic of "*Rasseschutz*" ("race protection"), referred in considerable detail to the American legislation and practice; they also referred, mostly approvingly, to the Prussian Memorandum's proposals of offences regarding "attacks on the race" ("Angriffe auf die Rasse") (Preußischer Justizminister, 1933, p 47–9) which itself referred to the American race legislation several times (ibid, eg p 48, 62, 143). See also Whitman (2017), p 1–2, 93 ff, who concludes regarding the 5 June meeting that "the participants clearly took a serious interest in what they could learn from the laws of the American states, and…the American example was pushed hardest by the radical faction" (p 112); on the Prussian Memorandum insofar ibid, p 76, 83 ff.

tradition in German thinking and was made a main building block of NS legal policy and science.[95] The Nazis invoked the *Volksgemeinschaft* in an inflationary fashion, increasingly displacing the original idea of *Gemeinschaft*.[96] German (Aryan, Nordic) thinking was framed in a propagandistic manner as organic, concrete, life- and people-based and so forth and contrasted with "Roman-Jewish" thinking as liberal, rational, positivist, abstract-conceptual, individualistic and so on.[97] We will return to these opposing qualifiers throughout the text. According to Freisler, the NS criminal law "mirrors the spiritual attitude of the people" ("ein Spiegelbild der seelischen Haltung des Volkes"), it serves to "protect the people themselves, their community of blood and fate",[98] their "racial honour",[99] which is why "keeping foreign blood at bay and eliminating degenerate blood" are the "highest imperative"[100] and corresponding "measures to safeguard the survival of the people need to be taken".[101] The Nuremberg "Law on the Protection of German Blood and German Honor" ("*Gesetz zum Schutz des deutschen Blutes und der deutschen Ehre*")[102] was perhaps the most drastic legal measure in this regard. Similarly, the state—as the peo-

95 *Cf* Stolleis (2016), p 94 ff.

96 Ibid, p 115–6 (with legislative examples).

97 Ibid, p 114.

98 Freisler, in Preußischer Justizminister (1933), p 6 ("Schutz des Volkes selbst, seiner Bluts- und Schicksalsgemeinschaft"); also see Freisler, in Frank (1934), p 7–8 ("blood-based guiding ideas" as the "precondition for rising or falling within the life of the people" ["bluthafte Gestaltung der richtunggebenden Ideen", "Vorbedingung für Auf- oder Abstieg im Volksleben"]) and 8 (protection of "blood and soil" ["Blut und Boden"]); Thierack, in Frank (1934), p 25–6 ("Blood and soil as the sacred goods of the German people" ["Blut und Boden als heilige Güter des deutschen Volkes"], "blood" as the "source of life" creating a "community of blood" ["Blut", "Lebensquell", "Blutsgemeinschaft"]); on the law as "expressing the thought of a blood-based community" ("Ausdruck eines bluthaften Gemeinschaftsdenkens"), see Dahm (1935a), p 17.

99 Thierack, in Frank (1934), p 26 ("Rassenehre"; "racial purity requires racial consciousness, racial pride" ["Rassereinheit fordert Rassebewußtsein, Rassestolz"] and protection under criminal law).

100 Freisler, in Frank (1934), p 8 ("Fernhalten fremden Blutes und Ausschaltung entarteten Blutes...höchstes Gebot"); similarly Preußischer Justizminister (1933), p 22 ("keeping the German blood community pure" ["Reinhaltung der deutschen Blutsgemeinschaft"]); Thierack, in Frank (1934), p 26 ("foreign blood is to be kept at bay, hereditarily defective..., degenerate...and polluted [blood]...must be eradicated" ["Artfremdes Blut ist fernzuhalten, erbrankes..., entartetes...oder verseuchtes...ist auszumerzen"]).

101 Freisler, in Frank (1934), p 8 ("Maßnahmen zur Sicherung des Volksbestandes zu treffen"). He mentions the "fight against abortion, girl trafficking, the protection of motherhood" ("Kampf gegen Abtreibung, Mädchenhandel, Schutz der Mutterschaft"). Similarly Thierack, in Frank (1934), p 26.

102 RGBl I 1146.

ple's "external form"—and the NS movement (NSDAP)—as "bearer of the idea of the state"— must be protected.[103]

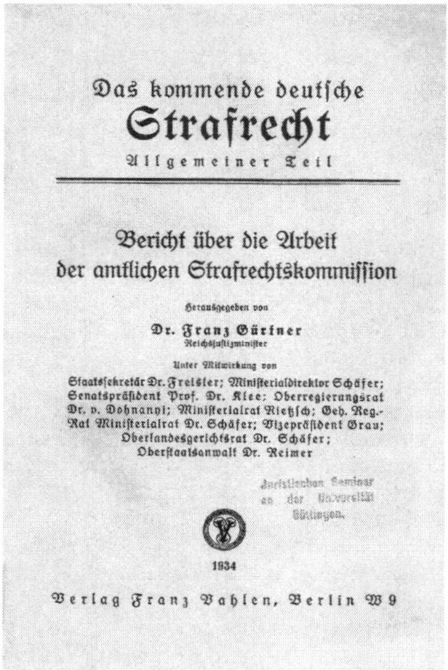

Figure 5: The Report on the work of the official Criminal Law Commission, headed by Reich Minister of Justice Gürtner, volume I on the General Part (Gürtner, 1934; vol. II on the Special Part was published in 1935)

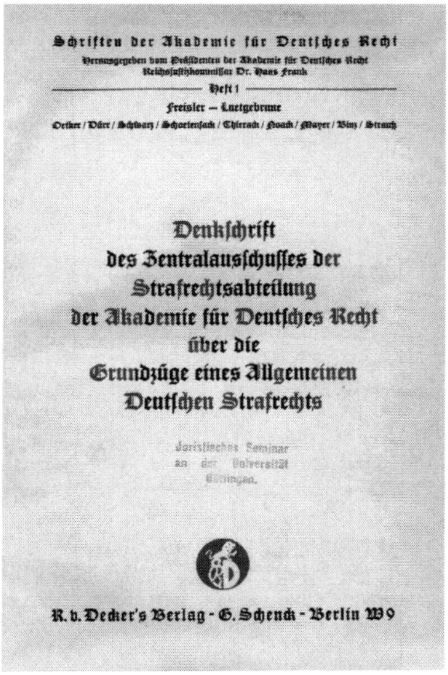

Figure 6: Memorandum of the Central Committee of the Criminal Law Section of the (NS) Academy for German Law on the Main Features of German Criminal Law (Frank, 1934)

103 Freisler, in Frank (1934), p 8 f ("äußere Form", "Trägerin des Staatsgedankens"). The NSDAP is "inextricably bound up with the state" ("unlöslich mit dem Staat verbunden"), but "by no means an organ of the state" ("keineswegs Staatsorgan"). The Memorandum of the Preußischer Justizminister (1933), p 13 ff took account of this increased protection of the state by starting with crimes against the state. This had been one of the main demands of the anti-liberal movement, *cf* Marxen (1975), p 124–5.

Helmut Nicolai attempted to underpin NS racial doctrine in vulgar philosophical terms[104] and (rather astonishingly) was applauded for doing so by Erik Wolf.[105] Nicolai sees the crime rate as dependent upon ethnicity and thus wants to direct criminal law against those who do not belong to the Nordic and Germanic population.[106] We can see here that National Socialism instrumentalised—certainly existing[107]—earlier criminological approaches based upon criminal biology and social Darwinism[108] in an at-

---

104 Nicolai (1932), p 42 ff (crime as a hereditary disposition, requiring "outlawing", that is, "excluding the criminal from the legal confraternity of the people, thus also making it impossible for him to procreate within it" ["Friedloslegung", "Ausschluß des Verbrechers aus der Rechtsgenossenschaft des Volkes, damit auch die Unmöglichkeit sich in dieser fortzupflanzen"]; "only he whose legal conscience is unadulterated can be a bearer of rights, a member of the legal community, a member of the ethnic community" ["Rechtsträger, Rechtsgenosse, Volksgenosse kann eben nur der sein, dessen Rechtsgewissen…unverfälscht ist"]; "eradication of dishonourable criminals" by a strict criminal law, as "humane" criminal law does not indicate "a high cultural status" ["Ausmerzung ehrloser Verbrecher", "humanes", "hohen Kulturzustand"]). On Nicolai's NS attitude, see Marxen (1975), p 90–1, 147 ff, 153; on his persecution in 1935 for alleged homosexuality Whitman (2017), p 74. On NS racial theory, also *cf* Hartl (2000), p 42–3 (for whom anti-Semitism forms its main centre).

105 Wolf not only included the text in the highly regarded *ZStW* literary review "Rechts- und Staatsphilosophie" (*ZStW* 53 (1934), 560, 572 ff) and thus put it on an equal footing with a series of significant contemporary legal-philosophical writings, but even praised it as a "bold and unbiased" ("unbefangen und unerschrocken") account of the NS idea of law and as the "beginning of National Socialist legal doctrine" ("Anfang nationalsozialistischer Rechtslehre"), containing merely some "unevenness", as "was inevitable" ("Unausgeglichenheiten", "nicht anders sein kann", 573–4; on selected criticisms of Nicolai's racial theory, see fn *in fine* below). Von Hentig, *MSchrKrimPsych* 24 (1933), 633 gives a similarly positive evaluation ("honest, well thought out, does justice to the system, and is...worth reading" ["ehrlich, durchdacht, systemgerecht und… lesenswert"]).

106 Nicolai (1932), p 43 (according to whom "crime rates show that criminality is lower the more Nordic and Germanic the population" ["die Kriminalität zeigt, daß die Straffälligkeit umso geringer ist, je nordischer und germanischer eine Bevölkerung ist"]); thereto also Zaffaroni (2017), p 147.

107 On such criminal biological and anthropological research during the *fin de siècle* and the Weimar Republic, Dölling, in: Dreier/Sellert (1989), p 195-6, 222-3; Vormbaum (2015), p 155 ff; Hilliger (2018), p 293 ff; also Ambos, in Dessecker et al (2019), p ##; earlier Wolf (1933), p 13 ff (referring in particular to the Italian positivists).

108 *Cf* eg Exner (1939), p 149 ff (significance of "genetic makeup" and "criminal predisposition" ["Erbgut", "Verbrecheranlage"]); also id (1949), p 272 ff (recognising environmental influence, but emphasising the particular importance of "predisposition" and "genetic makeup" ["Anlage", "Erbguts"]; Mezger (1934), p 18 (rejecting Lombroso's theory of the "born criminal", but recognising that there are "undeniably human beings who are destined to become criminals because of their innate predisposition" ["geborenen Verbrechers", "unleugbar Menschen, die vermöge ihrer angeborenen Anlage zum Verbrecher bestimmt sind"]), 54 (the particularly "pathological predisposition" of the "psychopathic criminal" ["krankhafte Veranlagung", "psychopathische Verbrecher"] that makes him particularly dangerous) 104 ff (emphasising "ancestral genetic

tempt to justify criminal law's discrimination against "foreign" elements[109] through racial biology;[110] however, the support provided by criminological research was limited.[111]

makeup" ["Erbgut der Ahnen"] within the context of a biologistic understanding of crime); on the biologistic view and (consequently) prevention of genetically defective children also Mezger (1942), p 79 ff, 269 ff; also see Dölling, in: Dreier/Sellert (1989), p 198, 202, 209. We should not overlook the fact that both Exner and Mezger in principle acknowledged a more complex interplay between predisposition and environment and thus rejected the crude genetic and racial determinism of Nazi ideologues such as Robert Ritter; see fn below; for a more detailed analysis see Ambos, in Dessecker et al (2019), p ##. On the impact of the US eugenics movement in this regard, see Whitman (2017), p 8–9 (referring in particular to Kühl's *The Nazi Connection*, 1994).

109 For a detailed account of the so-called *Fremdvolkstrafrechte* or "criminal laws for foreign peoples" (eg the *Polenstrafrecht*, the criminal law for Poles) and the special criminal law for Jews, *cf* Werle (1989), p 351 ff, 449 ff, 603 ff, 698 ff, 723–4, 725–6.

110 A one-sided emphasis on predisposition eg in Dahm, *MSchrKrimPsych* 24 (1933), 162, 172 ff, 176; Schaffstein (1934), p 19 ("superiority" of the NS "idea of race" due to "genetic dissimilarity" ["Überlegenheit", "Rassenidee", "erbbiologische Ungleichheit"]); Schaffstein, *ZStW* 55 (1936), 276, 282 ff (both passages criticise the overemphasis placed upon the idea of education and demand that "those impossible to educate" ["Unerziehbarer"] be neutralised). Also see Werle (1989), p 698, 700; Zaffaroni, in Zaffaroni (2009a), p 15 (NS perfects racist biologism).

111 *Cf* in greater detail Wetzell (2000), p 179 ff, whose analysis of writings by relevant authors proves that while NS needed research in criminal biology to underpin its eugenic-biologistic views, mainstream criminologists such as Mezger and Exner (ibid, p 209 ff) only provided limited support, as "genetically deterministic and racist explanations of crime did not predominate in criminal biology and criminology" and "mainstream criminology…was characterized by a continuing process of increasing methodological sophistication" (ibid, p 230). Then again, Nazi selection policy based on criminal biology found an advocate in Gustav Aschaffenburg, the founder and editor of the *Monatsschrift für Kriminalpsychologie und Strafrechtsreform* (today's *MSchrKrim*), whom the Nazis forced out of Germany because of his Jewish faith (186 ff); furthermore, jurists such as Helmuth Mayer criticised criminal-biological research (p 202 ff), meaning that neither a connection between "criminal biology and racism (including anti-Semitism)" (p 187) nor "a natural affinity between Nazi jurists and criminal biology" should be assumed (p 209); critically on Ritter and his research on "antisocials", especially gypsies, p 219 ff ("simplistic and methodologically backward quality of Ritter's research that accelerated his career in the Third Reich" [p 229]). However, Wetzell takes an overly positive view of Mezger; for more detail on Mezger, see ch IV 1. including fn 291 ff and main text below; for a more nuanced view on the role of German criminology during the NS regime see Ambos, in Dessecker et al (2019), p ##. – Arguing in favour of an interplay between predisposition and environment eg Wolf, *ZStW* 53 (1934), 573–4 (criticising Nicolai's pure, race-based predisposition theory in this regard); Gemmingen (1933), p 14 ff, is also surprisingly differentiated, claiming that Hitler himself emphasised the importance of the "milieu factor" ("Milieufaktors") and was thus certainly against any one-sided emphasis on predisposition.

Figure 7: Nicolai's Racist Legal Theory, 1932

Figure 8: Mezger's influential textbook on "Criminal Policy", first published in 1934 (our picture), the 2nd edition following in 1942; in 1931 Mezger also published a very influential textbook on criminal law, of which several editions appeared over the following years

In any case, the significance of this concept of the *Volksgemeinschaft*—understood as a community of race and blood—cannot be overstated: it forms the starting point and the purpose of National Socialist (criminal) law,[112] the main object it aims to protect[113] (ie keep "pure"),[114] especially

112 Zaffaroni (2017), p 72 ff. Also *cf* eg Gemmingen (1933), p 14, according to whom Hitler's "comprehensive goal" ("umfassende Ziel") was "educating the (liberalistically and atomistically conceived) society to become an (organically and ethnically conceived) community, that is, a *Volk* or 'people'" ("die Erziehung der (liberalistisch-atomistisch gedachten) Gesellschaft zur (organisch-völkisch gedachten) Gemeinschaft, also zum 'Volk'"). For a more recent summary *cf* Hartl (2000), p 43 ff.

113 *Cf* Preußischer Justizminister (1933), p 13 (where the protection of the *Volksgemeinschaft* comes right at the beginning of a possible new criminal code); on the relevant NS decrees/laws to protect the German people, state etc Werle (1989), p 64 ff, 700 ff.

114 *Cf* fn 100 above and the following section (2.) including fn 232.

by way of the infamous "Nuremberg Laws".[115] The concept of the *Volksgemeinschaft* further serves as the normative point of reference of any (criminal) law,[116] and even a source of law by way of the infamous concept of "*gesundes Volksempfinden*" ("healthy sentiment of the people").[117] Both the individual and the state are placed in the service of the *Volksgemeinschaft*. This deprives individuals of their status as ends in themselves[118] (and per-

115 Strictly speaking the "Nuremberg Laws" encompass the two laws adopted at the Nuremberg "Party Rally of Freedom" ("Reichsparteitag der Freiheit") on 15 September 1935, ie, the abovementioned "Blood and Honour Protection Law" (fn 102 above) and the *Reichsbürgergesetz* (Reich Citizenship Law, RGBl I 1146); thereto and on the influence of US immigration, naturalization and race legislation in this regard Whitman (2017), p 1–2, 29 ff, 73 ff (no "unmodified borrowing" but support for more radical Nazis [see already the quote in fn 94 above] and "obvious preeminent example of a 'race state'" [p 113]).

116 *Cf* eg Schaffstein, *ZStW* 53 (1934), 603, 624 ("For the National Socialist understanding of the state and the law, the people as a transpersonal whole constitute the highest and indeed only direct value, from which all other legal values arise indirectly" ["Für die nationalsozialistische Staats- und Rechtsauffassung ist das Volk als transpersonale Ganzheit höchster und einziger unmittelbarer Wert, aus dem sich alle anderen Rechtswerte mittelbar ergeben"]). Zaffaroni does not quote this article.

117 *Cf* Freisler, in Frank (1934), p 11 ("the people's consciousness of justice" as the "legal norm" ["Rechtsbewußtsein des Volkes", "Rechtsnorm"]); Freisler, *DJ* 97 (1935), 1251 (healthy sentiment of the people as the source of NS law); Schaffstein (1934), p 24 ("true source of law" ["wahre Rechtsquelle"], quoting the Memorandum of the Preußische Justizminister [1933]); Schaffstein, *ZStW* 53 (1934), 605, 607 ("the people's sense of justice" ["völkische Rechtsempfinden"] as the source of NS law); Henkel (1934b), p 28–9 ("values of the *Volksgemeinschaft*" as the "source of legal insight" ["Wertanschauungen der Volksgemeinschaft", "Rechtserkenntnisquelle"]); Mezger, *DJZ* 41 (1936), 602 ("healthy sentiment of the people" as an "independent form of expression of the living legal and moral order of the people", albeit supported by the "fundamental idea of a criminal law", that is, the first point of reference of the changed § 2 StGB ["gesundes Volksempfinden", "selbständige Äußerungsform der lebendigen völkischen Rechts- und Sittenordnung", "Grundgedanken eines Strafgesetzes"]). Also see Marxen (1975), p 70–1; Rückert, *ZRG-GA* 103 (1986), 222–3 (listing, at 214 ff, various NS sources [norms, case law, writers] where the concept was invoked); Werle (1989), p 145; Hartl (2000), p 54; Zaffaroni (2017), p 78 ff. – The *gesunde Volksempfinden* also served to define numerous individual issues of criminal theory, eg on omission *cf* ch V 4. including fn 580; on the irrelevance of mistakes of law when these cannot be reconciled with "healthy popular opinion on what is lawful and unlawful" ("gesunden Volksanschauung über Recht und Unrecht") ch IV 1. including fn 315 and main text below; on restrictions to the law on self-defence, Preußischer Justizminister (1933), p 137 and Freisler, in Frank (1934), p 17 (abuse of self-defence law "according to healthy popular opinion" ["nach gesunder Volksanschauung"]); many further examples can be found there.

118 *Cf* eg Preußischer Justizminister (1933), p 4–5 (the individual as part of the "organism of the people" ["Volksorganismus"], which is why he must be forced "to make the necessary allowances for the preservation of the nation and its wellbeing in all his actions" ["bei all seinem Handeln die notwendige Rücksicht auf die Erhaltung des Bestandes der Nation und ihre Wohles zu nehmen"]); Freisler, in Frank (1934), p 9 ("the individ-

haps even of their class identity),[119] binding them to loyalty;[120] at the same time, the state—overcoming the traditional separation between people and state—becomes a unique fascist state.[121]

This brings us to the **institutionalisation of the NS state**,[122] which focused upon realising the abovementioned *Volksgemeinschaft*. Here, Zaffaroni quotes at length from a famous speech given by Göring at the Academy for German Law in 1935,[123] where he emphasised that the NS state was not an end in itself, but a means to an end, the end of realising the "ho-

---

ual holds the position of custodian of the whole" ["Treuhänderstellung des Einzelnen in Bezug auf die Gesamtheit"]); similarly Thierack, in Frank (1934), p 28; also Gerland, *DJZ* 38 (1933), 860 ("Before the community, the individual only means as much as he means for it" ["Vor der Gemeinschaft bedeutet der Einzelne nur so viel, als er für sie bedeutet"]); Dahm (1935a), p 12 (individual as a "member of the *Volk*, as member of a concrete community" ["Volksgenosse, als Glied einer konkreten Gemeinschaft"]); for an non-criminal law author see Lange (1934), p 34 ("You are nothing, your people is everything" ["Du bist nichts, dein Volk ist alles"], "common good comes before self-interest" ["Gemeinnutz geht vor Eigennutz"]); thereto also eg Alexy, in: Säcker (1992), p 225 f; Hoyer, *GS Eckert* (2008), p 353 ("supremacy of the collective" ["Suprematie des Kollektivs"]); Rüping/Jerouschek (2011), p 98; on anti-individualism, anti-liberalism and community-related thinking, also Hartl (2000), p 47 ff; Murmann (2005), p 126 ff. – However, in 1933 Dahm was still of the opinion that "no German criminal law matching the idiosyncracy of our differentiated culture is conceivable that does not leave scope for the individual" ("kein deutsches, der Eigenart unserer differenzierten Kultur entsprechendes Strafrecht denkbar, das nicht dem Einzelnen Spielraum ließe", Dahm, *MSchrKrimPsych* 24 (1933), 162, 174).

119 Cf Hartung (1971), p 120–1 (arguing that the concept of *Volksgemeinschaft* removed to a great extent the discrimination of the lowest "fourth estate" ["vierten Standes"]).

120 Thierack, in Frank (1934), p 27 ("duty of loyalty towards the Führer, people and state" ["Treuepflicht gegenüber Führer, Volk und Staat"], loyalty as the "noblest German patrimony" ["vornehmstes deutsches Erbgut"]).

121 On the difference between NS Germany and fascist Italy in this regard, *cf* Dahm (1935a), p 6 ff, according to whom in the former the *Volksgemeinschaft* is the main focus and the state is to serve its purpose, while in the latter the nation is realised in the total state, which is why there is a "pronounced statism" ("ausgeprägter Etatismus", p 6) (similarly Grispigni [1941a], in Zaffaroni [2009a], p 70 including fn 12 [replacement of the "state" by the "people"]). By contrast, in the NS state there can be at most a total mobilisation in the sense of Jünger, but no total state, as the state is both "founded on and justified by nationhood" ("seine Grundlage und Rechtfertigung im Volkstum") (Dahm, 1935a, p 7). While Germans and Italians have different natures in any case, this implies a further "profound difference in character" ("tiefgreifenden Wesensunterschied", p 7). On the difference also *cf* Gúzman D., in Zaffaroni (2017), p 89 ("visión sustancialista" [NS] versus "supraindividual"); on the difference concerning the replacement of the "state" by the "people", also *cf* Grispigni (1941a), in Zaffaroni (2009a), p 70 including fn 12; Rückert, *ZRG-GA* 103 (1986), 206; id, *JZ* 2015, 797 (state less "völkisch").

122 Zaffaroni (2017), p 85 ff (ch 3).

123 Göring (1935).

mogenous" ("artgleich") *Volksgemeinschaft*.[124] Göring propagated the superiority of the Aryan race and of its Nordic-Germanic law over the people of the "South Seas", who were unable to understand this law and whose law in turn "we do not understand and reject".[125] Zaffaroni claims that this discrimination is directed not against Latin America, but against Italy.[126] This is doubtful, however. For one, discrimination against "South Sea islanders" was an expression of the colonial ("civilised") legal thinking directed against the "new world" that was prevalent at the time and is still occasionally found today. For another, Italian fascism served as a model for National Socialism in many regards.[127]

The *Volksgemeinschaft*, as the pivotal point around which the National Socialist project revolved, thus also forms the centre of Zaffaroni's subsequent reflections: he rightly emphasises several times that this "community of the people" was not an entity that existed *a priori*, but was a National Socialist *political project* that had yet to be realised.[128] And its realisation needed to be enforced through criminal law, for if a homogenous *Volksgemeinschaft* had already existed, this enforcement would have been completely unnecessary, as the "*Volksgenossen*" (Larenz, more thereto below), the ethnically homogenised members of the people, would have lived to-

124 Göring (1935), p 6 ("The Führer created the state for the people...Therefore our state is not a means in itself, but a means to an end" ["Unseren Staat hat der Führer für das Volk geschaffen...Unser Staat ist daher nicht Selbstzweck, sondern Mittel zum Zweck"]); thereto Zaffaroni (2017), p 85 f. Similarly Preußischer Justizminister (1933), p 4.

125 Göring (1935), p 13 ("And therefore those of the same blood and kind have their law and understand it. Down in the South Seas, you probably will not find anyone able to understand Nordic-Germanic law. The concept of the law understood there, that which every individual sees as eternal law, we do not understand and reject" ["Und darum haben die Blut- und Artgleichen ihr Recht und verstehen es. Sie werden vielleicht unten in der Südsee keinen Menschen finden, der nordisch-germanisches Recht verstünde. Das, was dort als Rechtsbegriff von jedem einzelnen aufgefaßt wird und als ewiges Recht gilt, wird von uns nicht verstanden und zurückgewiesen"]).

126 Zaffaroni (2017), p 86, 96.

127 Hitler admired Mussolini (thereto Nolte [1963], p 32-3, 50, 55, 291), and numerous Nazi symbols have their origins in Italian fascism (such as the Nazi salute, which is modelled on the "Roman salute", and the "Roman" standards of the NSDAP units; on the Roman Empire as a model ibid, p 500; on the similarities and differences between NS and Italian fascism ibid, p 343 f); on the punishability of the "Roman salute" as compared to § 86a StGB recently Caroli, *JJZ* 19 (2019), p 48 ff). Despite emphasising the differences elsewhere (fn 121 above), Dahm/Schaffstein cited Italian fascism as an example of the "nationalist and total understanding of the state" ("nationalen und totalen Staatsauffassung", see ch V 2. including fn 535 and main text below). In this sense also Grispigni (1941a), in Zaffaroni (2009a), p 70 including fn 12 ("doctrinas...completamente análogas").

128 See eg Zaffaroni (2017), p 128 ("no era más, que un proyecto politico para imponer"), 293 ("programa político por realizar o en vías de realización").

gether in perfect harmony and accepted the National Socialists' claim to leadership without further ado.[129] During his discussion of the *Volksgemeinschaft*, Zaffaroni—somewhat surprisingly—at several points refers to the "systemic conception of society" inherent in this idea of the "community of the people".[130] However, he sees this systemic conception in more organic terms, as an "ant society" ("sociedad hormiguero") in the sense defined by the Dominican monk Johannes Nider[131] and not in the sense of sociological systems theory. Zaffaroni finally states explicitly: "The *Volksgemeinschaft* was a systemic concept, but not a simple systemic sociology, from which it must be clearly differentiated."[132] Ultimately, Zaffaroni thus understands "systemic" in the sense of an "organic conception of society".[133] However, we should not overlook the fact that National Socialism understood *Volk* and *Volksgemeinschaft* as the antithesis of the systemic concept of society defined above.[134] The concept of the *Volk* "constituted the state to the same degree that it destroyed the individual".[135]

In parallel, those citizens who did not belong to the "Aryan *Volksgemeinschaft*" were **depersonalised** and thus *deprived of their rights*.[136] In this regard, Zaffaroni makes accurate reference to the justifications formulated by Karl Larenz—which consciously rejected the "subjective-ethical individualism of late natural law"[137] and embraced "law as a form of life of the *Volksgemeinschaft*"[138]—for restricting full participation in legal relations to "*Volksgenossen*", as only they were members of the German people and of

---

129 Zaffaroni (2017), p 127–8 ("si la sociedad estaba tan integrada éticamente como se pretendía, no se explica por qué fueron necesarias leyes penales tan draconianas y extremas y un ejercicio de poder punitive tan fuertemente verticalizador").

130 Zaffaroni (2017), p 72, 78, 80–1, 214–5, 217, 290, 302.

131 Nider (1473); thereto Zaffaroni (2017), p 37 ff.

132 Zaffaroni (2017), p 290 ("La *comunidad del pueblo* era un concepto sistemico, pero no una simple sociología sistémica, de la cual se la debe distinguir cuidadosamente" [Translation K.A., italics in the original]).

133 Zaffaroni (2017), p 291 ("concepción orgánica de la sociedad").

134 *Cf* Freisler, *DJZ* 97 (1935), 1247, 1248 (organic concept of society); as a secondary source Rüping (1989), p 180; Murmann (2005), p 129 ff.

135 Murmann (2005), p 130 ("für den Staat ebenso konstitutiv wie er für den Einzelnen vernichtend").

136 Zaffaroni (2017), p 97 ff. On "Entrechtlichung" as one of the NS strategies, see also recently Gusy, *ZDRW* 1 (2019), 8.

137 Larenz, in Dahm et al (1935), p 225, 228 ("subjektiv-ethischen Individualismus des späten Naturrechts"). On the combatting of subjective law, drawing upon Germanic law (whose orientation was supposedly social and communal, in contrast to the supposedly individualistic Roman law) Klippel, in Rückert/Willoweit (1995), p 39 ff (49 ff); Luig, in Rückert/Willoweit (1995), p 95 ff. On recoursing to Germanic criminal law to justify the idea of the community, Dahm (1935a), p 6.

138 Larenz, in Dahm et al (1935), p 238–9 ("Recht als Lebensform der Volksgemeinschaft"). Here, the significance of "*völkisch* legal thinking" ("völkisches Rechtsdenken")

German blood and thus could be recognised as full members of the legal community, full "legal persons" ("*Rechtsgenossen*").[139] This of course meant that only *Volksgenossen* had full duties towards the *Volksgemeinschaft* and Führer—ultimately, they no longer had rights, only duties.[140]

In this model, the **role of judges**, too, was to serve the *Volksgemeinschaft* and thus the Führer; accordingly, their task was not to independently restrict the new state's punitive powers, but—as National Socialist leaders

---

and the thinking in "concrete and general basic concepts" ("konkret-allgemeinen Grundbegriffen") (kaB)—based upon Schmitt's "thinking in terms of (social) order" ("*Ordnungsdenken*") (fn 339 below)—becomes clear, *cf* Larenz (1933), p 9, 43 ff, 52. In National Socialism's shaping of social reality in line with the racist definition of the *Volksgemeinschaft*, the function of this thinking lay in the "*völkisch* renewal of the law" ("völkischen Rechtserneuerung") through conceptual change; thereto Rüthers (1989), p 58–9, 76 ff, 95 ff including further references; on "law as the right of the real life" ["Recht als Lebensrecht"] and concrete *Ordnungsdenken* from the perspective of legal history, Rückert, in Rückert/Willoweit (1995), p 177 ff (concluding that NS law abandoned "the old legal source theory's liberal framework oriented towards the rule of law" ["den rechtsstaatlich liberalen Rahmen der alten Rechtsquellenlehre"] and openly propagated "the respective concrete order's permanent access to all areas of life" ["den permanenten Lebensdurchgriff in die jeweilige konkrete Ordnung"], p 234–5); also Rückert, in id (2018a), p 274 ff (on Schmitt and Larenz).

139 Larenz (1935), p 241 ("Only those who are members of the community of the people can be members of the legal community; and only those of German blood are members of the community of the people" ["Rechtsgenosse ist nur, wer Volksgenosse ist; Volksgenosse ist, wer deutschen Blutes ist"]). This aimed to replace § 1 BGB (German Civil Code), which recognised that "every human being" possessed legal capacity (ibid). According to Larenz, foreigners outside the *Volksgemeinschaft* only enjoy a "limited legal capacity" ("beschränkte Rechtsfähigkeit") granted to them by the *Volksgemeinschaft* and are "regarded as guests" ("als Gast geachtet", p 241–2). From here, it is only a small step to depriving Jewish citizens and other citizens regarded as non-Aryan of their rights, for more detail *cf* Rüthers (1989), p 88 ff (91: "instrument to revoke rights linked to citizenship" ["Instrument zur Aberkennung staatsbürgerlicher Rechte"]); in greater detail on Larenz's career and criminal theory, Schild, in Asholt et al (2014), p 122 ff (even though Larenz was a member of numerous NS associations, he was no "crown jurist" of the Third Reich, as he was "largely ineffective" ["weitgehend wirkungslos", 126]), 128 ff (complex relationship to Hegel's philosophy), 142 ff (Larenz's criminal theory is oriented towards the "way of life of the *Volksgenossen*" ["Lebensordnung der Volksgenossen"]—as "members of the same race" ["Rassegenossen"]—and understands crime as "unlawful under the law of the community" ["Gemeinschaftsrechtswidrigkeit"], leading to the offender's exclusion from the community and the loss of his honour; "building upon the…life of the people, understood in terms of race and fate, in which those foreign to the race have no legal status and indeed cannot have any legal status" ["auf ein…Leben eines rassistisch und schicksalhaft aufgefassten Volkes aufgebaut, in der die Rassefremden keinerlei Rechtsstellung haben und haben können", 153]).

140 Zaffaroni (2017), p 101.

themselves[141]—to act with the goal of implementing the Nazi state,[142] only to the detriment of the alleged criminals, of course.[143] More concretely, in line with the guidelines formulated by Dahm et al,[144] the judge, as a "member of the living community of the German people" ("Glied in der lebendigen Gemeinschaft des deutschen Volkes"), has "to preserve the concrete order of the *völkisch* community, eradicate harmful elements, punish anti-communal conduct" ("die konkrete völkische Gemeinschaftsordnung zu wahren, Schädlinge auszumerzen, gemeinschaftswidriges Verhalten zu ahnden"). And this is to be done based on the "National Socialist *Weltanschauung*" as expressed in the program of the party (itself a legal source)[145] and the declarations of the *Führer*, whose decisions can never be challenged ("kein Prüfungsrecht").[146] Norms preceding the "National Socialist revolution" "must not be applied" if they "would fly in the face of the current healthy sentiment of the people".[147] Ironically, these guidelines end with a call for the "independence" ("Unabhängigkeit") of judges and their freedom from instructions ("nicht an Weisungen gebunden"),[148] blatantly ignoring the regime's multiple interferences with the administration of

141 *Cf* Vormbaum (2015), p 205 ff.

142 *Cf* eg Siegert (1934), p 19, according to whom, if there is no law or customary law concerning the matter at hand, the judge must "act in the spirit of the people and the leadership" ("im Geist des Volkes und der Führung zu handeln"); similarly Gürtner (1936), p 11 f (judges should "fill the remaining gaps" by drawing upon "the requirements of the life of the people" and the Führer principle ["Ausfüllung verbliebener Lücken", "die Forderungen des völkischen Lebens"]). On Hitler as "judge" ("Gerichtsherr") and the resulting judicial orientation towards the will of the Führer ("enfeoffment" ["Belehnung"]) and its unconditional implementation, Werle (1989), p 19 ff, 151, 270 ff, 577 ff, 602, 682, 690–1, 692 ff, 715; also see Rüping (1989), p 182; Maus (1989), p 88 ff; Hartl (2000), p 53 ff, 262 ff; Rückert, *JZ* 2015, 804; Zaffaroni (2017), p 101 ff; Arnedo, in Zaffaroni (2017), p 63 ff.

143 *Cf* eg Dahm, *DStR* 80 (1934), 88, where he expresses concern in regard to the "expansion of judicial discretion" ("Erweiterung des richterlichen Ermessens") concerning the grounds for ruling out unlawfulness and culpability, because the effects of this "one-sidedly favour the perpetrator" ("einseitig zugunsten des Täters auswirke").

144 Dahm et al, *DRWis* 1 (1936), 123–4; thereto Rüping (1989), p 182.

145 Thus, the party program appears as legal text no. 1, even before the Weimar Constitution, in the leading collection of legal texts called "Schönfelder" published by C.H. Beck; cf Rückert, *JZ* 2015, 801.

146 The judge is bound by any decision of the Führer which has been "unambiguously" ("unzweideutig") issued with a view to "set the law" ("Recht zu setzen") (Dahm et al, *DRWis* 1 (1936), 124).

147 Ibid ("…dürfen nicht angewandt werden, wenn ihre Anwendung dem heutigen gesunden Volksempfinden ins Gesicht schlagen würde").

148 Ibid.

justice[149] and its detailed directives, for example by way of the infamous "Judges' Letters" (*Richterbriefe*) published by the Reich Ministry of Justice from 1942 onwards.[150] At any rate, the judges had a broad power to (re-)interpret the law or even bring it into line with the NS-*Weltanschauung*[151]—indeed, it served as an interpretative guideline for all judicial actors (*Rechtswahrer*)[152]—and many judges took this new, active role seriously and contributed to the implementation of the NS project.[153] In this sense, there is some truth to the famous, albeit somewhat overstated *dictum* of the Nuremberg Jurists' trial—"[T]he dagger of the assassin was concealed beneath the robe of the jurist"[154]—and the judiciary cannot, contrary to Eberhard Schmidt,[155] be fully exonerated, attributing all responsibility to

---

149 From an inside perspective, see Hartung (1971), p 107 ff (recalling, *inter alia*, Hitler's direct attack on the independence of the judiciary in his infamous speech of 26 April 1942 at the "*Großdeutschen Reichstage*" ["Greater German Diet"]).

150 See Maus (1989), p 90; Kroeschell (1992), p 113–4; Rüping/Jerouschek (2011), p 105.

151 *Cf* the fundamental work of Rüthers on the "unlimited interpretation" (1968/2017, p 175–6; also id, 2017, p 47, 54) where he coined the concept of the "(subjective) re-interpretation" ("(subjektive) Einlegung") in order to characterize the broad interpretative power of the judge with a view to implement the NS-*Weltanschauung*. Concurring Stolleis (2016), p 11.

152 *Cf* rules 20, 21 and 23 of the 1942 draft of a "Volksgesetzbuch" ("people's code"), proposed as a working paper of the "Academy of German Law", calling upon judges, notaries and lawyers to always follow the "National Socialist *Weltanschauung*"; quoted in Rückert, in: Lück/Holänd (2011), p 122–3.

153 *Cf* eg Falk (2017), p 4–5 (the judiciary not only not opposed the Nazis, but "often submissively made their own constitutive contribution to the establishment and continuance of the unjust state" ["vielfach willfährig ihren konstitutiven Beitrag zu Errichtung und Fortdauer des Unrechtsstaates geleistet"]; the resistance of the labour movement "was eliminated almost completely with significant help from the judiciary" ["mit maßgeblicher Hilfe der Justiz…fast vollständig ausgeschaltet"]; judges fulfilled Nazi expectations "in discriminating against and persecuting the Jewish population and other…minorities" ["bei Diskriminierung und Verfolgung der jüdischen Bevölkerung und anderer…Minderheiten"]; judiciary was an "essential element" ["essentieller Bestandteil"] of the NS state until its end); similarly with a focus on the traditionally conservative and anti-republican attitude of the judiciary Braun/Falk, in: Form et al (2015), p 21 ff. For a more positive account Graver, *GLJ* 19 (2018), 845 ff (according to whom the judiciary's independence was initially preserved [853], which had to do with German tradition [Graver explains this using the theories of "path dependency" and "habitus", 871 ff]; while there was no organised "resistance", there was occasional "opposition" and "dissent" [864, examples on 853 ff]); similarly, Hoefer, *JCL&Crim* 35 (1945), 392 f ("certain degree of independence" during the first years of NS rule, which the Nazis were set on breaking). For a cautious summary with multiple references Kroeschell (1992), p 113 ff., 241 ff; more critically Rüping/Jerouschek (2011), p 101 ff., 107; Stolleis (2016), p 23–4.

154 *U.S. v. Altstoetter et al.* ("The Justice Case"), in TWC III (1951), p 985.

155 Schmidt (1947a), p 231 ("not the judiciary, but the legislator alone had abandoned the flag of justice" ["nicht die Justiz, sondern ganz alleine der Gesetzgeber hatte die Fahne des Rechts verlassen"]).

the legislature. It is also true however that further research is necessary.[156] As we will see below (ch V 3.), the major role of the judges in realising the NS project was recognised and justified by the Kiel School in particular.[157]

156 For example, the role of the *Reichsgericht* is still controversial: while Schmidt-Leichner, *DStR* 9 (1942), 14–5 shows how the case law, including that of the RG, contributed to the breakthrough of the NS material concept of justice, Hartung (1971), p 106 ff and Zimmer, in: HRG IV (1990) 578–9 provide a positive, albeit brief account ("many judges…no National Socialists", "adjudicated as far as possible according to rule of law principles" ["viele Richter…keine Nationalsozialisten", "soweit irgend möglich weiter nach rechtsstaatlichen Grundsätzen judizierten"] ibid, 579).

157 Not only the "Kiel scholars", but also the "Marburg scholars" Schwinge and Zimmerl emphasised the judges' serving role, *cf* ch IV 2. including fn 345, 374 and main text below. Furthermore, two texts by Henkel should be pointed out (1934a and 1934b), in which he stresses that judges are "bound to the leading principles of the *völkisch* Führer state" ("Bindung an die leitenden Grundsätze des völkischen Führerstaats", 1934b, p 21) and sees their task as "interpreting the valid law according to the legal views of the time wherever possible" ("dem geltenden Gesetz nach Möglichkeit eine der gegenwärtigen Rechtsanschauung entsprechende Auslegung zu geben", ibid, p 28); in doing so, they must "express the guiding principles of the state leadership in [their] discretionary practice" ("in seiner Ermessenspraxis die leitenden Grundsätze der Staatsführung zum Ausdruck", ibid, p 31). Thereto also Werle (1989), p 147 ff; Jeßberger, in: Jeßberger/Kotzur/Repgen (2019), p 240 ff. – Critically on **Henkel's involvement with National Socialism** Wolf, *JuS* 1996, 189; for a more detailed and differentiated account, see Jeßberger, in: Jeßberger/Kotzur/Repgen (2019), p 236-7, 251 ff (making a distinction between the "early Henkel"—who was "deeply involved in the 'project' of the National Socialist renewal of the law", a "radical partisan" [Diestelkamp] and classed as a "follower"—and the "Hamburg Henkel", who among other things advocated extending the statute of limitations in regard to NS crimes ["tief in das 'Projekt' nationalsozialistischer Rechtserneuerung verstrickt", "radikaler Parteigänger", "Mitläufer"]). Another interesting fact concerning the "late Henkel" is that there was a lot of debate on NS crimes in his seminar (*cf* Duve, Ein Gespräch mit Claus Roxin (15 May 2006), <www.forhistiur.de/2006-05-duve/>, mn 6), and his students Roxin (GA 1963, 193) and Jäger (1967)—supported by Henkel—both made major contributions to investigating and dealing with criminal law's NS past. While Jäger confirmed Henkel's "affinity to National Socialist thought" ("Nähe zu nationalsozialistischem Gedankengut"), "looking back" ("im Rückblick") he did not think him capable of anything "truly evil" ("wirklich Böses"); while Henkel had given him a "very gentle warning" ("ganz vorsichtig gewarnt") before he embarked upon his NS-related habilitation project, he had later "strongly supported it" ("sehr unterstützt") (Jäger, in Horstmann/Litzinger, 2006, p 47, 49).

Figure 9a: Trial re 20 July 1944; from left to right: Hermann Reinicke (general, assisting judge), Roland Freisler (presiding judge) and Heinrich Lautz (prosecutor)

Figure 9b: Trial re 20 July 1944; from left to right: Hermann Reinicke (general, assisting judge), Roland Freisler (presiding judge) and Heinrich Lautz (prosecutor)

Figure 9c: Trial re 20 July 1944, Berthold von Stauffenberg second from right

Figure 9d: Ruins of the Volksgerichtshof (People`s Court of Justice), Berlin, 1951

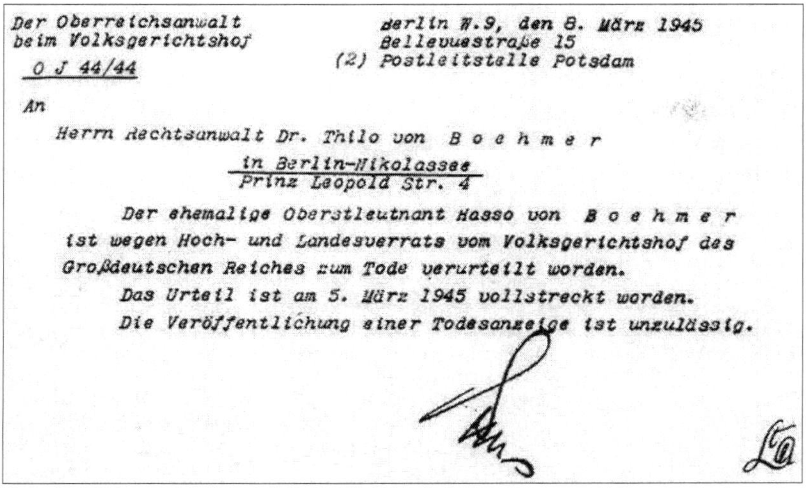

Der Oberreichsanwalt
beim Volksgerichtshof
O J 44/44

Berlin W.9, den 8. März 1945
Bellevuestraße 15
(2) Postleitstelle Potsdam

An

Herrn Rechtsanwalt Dr. Thilo von Boehmer
in Berlin-Nikolassee
Prinz Leopold Str. 4

Der ehemalige Oberstleutnant Hasso von Boehmer ist wegen Hoch- und Landesverrats vom Volksgerichtshof des Großdeutschen Reiches zum Tode verurteilt worden.

Das Urteil ist am 5. März 1945 vollstreckt worden.

Die Veröffentlichung einer Todesanzeige ist unzulässig.

Figure 10: Execution notice from the Prosecutor at the Volksgerichtshof re Hasso von Boehmer; the execution took place on March 1945; the publication of and obituary was prohibited

Finally, Zaffaroni sees Ernst Rudolf Huber, Ernst Forsthoff and Carl Schmitt, the leading representatives of the "new right" within the German constitutional law scholars (*Staatsrechtslehrer*) of the time,[158] as the pioneers of the **Führer state** in terms of constitutional law.[159] Among other things (such as his anti-Semitism[160]), Zaffaroni[161] charges Schmitt with replacing the principle of *nulla poena sine lege* with *nullum crimen sine poena*.[162] However, Schmitt's aims went far beyond this: his goal was to replace the liberal concept of the *Rechtsstaat* by a National Socialist, material concept—a goal that in fact entailed a perversion of the very idea of the

158 Thereto and on the different (four) strands within the association of *Staatsrechtslehrer* (public law scholars) Stolleis (2016), p 130 ff. (133); on Schmitt, Cattaneo (2001), p 181 ff. Priemel (2016), p 260 ff gives an instructive account of these theorists and German "geojurisprudence"; thereto Ambos, *CLF* 29 (2018), 39 ff.

159 Zaffaroni (2017), p 87–8.

160 Zaffaroni (2017), p 66 ff.

161 Zaffaroni (2017), p 92.

162 Schmitt, *JW* 63 (1934), 713; also ibid, *DJZ* 39 (1934), col 691 (693). Thereto also Walther, in: Dreier/Sellert (1989), p 323, 337–8; Cattaneo (2001), p 206 ff; Vormbaum (2015), p 180 including fn 198.

Rechtsstaat.[163] Schmitt propagated the Führer state and the cult of the Führer, along with the *Führer principle*.[164] Zaffaroni correctly identifies a contradiction between the people's weakened sense of justice and the legitimation that this provided for the NS state and the Führer.[165] From the NS perspective, this contradiction was to be resolved through the close, intrinsic connection between the Führer and the people that made the Führer the mediator of the people's will.[166]

---

163 Schmitt, *JW* 63 (1934), 715-6 ("Our definition of National Socialism does not start from a precedent concept of the rule of law; rather, we take the opposite approach, taking National Socialism as the starting point for our definition of the rule of law" ["Wir bestimmen also nicht den Nationalsozialismus von einem ihm vorgehenden Begriff des Rechtsstaates, sondern umgekehrt den Rechtsstaat vom Nationalsozialismus her", 716]). The rejection of the principle of legality then follows from replacing a (in Schmitt's words) formal, positivist concept of the law with a material—that is, a National Socialist—one, from which it follows, among other things, that all undefined legal concepts and blanket clauses must be interpreted "absolutely and unconditionally in a National Socialist sense" ("unbedingt und vorbehaltlos im nationalsozialistischen Sinne", 717); on the respective reinterpretation or perversion of legal concepts see Rückert, *JZ* 2015, 802; id, *ZDRW* 2019, 31, 35–6 ("Umdenken der Rechtsbegriffe"). Schmitt further argues that no state "is able to truly guarantee legal certainty and predictability to the same extent as the strong National Socialist state", but the NS state cannot be expected "to subject itself to the 'calculations and expectations' of its opponents" ("in gleichem Maße wie der starke nationalsozialistische Staat imstande, wirklich Rechtssicherheit und Berechenbarkeit zu gewährleisten", "daß er sich den 'Berechnungen und Erwartungen' seiner Gegner unterwerfe", Schmitt, *DJZ* 39 [1934], col 695). – The similarity between Schmitt's position and contemporary authoritarian and dictatorial understandings of the rule of law is striking, for example the "rule of law" concept propagated and defined by the Chinese Communist Party, which was presented by "Leader" Xi Jinping at the 19th National Congress on 18 October 2017 (the English translation of the official Xinhua New Agency is available at <http://www.xinhuanet.com/english/special/2017-11/03/c_136725942.htm>), and as can be found in the Party's constitution and a recent Central Committee resolution (English translations by the state Central Compilation and Translation Bureau, available at <http://book.theorychina.org/upload/2017-19D-EN-2/> and <http://book.theorychina.org/upload/ae0b0b63-7c4a-4f50-b978-3ddceafabb89/>); all last accessed on 9 August 2019.

164 Schmitt, *DJZ* 39 (1934), col 934; also id, *DJZ* 39 (1934), col 695 (the "will of the Führer" ["Wille des Führers"] as a legal basis); Freisler, *DJ* 98 (1936), 155 adopts a more melodramatic tone (Führer "as the central organ of the will" ["als das zentrale Willensorgan"], the "laws of the Führer" as "expressions of this his will and as such the holiest of ways, means of formally conveying the order of the Führer" ["Gesetze des Führers", "Äußerungen dieses seines Willens und als solche heiligste Arten, Formenübertragungsmittel des Führerbefehls"]) and id, *DJ 96* (1934), 850 (enthusiastically justifying the Röhm purge). On the Führer, *Führertum* (leadership) and the Führer principle from a legal history perspective, Kroeschell, in: Rückert/Willoweit (1995), p 55 ff; a summary account is provided by Hartl (2000), p 45–6.

165 Zaffaroni (2017), p 97.

166 *Cf* Marxen (1975), p 65, 213, 253; on the "Führer's" role as a mediator also *cf* Rüping (1989), p 181–2 (the will of the people "is revealed and continued in the will of the Führer", whose "historic greatness guarantees that he will always unerringly identify the 'true' will of the people" ["offenbart sich fortgesetzt im Willen des Führers", "his-

2. *The material concept of justice and wrongdoing, ethicisation, "total" criminal law and deformalisation*

The race- and blood-based concept of the *Volksgemeinschaft*, the Führer state and the Führer principle formed the guidelines of the **"political" criminal law science** already mentioned above. Accordingly, they were propagated by Nazi criminal law scholars[167] such as Hans Frank, (the abovementioned) Roland Freisler and Karl Siegert,[168] the successor of (the Jewish) Richard Honig,[169] who was forced out of the Faculty of Law and Political Science at Göttingen University.[170] In his opening speech at the 11th International Criminal Law and Prisons Conference in 1935,[171] Reich Minister of Justice Franz Gürtner advocated replacing formal legality by a substantive or **material concept of justice** and wrongdoing, the content of which was to be defined by judges based upon the "demands of the life of the people" and the "Führer principle".[172] A few years later a leading civil servant in the Ministry wrote about the "breakthrough" ("Durchbruch") of the material concept of justice, basing his understanding on the final words of the *Führer* in the 1924 Munich treason trial, which alluded

---

torische Größe garantiert, den 'wirklichen' Willen des Volkes stets unfehlbar zu finden"]); Werle (1989), p 146–7, 691; Murmann (2005), p 134.

167 "Nazi jurists" or "juristic Nazis" (not just "National Socialist jurists") in the sense of Batista, in Zaffaroni (2017), p 103 (already referred to in ch I 2. including fn 69 above).

168 Siegert had made a particular name for himself in the "Aryanisation" of the Göttingen Faculty; thereto Schumann, in: Schumann (2008), p 89–90, 96–7 (using the example of Siegert's role in removing the economist Richard Passow), 100 ff (on his "suggestions for increasing the academic staff" at the Göttingen Faculty ["Vorschläge zum Ausbau des Lehrkörpers"]), 103 ff (on the "terrorist group" ["Terroristengruppe"] Schürmann-Rath-Siegert, also *cf* ibid, p 95).

169 Honig was initially suspended on 25 April 1933 (Siegert took over his chair on 1 November 1933) and then forcibly retired on 31 December 1933 (pursuant to § 3(1) of the Law for the Restoration of the Professional Civil Service of 7 April 1933, RGBl 1933 I, 175). Honig went into exile, first at the University of Istanbul (1933–1939) and then in the United States, where (among other works) he produced a seminal essay on US criminal law in an anthology edited by Mezger (!) among others (in: Mezger/Schönke/Jescheck (1962), vol IV, p 7). After 1945, he refused to return to his old chair in Göttingen, but held guest lectures there from 1954 onwards. Today, his picture hangs in the criminal law section of the law library at the Göttingen Faculty. For more detail, Schumann, in: id (2008), p 65, 89, 108, 110 f.

170 Zaffaroni (2017), p 93 ff. For more detail on the anti-liberal criminal law movement's criticism of the liberal understanding of the state, Marxen (1975), p 56 ff. including further references.

171 Gürtner (1936), p 4 ff.

172 Gürtner (1936), p 9 ff ("Forderungen des völkischen Lebens", "Führerprinzip"). Also *cf* Frank (1935), p 13, 16 (guidelines 9, 11, 26) (orientation towards the idea of "substantive justice" ["materiellen Gerechtigkeit"]).

to an eternal, divine justice[173] and contrasted it with a formal concept of justice, represented especially by the *nulla poena* principle.[174] Roland Freisler likewise propagated a free, substantive concept of law and wrongdoing without formal constraints that was "rooted" in the "moral order of the people",[175] drawing its content from "healthy sentiment of the people",[176] now recognised "as a legal source".[177]

In this concept of law there is no longer any separation between morals and law[178] and—besides further consequences for "*Tatbestandstechnik*", the technique of interpreting the elements of the *actus reus*[179]—**analogy** is now admissible.[180] It should be noted however that the 1935 version of the re-

173 According to Schmidt-Leichner, *DStR* 9 (1942), 2 Hitler stated (*inter alia*): "Nicht Sie, meine Herren, sprechen das Urteil über uns, das Urteil spricht das ewige Gericht der Geschichte…Aber jenes Gericht wird uns nicht fragen: Habt Ihr Hochverrat getrieben oder nicht?…Mögen Sie uns tausendmal schuldig sprechen, die Göttin des ewigen Gerichts der Geschichte wird lächelnd…das Urteil des Gerichts zerreißen; denn sie spricht uns frei." ("Not you, sirs, will pronounce judgment upon us, that judgment will be pronounced by the eternal court of history…but that court will not ask us: did you commit high treason or not?...You may pronounce us guilty a thousand times, the goddess of the eternal court of history will tear up the court's judgment with a smile; for she will acquit us.").

174 Schmidt-Leichner, *DStR* 9 (1942), 2 ff.

175 Freisler, *Willensstrafrecht* (1935), p 32 ("völkischen Sittenordnung…wurzelt").

176 Freisler, *DJ* 97 (1935), 1251.

177 *Cf* ch II 1. including fn 117 above ("als Rechtsquelle").

178 Freisler, *DJ* 97 (1935), 1250.

179 Freisler, *DJ* 97 (1935), 1251 ("Normative elements of crime, blanket clauses...recognition of the healthy sentiment of the people as a legal source and admission of the direct insights of this law" ["Normative Tatbestände, Generalklauseln…, Anerkennung des gesunden Volksempfindens als Rechtsquelle und Zulassung der unmittelbaren Erkenntnis dieses Rechts"]). In detail on the undefined concepts in NS legislation, Werle (1989), p 716 ff.

180 In more detail Freisler, in Frank (1934), p 10 ff (punishment of any "conduct harmful to the people" ["volksschädliches Verhalten"] through the admission of "legal analogy" ["Rechtsanalogie"], that is, "decisions according to the correctly understood spirit of National Socialist criminal law" ["Entscheidung nach dem richtig erfaßten Geiste nationalsozialistischen Strafrechts"]); briefly Freisler, *DJ* 97 (1935), 1251; similarly Preußischer Justizminister (1933), p 127 (acts are punishable if they are "morally reprehensible according to the healthy sentiment of the people" and punishment "is required according to the legal notion that forms the basis of a certain criminal law" ["Handlung nach gesunder Volksanschauung sittlich verwerflich und…von dem einem bestimmten Strafgesetz zugrunde liegenden Rechtsgedanken gefordert"]); Luetgebrune, in Frank (1934), p 42 ff (applicable criminal laws also include the "criminal law principles born of German National Socialist popular opinion and ascertained through the approximation of the law [by judges]" ["aus der deutschen nationalsozialistischen Volksanschauung geborene und durch Gesetzes- und Rechtsangleichung [vom Richter] gefundene strafrechtliche Rechtssatz", p 43]).

spective § 2 RStGB still had a statutory reference[181] and thus constituted more of a *relaxation* than a complete abolition of the analogy prohibition. Insofar the more radical view represented by Freisler and other hardcore Nazi voices focusing on the "healthy sentiment of the people" alone[182] had to give way to a more moderate line of thought for which a statutory reference was indispensable since the "statute is as much part of the legal professional as the weapon is of the soldier."[183] At any rate, precisely this relaxation of the analogy prohibition serves as a good example of future-oriented **continuity** in existing German criminal law, either in the form of the authorisations of analogy (see eg § 315b(1)(3) StGB, which requires a "a similar act of interference of equal dangerousness") or the so-called "rule-examples" or *Regelbeispiele* (which include, besides the unnamed "especially serious case" of § 243 StGB, cases that are completely undefined, eg § 212(2) StGB).[184] Apart from these rather sophisticated doctrinal considerations we should also recall that immediately after the reintroduction of the analogy prohibition by the Allies, German authors tried to find substitutes, calling for punishment on the basis of custom[185] or pursuant to a broad, "generous" interpretation.[186]

181 § 2 RStGB, amended by the Act to Change the Criminal Code of 28 June 1935 (RGBl I 839), fulfilling one of the "key demands of the National Socialist criminal law reform programme" ("wesentlichen Forderungen des nationalsozialistischen Strafrechtsreformprogramms"), reads:
"Whosoever commits an act declared punishable by the law, or that merits punishment according to the *fundamental idea of a criminal statute* and according to the *healthy sentiment of the people*, will be punished" ("Bestraft wird, wer eine Tat begeht, die das Gesetz für strafbar erklärt oder die nach dem *Grundgedanken eines Strafgesetzes* und nach *gesundem Volksempfinden* Bestrafung verdient." [Italics K.A.])
Thereto see also Cavaleiro de Ferreira (1938), p 76–7; Marxen (1975), p 192 ff; Schreiber, in: Dreier/Sellert (1989), p 160 ff.; Werle (1989), p 16–7, 141 ff, 715–6 (rightly emphasising that there could be no legality in the NS state with its abolition of the separation between law and justice ["Gesetz und Recht"] and political control of the law); Hartl (2000), p 297 ff.

182 Fn 180 above.

183 Schmidt-Leichner, *DStR* 9 (1942), 10–1, 18 ("Das Gesetz gehört so sehr zum Rechtswahrer wie die Waffe zum Soldaten").

184 *Cf* Hoyer, *GS Eckert* (2008), p 365–6; for a fundamental, critical account of *Regelbeispiele* Hirsch, *FS Gössel* (2002), 287 ff ("faulty legal construction" ["juristische Fehlkonstruktion"] that contradicts the basic principles of criminal law, particularly the principle of legality, which the "relabelling" ["Umetikettierung"] of qualified offence elements in sentencing rules aimed to undermine [302]; particularly critically on their increased use during the NS period [288, 300]).

185 *Cf* Mayer, *SJZ* 2 (1947), 19 ("strafbegründendes Gewohnheitsrecht", invoking, *inter alia*, the common law).

186 Meister (1949), p 31–2.

Returning to the material concept of justice, justice is ultimately equated with the will of the people: "Just is that which benefits the German people" ("Gerecht ist, was dem deutschen Volke frommt").[187] Of course, "the content of this popular will" must correspond ("healthily") to the "National Socialist idea of justice",[188] which is defined by the NS leadership and thus ultimately is at the mercy of the Führer's whims.[189] Accordingly, Freisler's criminal law doctrine revolves around the people (defined by race and blood), the Führer and the Party.[190] For Siegert, NS law was based upon a combination of "the spirit of the people and leadership" ("Volksgeist und Führung"). However, the National Socialist citizen—the *Volksgenosse*, to use Larenz's terminology—must always "follow the leadership's laws" and "interpret them in the spirit of the leadership and the people".[191] The "National Socialist Guidelines for a New German Criminal Law" ("Nationalsozialistische Leitsätze für ein neues deutsches Strafrecht") presented the same year emphasised the preservation of the blood-based *Volksgemeinschaft* as the main aim of criminal law; thus the law is dominated by the ideas "of the *Volksgemeinschaft*, loyalty, duty, honour and just atonement".[192] As we will see below (ch V 4.), all these concepts were further theoretically elaborated, were interrelated and implied a binding nor-

---

187 Freisler, *DJ* 98 (1936), p 1630.

188 Dahm, *DStR* 80 (1934), 91 ("The only view of the law that can be regarded as 'healthy' is one that corresponds to the German and National Socialist idea of the law" ["Als 'gesund' kann...nur die Rechtsanschauung gelten, die der deutschen und nationalsozialistischen Rechtsidee entspricht"]).

189 Radbruch rephrased Freisler's pronouncement as "Law is that which is useful to the people" ("Recht ist, was dem Volke nützt") and criticised it in his "Five-Minute Legal Philosophy" ("Fünf Minuten Rechtsphilosophie", 1945) under "Second Minute", as thus "caprice, breach of contract, unlawfulness", "whatever seems of communal benefit to those invested with state power,...every whim of the despot, punishment without law and judgment, lawless murder" become law, meaning that the *Rechtsstaat*, the state under the rule of law, is transformed into an *Unrechtsstaat*, a "state of injustice" ("Willkür, Vertragsbruch, Gesetzeswidrigkeit", "was den Inhaber der Staatsgewalt gemeinnützig dünkt, ... jede Laune des Despoten, Strafe ohne Gesetz und Urteil, gesetzloser Mord", "Rechtsstaat in einen Unrechtsstaat verwandelt"). Therefore, the correct statement would be: "only what is lawful benefits the people" ("nur was Recht ist, nützt dem Volke", in Dreier/Paulson [1999], p 209). Werle (1989), p 697–8 is critical likewise (the "'usefulness to the people'"—which is not defined—"leads back to the Führer" ["'Volksnutzen' führt zum Führer zurück", quoting Eb. Schmidt]).

190 Also *cf* Arnedo, in Zaffaroni (2017), p 41 (including fn 77), 43.

191 Siegert (1934), p 19 ("Gesetzen der Führung folgen", "im Geiste der Führung und des Volkes auslegen"). Zaffaroni (2017), p 146–7 rightly speaks of Siegert's lack of coherence and increasing confusion here.

192 Frank (1935), p 11 ("If the blood is tainted, the people will die; if loyalty is extinguished, the community will fall apart" ["Verdirbt das Blut, dann stirbt das Volk; erlischt die Treue, dann zerfällt die Gemeinschaft", printed in bold in the original]). The following principles (p 12 ff) consist of (nine) introductory principles and (28) conclu-

mative command. A striking and paradigmatic example is the inscription on the padlocks of the Waffen-SS: "Meine Ehre heißt Treue" ("Loyalty is my honour").

Figure 11: Siegert's main contribution to the NS criminal law "in the new State"

Figure 12: NS Guiding Principles for a new German Criminal Law, First Part (General Part) (Frank, 1935); the Second Part on the Special Part was published in 1936

sions, four for the criminal laws, 13 for crimes and 11 for punishments, as well as a final conclusion. This final conclusion states that the "re-awakening of the German idea of loyalty in the hearts of all *Volksgenossen* and their education to fulfil their duty" by "the National Socialist movement as the greatest *völkisch* driving force" are the precondition for effective protection through criminal law. The second part of the principles, published in 1936, refers to the Special Part. Also *cf* Thierack, in Frank (1934), p 30 ("honour, loyalty, moral purity" as "ethical values" and "the highest goods of the people" ["Ehre, Treue, Sittenreinheit", "ethische Werte", "höchste Volksgüter"]; honour as the "noblest good of the people", breaches of the law as "dishonourable conduct" that "excludes [the perpetrator] from the community" as "the honourable *Volksgenosse* cannot be expected to tolerate" the perpetrator's continued presence ["ehrloses Verhalten", "aus der Gemeinschaft ausschaltet", "dem ehrhaften Volksgenossen nicht zuzumuten ist"]).

As a consequence, the dualism of morality and law was rejected[193] and instead a complete **ethicisation** of (criminal) law advocated.[194] In a nutshell, the aim was an anti-positivist (substantive) justification of the law charged with ethicising, *völkisch* ideals[195]—that is, based upon a mystical understanding of the German nation and race and a metaphysical, being- and life-oriented conceptualisation[196] (to be discussed in more depth in ch IV 4. with regard to the role and influence of Neo-Kantianism)—and founded upon the healthy sentiment of the people mediated by the Führer.[197] Against this background, it hardly seems surprising that the Nazi lawyers were attracted by American (common law) legal culture, well beyond its racist undertones: it offered a similarly flexible and informal approach to the law[198] and additionally in legal realism provided a theory that came close to the NS idea of a law rooted in the reality of the popular (*völkisch*)

---

193 *Cf* Frank (1935), p 12 (principle 3): "In German thinking, moral judgement, the sense of duty and the sense of justice are in harmony" ("Für deutsches Denken besteht Einklang zwischen sittlicher Wertung, Pflichtgefühl und Rechtsempfinden").

194 Beyer (1947), p 49 was already critical ("ethics and politics are mixed up with law" ["Ethik und Politik werden mit dem Recht vermischt"]); from today's perspective Hartl (2000), p 50 ff; Vogel (2004), p 72 ff; Murmann (2005), p 136; Hoyer, *GS Eckert* (2008), p 357–8. However, also *cf* Marxen (1975), p 71 ff (73), for whom this dualism continued to exist "in disguised form" ("in verschleierter Form"), for any judgement of reality as "meaningful" ("sinnvoll") or of popular opinion as "healthy" ("gesund") requires benchmarks that necessarily must be external to this reality. See thereto also in regard to the Kiel School ch V 2. including fn 556–10 below. – Critically on ethicising tendencies in today's law (as a further example of future-oriented **continuity**) Hoyer, *GS Eckert* (2008), p 366 ff (eg elements of murder, reference to morals in § 228 StGB and the "reprehensibility clause" [*Verwerflichkeitsklausel*] in § 240 StGB); Wolf, *JuS* 1996, 191–2 is also critical of § 240 StGB. Its *Verwerflichkeitsklausel* replaced the infamous Nazi "healthy sentiment of the people" ("gesunde Volksempfinden") and the Supreme Court (BGHSt 5, 254 (256) considered this only a change in terminology, since the judge still has "to respect the legal sentiment of the people" ("das Rechtsempfinden des Volkes zu achten").

195 On this new (anti-liberal) substantive concept of crime and the earlier approaches, also *cf* Marxen (1975), p 172 ff, 182 ff; Werle (1989), p 145–6; Hoyer, *GS Eckert* (2008), p 354 ff.

196 *Cf* Rückert, *JZ* 2015, 801 (NS thinking as "classical and metaphysical, not critical-rational-conceptual, but holistic-experiential-feeling-beholding-substantial" ["klassisch-metaphysisch, nicht kritisch-rational-begrifflich, sondern ganzheitlich-erlebend-erfühlend-anschauend-substantiell"]).

197 Also *cf* Murmann (2005), p 133 ff; on the Führer's role as a mediator, see ch I including fn 99 and main text above.

198 *Cf* Whitman (2017), p 146 ff. (referring to common law's "flexibility", "open-endedness" and "pragmatism" as opposed to German law's legal positivism and formalism).

life, the concrete *Wesensschau*,[199] that is, a theory which replaces "formal law" with "life-law".[200]

Renowned criminal law scholars aligned themselves with these ideas. In 1934, Edmund Mezger thus refers to the "total understanding of the state" and the "*totality* of the legal community", distinguishing them from the outdated "liberalist understanding" in order to justify his claim that criminal law's reaction to the "psychopathic offender" "can in no way be derived from the individual and his individual constitution", but instead must take the abovementioned "totality of the legal community" as its "starting point".[201] In a total state such as this, adherence to the principle of legality becomes a "question of expediency" and a "moderate relaxation" of the prohibition of analogy raises "no significant concerns".[202] "Substantive unlawfulness" should be understood as "acting against the German National Socialist worldview".[203] Hans Welzel, Mezger's great antagonist in terms of the overcoming of the (neo)classical theory of crime by finalist thinking,[204] also had considerable sympathy with the Nazi's ethicising renewal of the criminal law and clearly commits himself to the NS *Weltanschauung* in various writings, as we will see in detail below (ch VII 2.). Erik Wolf, to whom we will return in greater detail later (ch VI), similarly sees the "substantive content of justice...as given by National Socialism".[205] Friedrich Schaffstein, to whom we will likewise return (ch V 1.), also demanded that criminal law commit itself unequivocally to National Socialist values and the NS state that implemented them in his 1934 seminal text on "political criminal law science".[206] In a treatise appearing at the same

199 Thereto ch IV section 5.

200 *Cf* Whitman (2017), p 115, 153 ff (finding "almost identical" approaches between American legal realists and NS lawyers, with both focusing on "[B]ringing law back in line with 'life' and 'social realities'" [p 155]).

201 Mezger (1934), p 65–6 ("totale Staatsauffassung", "Totalität der Rechtsgemeinschaft", "liberalistische Auffassung", "psychopathischen Verbrecher", "unmöglich...vom Individuum und seiner individuellen Beschaffenheit hergeleitet werden", "Totalität der Rechtsgemeinschaft", "Ausgangspunkt").

202 Mezger, *DJZ* 39 (1934), col 100–1 ("Zweckmäßigkeitsfrage", "maßvolle Auflockerung", "keinem wesentlichen Bedenken"), referring explicitly to the abovementioned suggestion in the Memorandum of the Preußischer Justizminister , fn above.

203 Mezger, *ZStW* 55 (1936), 1, 9 ("Materielle Rechtswidrigkeit", "Handeln gegen die deutsche nationalsozialistische Weltanschauung").

204 See already fn 34 above *in fine*.

205 Wolf, *DRWis* 4 (1939), 177 ("materiellen Inhalte der Gerechtigkeit...durch den Nationalsozialismus gegeben").

206 Schaffstein (1934), p 15 ff, 23 ff. In this totalitarian state, the only concern is the "implementation of the 'correct' National Socialism" ("Durchsetzung des 'richtigen' Nationalsozialismus", p 23–4).

time, he—like Mezger—propagated the National Socialist substantive[207] and "total state",[208] in which "the individual's desire for legal certainty" becomes secondary to "the pursuit of substantive justice"[209] and—as he wrote one year later—"the recovered unity of criminal law and the *völkisch* moral order" prevails.[210] The substantive concept of wrongdoing thus established has as its "natural and at the same time most practically significant consequence" the "abolition of the prohibition of analogy"—in line with Schmitt's *nullum crimen sine poena*.[211]

In other words, the aim is to overcome the **formal constraints of positivism**[212] through an understanding of natural law that is charged with

207 Schaffstein, *ZStW* 53 (1934), 606 ("organic understanding of National Socialism, which...defines the concept of the state in substantive terms and understands it as the people's way of life and way of shaping the law" ["organische Auffassung des Nationalsozialismus, welche...den Begriff Staat materiell bestimmt und ihn als Lebens- und rechtliche Gestaltungsform des Volkes begreift"]). On "materialisation", also *cf* Vogel (2004), p 58 ff.

208 Schaffstein, *ZStW* 53 (1934), 607, 621 ("in the total state, not only the civil servant, but ultimately everyone somehow appears as a trustee and official of the people as a whole" ["im totalen Staat erscheint nicht nur der Beamte, sondern letztlich jeder irgendwie als Treuhänder und Amtsträger der Volksgesamtheit"]). On the (controversial) relation between the authoritarian, total state and its implementation, Marxen (1975), p 66–7, 139–40, 171–2; also Vogel (2004), p 73 ("total politicisation or ideologisation of law and criminal law" ["totale Politisierung oder Ideologisierung von Recht und Strafrecht"]), 623 ("protection of the total state" ["Schutz des totalen Staates"]).

209 Schaffstein, *ZStW* 53 (1934), 607 ("das Verlangen nach Rechtssicherheit für das Individuum...hinter dem Streben nach materieller Gerechtigkeit"); for an NS-inspired substantive concept of wrongdoing also Schaffstein, *DR* 4 (1934), 349, 350 (the "National Socialist revolution" has "also taken hold of legal thought" ["auch das Rechtsdenken ergriffen"], and "endeavoured" to "uncover its ideological and political foundations [that lie] beneath the surface of legal terminology" ["bemüht... unter der Oberfläche juristischer Begriffe deren weltanschauliche und politische Grundlagen aufzudecken"], which is why there is now "some hope" ["einige Hoffnung"] that it will be possible to "finally" eradicate liberal "evil at the roots" ["Uebel endlich an der Wurzel"]).

210 Schaffstein, in: Dahm et al (1935), p 110 ("wiedergefundene Einheit von Strafrecht und völkischer Sittenordnung").

211 Schaffstein, *ZStW* 53 (1934), 607 ("selbstverständliche und zugleich praktisch bedeutsamste Folge", "Beseitigung des Analogie-Verbots"); on the relaxation of the prohibition of analogy by reference to the "healthy sentiment of the people" Schaffstein, *DR* 1934, 349, 352; also see ch IV 2. including fn 543 ff and main text below. At least Schaffstein sees "the threat to legal certainty" as alarming "from the point of view of the norm addressee", but immediately relativises this by adding that this viewpoint "no longer carries the same weight in the new state as in former times" (*ZStW* 54, 1934, 608). His aim is to replace liberal formalism with National Socialist formal requirements, see Schaffstein, *DR* 4 (1934), 349 ff and ch IV 3. including fn 562 ff and main text below. Emphasising the differences to the fascist state (Italy) in this regard, Dahm (1935b), p 11 ff (according to whom there is a tendency in Italy towards preserving the principle of legality, as the law is the expression of state fascist authority and no extralegal will of the people is recognised, which is why punishment restores the violated authority of the state).

racist, *völkisch* ideas and oriented towards the will of the Führer[213] (which is itself equated with the law[214]).[215] For Schaffstein, the "broad definition of crimes" that raises concerns from a liberal perspective mindful of the rule of law is a "necessary and inevitable evil" of NS criminal law,[216] the law becoming merely a "guideline for interpretation";[217] an "unlimited interpretation" in line with the NS *Weltanschauung* is called for,[218] the end to the "enslavement by paragraphs" ("Paragraphen-Sklaverei").[219] According to Larenz, the legislature is to be freed from "normative constraints" ("normativen Bindungen") of any kind and only to be guided by the "*völkisch* idea of the law" ("völkische Rechtsidee") and the "spirit of the people" ("Volksgeist").[220] Positivism leads to a "renunciation of creative transformation in the life of the law" ("Verzicht auf schöpferische Umgestaltung im Rechtsleben"), paralyses "the judge's eagerness to take responsibility" ("die Verantwortungsfreudigkeit des Richters") and thus aggravates the "gap between written law and moral conscience."[221] Last but not least,

---

212 On the NS rejection of positivism "as its nature is essentially the same as that of liberalism" ("wegen seiner Wesensgleichheit mit dem Liberalismus") Beyer (1947), p 48; on National Socialism's battle against positivism also Walther, in: Dreier/Sellert (1989), p 336–7.

213 Schaffstein (1934), p 24 ("subjection to the will of the Führer embodied in the law" ["Unterwerfung unter den im Gesetz verkörperten Führerwillen"]). On the—legally binding—will of the Führer as the starting point of NS law combatting crime and as the expression of the primacy of political leadership, Werle (1989), p 681 ff, 690, 715, 720 ("criminal law...nothing other than a 'domestic political executive'" ["Strafrecht... nichts anderes als 'innenpolitische Exekutive'", 690, quoting Naucke]).

214 On the equation of the (mere) will of the Führer with the law and thus the replacement of the principle of the "reservation of the law" (*Vorbehalt des Gesetzes*), Maunz, in: Huber (1943), p 27 ("This system has necessarily and logically replaced the old principle of legality as the will of the Führer has taken the place of the old law by" ["Dieses System hat notwendigerweise und folgerichtig den alten Gesetzmäßigkeitsgrundsatz ersetzt, seitdem an die Stelle des alten Gesetzes der Wille des Führers getreten ist"]).

215 National Socialism's orientation towards the vulgar natural law of blood, *Volk* and race was already criticised by Beyer (1947), p 47 ff (ultimately "natural law with a strong political colouring" ["stark politisch gefärbtes Naturrecht", 51]). On National Socialism's battle against the natural law of reason of the Enlightenment, Walther, in: Dreier/Sellert (1989), p 337.

216 Schaffstein, *ZStW* 53 (1934), 623 ("weite Fassung der Tatbestände", "notwendiges und unvermeidliches Übel").

217 Dahm (1935b), p 14 ("bloßen Richtlinie für die Auslegung"); also Dahm (1935a), p 17 (legislator should restrict itself to "general guidelines" ["allgemeinen Richtlinien"]).

218 *Cf* Rüthers (1986/2017) already quoted fn 151 above; concurring Gusy *ZDRW* 1 (2019), 9.

219 See the respective Nazi pamphlet by Heuber (1937[?]); thereto Rückert, in: Lück/Holänd, p 124 ff.

220 Larenz, *ZKph* 1 (1935), 60.

221 Larenz (1934), p 13 ("Kluft zwischen geschriebenem Recht und sittlichem Bewusstein").

Henkel provides an innovative doctrinal justification for this deformalisation and materialisation in his theory of the "danger zone" indicated by definitions of crimes,[222] which was later taken up by Minister of Justice Gürtner.[223]

3. *General preventive and atonement-focused Willensstrafrecht (criminal law of the will)*

As far as the **purposes of punishment** are concerned, NS authors display a range of positions. In line with the all-encompassing project of the *Volksgemeinschaft*, punishment should be guided by the way that it impacts upon said *Volksgemeinschaft* and its cohesion; its aim is the "atonement-focused protection of the *Volksgemeinschaft*".[224] From this arises the particular significance of shame sanctions, which put an end to one's life as a citizen.[225] Siegert advocates an "interplay" of all possible punishment purposes—retribution,[226] negative general prevention, special prevention, integration and "expulsion from the *Volksgemeinschaft*"[227] — as only in this way will

222 Henkel (1934a), p 68 ("a certain 'danger zone' that surrounds the elements of the criminal *actus reus*" as expressing a "view of criminal law oriented towards the legality of the life of the people and the state as a whole" ["eine gewisse 'Gefahrenzone', die sich um die strafgesetzlichen Tatbestände herumlegt", "an der Lebensgesetzlichkeit des Volks- und Staatsganzen orientierten Strafrechtsbetrachtung"]). Even after the war, Henkel held fast to this idea, *cf* Henkel (1977), p 439–40 ("danger zone" of crime definitions "to make the comprehensive inclusion of disapproved-of perpetrator conduct possible" ["Gefahrenzone", "um ein mißbilligtes…Täterverhalten umfassend…einbeziehen zu können"]; rejecting such a "zone" places "utopian demands" ["utopische Forderung"] upon legal certainty). Critically Marxen (1975), p 173–4; Cattaneo (2001), p 215–6, 231–2; Hoyer, *GS Eckert* (2008), p 355; on Henkel's involvement with National Socialism, see ch II 1. including fn 157 above.

223 Gürtner (1936), p 11–2 ("By instructing judges to base their decisions not only upon the wording of the law, but upon the legal ideas that inform it, we create...a danger zone around each criminal law...those who move within this zone...risk being punished" ["Indem wir den Richter anweisen, nicht nur nach dem Wortlaut des Gesetzes, sondern nach seinen Rechtsgedanken zu entscheiden, legen wir…um jede Strafvorschrift eine Gefahrenzone…wer sich in dieser Sphäre bewegt…wird riskieren, der Strafe zu verfallen").

224 Seidenstücker (1938), p 45 ff ("sühnende Schutz der Volksgemeinschaft").

225 Also *cf* ch V 4. including fn 591 and ch VI 2. including fn 743, with the respective main text below. Thereto and on the system of sanctions Freisler, in Frank (1934), p 19 ff (21); Hartl (2000), p 237 ff (240 ff).

226 According to Gemmingen (1933), p 23 "the idea of retribution is deeply rooted in Adolf Hitler's thinking" ("Denken Adolf Hitlers…der Vergeltungsgedanke tief verankert").

227 Siegert (1934), p 74 ("Ausstoßung aus der Volksgemeinschaft"). Thus Siegert, ibid, also argues in favour of "killing" the "degenerate *Volksgenossen*" and "exterminating life un-

"National Socialist criminal law [achieve its] full clout in the fight for Germany".[228] Overall, however, general preventive considerations prevail.[229]

Freisler's concept of **Willensstrafrecht** or the criminal law of the will also leaned towards general prevention.[230] The purpose of *Willensstrafrecht* —as the "mirror image of the National Socialist German worldview"[231]— was the constant self-cleansing of the *Volkskörper* (the "body of the people")[232] and its education in the spirit of National Socialism.[233] As a "law of combat" or the "armoury of the *Volksgemeinschaft*",[234] it needed to "de-

---

worthy of living" ("Tötung", "entarteten Volksgenossen", "Vernichtung lebensunwerten Lebens").

228 Siegert (1934), p 15–6 ("dem nationalsozialistischen Strafrecht die volle Schlagkraft im Kampfe für Deutschland"). Zaffaroni (2017), p 146–7 fails to provide page numbers here.

229 *Cf* ch V 2. including fn 537 ff below.

230 Freisler, in: Gürtner (1934), p 11 ff; also Gürtner (1936), p 14 ff. Also *cf* Zaffaroni (2017), p 153 ff (155 ff), some parts quoted imprecisely; Spanish translation in Zaffaroni, ed. (2017), p 113 ff with critical comments by Arnedo (in particular p 72 ff), Guzmán D. and Batista; concurring in principle Cavaleiro de Ferreira (1938), p 77–8. — On the legislative development and debate, Hartl (2000), p 65 ff (referring to the Memoranda of the Preußischer Justizminister [1933], the Academy for German Law [1934], the NS guiding principles [Frank, 1935] and the work of the official criminal law commission [Gürtner, 1935]); on fundamental ideas and motives Hartl (2000), p 89 ff, 96 ff.

231 Freisler, in: Gürtner (1934).

232 Freisler, in: Gürtner (1934), p 13–4 (criminal law as the "apparatus through which the body of the people cleanses itself" ["Selbstreinigungsapparatur des Volkskörpers"]); thereto also Werle (1989), p 705 ff. – In this regard, abolishing the prohibition against extraditing Germans—as suggested by the Memorandum of the Preußischer Justizminister (1933) —is a logical step, as in this way "degenerate and sick parts of the people...can be shed if possible to avoid both the unprofitable expenditure of energy and costs and any further threat to the whole body of the people" ("entartete und kranke Volksbestandteile...zur Vermeidung unnützen Kraft- und Kostenaufwandes und weiterer Gefährdung des ganzen Volkskörpers möglichst abgestoßen werden", Schaffstein, *ZStW* 53 [1934], 614). Also see Schaffstein, *ZStW* 55 (1936), 285 (if necessary, sacrificing a "sick but still curable limb" of the community "if the threat to the organism as a whole appears to exceed a certain minimum" ["heilbare kranke Glied", "wenn die Gefahr für den Gesamtorganismus ein gewisses Mindestmaß zu überschreiten scheint"]), 286 (general preventive effect of punishment to "cleanse and...restore the community" ["Reinigung und...Wiederherstellung der Gemeinschaft"]). However, according to Gemmingen (1933), p 15–6. Hitler himself did not consider punishment an "appropriate means for the—in itself desirable—elimination of racially foreign elements from the body of the people" ("angemessene Mittel für die—an sich erstrebenswerte—Ausscheidung des rassisch Fremden aus dem Volkskörper").

233 Freisler, in: Gürtner (1934), p 18 ("The anti-socialist will must be deprived of its breeding ground through National Socialist education and social work" ["Dem antisozialistischen Willen muß der Nährboden entzogen werden durch nationalsozialistische Erziehungs- und Sozialarbeit"]); thereto also Hartl (2000), p 99–100.

234 Freisler, *DJ* 97 (1935), 1251 ("Kampfrecht", "Rüstzeug der Volksgemeinschaft"). On "law of combat", also Hartl (2000), p 96–7.

stroy" the "type of the disturber of the peace within the *Volk*", that is, those who "threaten [the people] from within".[235] Because National Socialism believed that "the will [was] that which moved the world", the "will of the disturber of the peace" already constituted the "enemy",[236] which needed "already to be nipped in the bud".[237] Thus the NS criminal law of the will, while drawing on some predecessors,[238] clearly amounted to a radicalisation of the former subjectivisation attempts.[239]

Freisler's reference to the "*activation* of the will",[240] that is, the external manifestation of the will, did not mean to restrict criminal liability, since Freisler in fact intended to replace the requirement for a result achieved in the world, or for a completed action, by his will requirement. Thus, Freisler formulated it as a mere procedural concession—for, after all, how is a will that has not been "activated" to be identified and thus prosecuted?[241] At least an element of the criminal law of the act—in the sense of an

235 Freisler, in: Gürtner (1934), p 12 ("Thypus des Friedensstörers im Volke", "von innen aus bedroht", "vernichten").

236 Freisler, in: Gürtner (1934), p 13 ("das die Welt Bewegende der Wille", "Wille des Friedensstörers", "Feind"). In this regard, also see Frank (1935), p 14 ff (referring specifically to the criminal, evil will in principles 16, 19, 28); Gürtner (1936), p 15 (adapting punishment to the "intensity of the criminal will" ["Intensität des verbrecherischen Willens"]). Emphasising the difference to the fascist (result-focused) criminal law (of Italy) in this regard, Dahm (1935b), p 17 ff (to which "such a criminal law of the will is foreign" ["ein solches Willensstrafrecht fremd", 19], as Italian law does not focus upon the *Volksgemeinschaft* and the individual as its member, see ch II 1. including fn 121 above); rudimentarily also Dahm (1935a), p 11.

237 Freisler, in: Frank (1934), p 13 ("bereits im Keime erstickt werden").

238 See Hartl (2000), p 56 ff (drawing particular attention to § 49a RStGB, the subjective theory of attempt advocated by the *Reichsgericht*, the Supreme Court of the Reich ["forerunner" ("Wegbereiter"), p 60, 184 ff], Karl Klee's preliminary work on *dolus indirectus* [p 60 ff] and the 1922/1925 Drafts of the StGB [p 64]).

239 Cf Hartl (2000), p 64–5 ("no comparable equivalent existed" ["kein vergleichbares Äquivalent existierte"]); in this regard, Hartl takes a similar view to Marxen, *KritV* 73 (1990), 294 ("apex", "extreme" ["Höhepunkt", "Extrem"]).

240 Freisler, in: Frank (1934), p 13 ("activated criminal will...forms the foundation" ["betätigte verbrecherische Wille...zugrund zu legen"]); Freisler, in: Gürtner (1934), p 30 ("the result achieved through the activation of the will or the completion of the activation of the will...is merely replaced by the activation of the will focused upon achieving the result or the completion" ["nur an die Stelle des durch die Willensbetätigung herbeigeführten Erfolges oder an die Stelle der Vollendung der Willensbetätigung tritt... die auf die Herbeiführung des Erfolges oder die Vollendung...gerichtete Willensbetätigung"]).

241 See Freisler, in: Gürtner (1934), p 31, where he explicitly rejects "evidentiary problems" ("Beweis- schwierigkeiten"), precisely because it is not the "non-activated will" ("nicht betätigten Willen") that is at stake here. Earlier Gemmingen, *JW* 62 (1933), 2373 ("proof of the likelihood of a result on the basis that a will has been identified" ["Beweis der Erfolgswahrscheinlichkeit anhand eines Willensbefundes"]). Mezger, *DJZ* 39 (1934), col 102–3 also cites evidentiary difficulties concerning *Willensstrafrecht*.

act-oriented subjectivisation—can be identified in the reference to the act,[242] which was subsequently abandoned, however, within the context of the theory of perpetrator types—in the sense of *agent*-oriented subjectivisation.[243] At any rate, the externalisation of the will confirms the threat inherent in the will, bringing together the at first glance contradictory theories of the (subjective) criminal law of the will and the (objective) criminal law of endangerment.[244]

Furthermore, Freisler links his concept of *Willensstrafrecht* to the idea of **atonement** ("*Sühne*"). The meaning of criminal law consists of "atonement", which is "as ancient for us Germans as our people is ancient"; there is no need for a rational or philosophical justification for it, as it "lives in us".[245] However, as guilt is already attributed to the will, the need for atonement requires a criminal law of the will.[246]

Developed consistently, the criminal law of the will necessarily impacted upon numerous questions of *Verbrechenslehre*, the **theory of crime**,[247] in regard to intentional offences.[248] Thus the distinction between attempt and completion becomes insignificant, as the criminal will is already expressed in the attempt.[249] Nor is it possible to retain the distinction between perpetration and secondary participation, or the (strict) accessori-

242 See also Hartl (2000), p 138 (interpreting Freisler's demand for an "activation of the will" as confirming the criminal law of the will's requirement of a conduct element).

243 *Cf* Vogel (2001), p 84. See on this further development towards a pure criminal law of the will or attitude ch V 5. with fn 639 ff and ch VI 1.

244 *Cf* Gemmingen, *JW* 62 (1933), 2371 ff; Mezger, *DJZ* 39 (1934), col 97 ff; as a secondary source Hartl (2000), p 266 ff (*Willensstrafrecht's* expansion of criminal liability by way of independent preparatory offences because of the increased dangerousness of certain actions); Vogel (2004), p. 81.

245 Freisler, in: Gürtner (1934), p 15–6 ("für uns Deutsche so alt wie unser Volk alt ist", "lebt in uns"); also *cf* Frank (1935), p 11 ff (with specific reference to atonement in principles 6, 10); thereto also Hartl (2000), p 97–8.

246 Freisler, in: Gürtner (1934), p 16–7.

247 In detail Hartl (2000), p 137 ff, 378 (discussing not only the areas that will be mentioned shortly, but also "improper" omission or commission by omission ["*unechtes Unterlassen*"], the dispensability of causality, unlawfulness [in particular self-defence], guilt [including intent and negligence], punishment and sentencing, and concurrence). We will return to most of these areas below.

248 Freisler, in: Gürtner (1934), p 13 (it is only possible to speak of a "criminal law of the will" in the case of "consciously" carried out disturbances of the peace ["bewußt"]), 15 (attribution of guilt to the will "except in cases of carelessness" ["von den Fällen der Unachtsamkeit abgesehen"], 29 ("the punishment of negligence in itself cannot link to the will" ["kann die Nachlässigkeitsbestrafung an sich schon nicht an den Willen… anknüpfen"]), 32 (*Willensstrafrecht* as far as it does not concern the "punishment of negligence" ["Nachlässigkeitsbestrafung"]). Thereto also Hartl (2000), p 149, 150–1.

249 Freisler, in: Frank (1934), p 13–4; Freisler, in: Gürtner (1934), p 32–3; also Mezger, *DJZ* 39 (1934), col 102, 103–4; Schaffstein, *DRWis* 1 (1936), 48–9; as secondary sources Marxen (1975), p 228–9; Werle (1989), p 710; Hoyer, *GS Eckert* (2008), p 357; Zaffaroni

ness of the latter to the former, for the guilt of the will is to be determined independently for each individual and does not depend upon the main act;[250] accordingly, the case is made for an extensive concept of the perpetrator (in the sense of a unified model of perpetration), with fundamentally the same punishment applied to both perpetrator and secondary participant.[251] As far as the Special Part was concerned, the criminal law of the

---

(2017), p 158 ff; in detail on the debate, reform attempts and reforms, Hartl (2000), p 77, 189 ff (attempted participation), 197 ff (attempt), 322–3 (liability for attempted participation through § 49a RStGB), 329 ff (expansion of liability for attempt through Art. 4 Harmonisation Decree [*Angleichungsverordnung*]; thereto Schröder (2016), p 22). – In this context, it is worth mentioning that the general definition of the "***Unternehmen***" or **undertaking** of an act (§ 11(1)(6) StGB) was introduced in the exact same wording by the NS regime in § 87 StGB as part of the treason offences (RGBl I 1934 341 ff; Hartl, 2000, p 285–6; Wolters, 2001, p 60–1; Rüping/Jerouschek (2011), p 100; on the general deliberations and the further expansion of the law on the protection of the state, also see Preußischer Justizminister (1933), p 133–4; Freisler, in: Frank (1934), p 13; Freisler, in: Gürtner (1934), p 32; Mezger, *DJZ* 39 (1934), col 102; as a secondary source, Hartl (2002), p 200 ff, 284 ff). This led to a renaissance and expansion of this concept following its rejection during the Weimar Republic (Wolters, 2001, p 65). § 87 StGB, which was initially abolished in 1950, was reintroduced in identical form in 1951 (BGBl. I, p 739 ff; Wolters, 2001, p 66). While we should not overlook that the concept of "undertaking" was already used in the late 18th century within the context of crimes against the state (ibid, p 48 ff) and that today's version originated in § 61(1) of the Prussian Criminal Code (ibid, p 54–5), many NS jurists regarded it as a "flawless implementation" of the criminal law of the will in terms of "legislative technique" ("gesetzestechnisch einwandfreie Verwirklichung", Mezger, *DJZ* 39 [1934], col 99).

250 *Cf* Frank (1935), p 34 f (punishment based only on the "criminal will...regardless of the other party's punishment" ["verbrecherischen Willen...ohne daß es auf die Bestrafung des anderen ankommt"], for the "controversial issues hitherto concerning forms of perpetration and their relationship to one another" "no longer [have] any significance" ["bisherigen Streitfragen über die Täterschaftsformen und deren Verhältnis zueinander", "keine Bedeutung mehr"], as it "is up to the judge to take the degree of the criminal will into account when sentencing individual cases" ["dem Richter überlassen, im Einzelfall den Grad des verbrecherischen Willens...bei der Strafzumessung zu berücksichtigen"]. Mitigated punishment is only possible if this criminal will "is only present to a negligible degree" ["nur in einem ganz unwesentlichen Umfange vorhanden"]).

251 *Cf* Freisler, in Frank (1934), p 22–3 (contribution is decisive, against accessoriness); similarly Mezger, *DJZ* 39 (1934), col 101–2. However, even among contemporary NS jurists this was by no means uncontroversial, eg Oetker, in Frank (1934), p 116 ff is in favour of retaining the traditional distinction while at the same time emphasising the element of the will; likewise in favour of retaining the distinction as "*volkstümlicher*", "more of the people" (with a generally lower liability for attempt) Zimmerl, *ZStW* 54 (1935), 575 ff (579, 581, 582), for whom the question of a restrictive or extensive concept of the perpetrator was merely a matter of "legal technique" ("rechtstechnische") and criminal law terminology ("Frage der strafrechtlichen Begriffsbildung", 577), which is why the "so-called criminal law of the will" ("sog. Willenstrafrecht") makes "not even the slightest" ("auch nur das Mindeste") contribution to answering both this question and the content-related question of the level of penalty applied for participation—much like NS ideology itself (577–8). As a detailed secondary source, Hartl

will resulted first and foremost in an expansion of criminal law through (subjectivising) anticipatory liability.[252]

(2000), p 77 ff, 163 ff including further references (extensive perpetrator concept, completely abandoning the distinction or at least still mentioning different forms of participation [reminiscent of the Austrian functional unified perpetrator model] and an approach independent of or with only minimal accessoriness). – In this regard, the criminal law of the will differs from the Kiel School's criminal law of the agent (*Täterstrafrecht*), *cf* ch V 5. including fn 641 and main text below. Overlooked by Stefanopolou, *JoJZG* 2010, 116.

252 *Cf* Hartl (2000), p 136, 266 ff, 379 (independent preparatory offences, liability for attempted participation and relaxation of the conditions of liability for dealing in stolen goods, *ex post* assistance to a committed offence and omitting to report a crime). Summarising the work of the NS criminal law commission, Freisler, in Gürtner (1935), p 9 ff. This source also contains reports on individual groups of offences, including by renowned criminal law scholars such as Dahm, Kohlrausch and Mezger.

Chapter III. Continuity and the "Schulenstreit" ("Dispute between the Schools") (?)

As already stated above,[253] Zaffaroni, too, embraces the theory of continuity concerning the classical and modern schools of criminal law. In his view, the so-called *Schulenstreit* or "dispute of the schools" between Binding and Liszt constructs an opposition that obscures the conservatism and authoritarianism both of these scholars have in common.[254] This theory, while certainly correct from the perspective of today's liberal criminal law, is not new; Marxen in particular provided evidence for the anti-liberal tendencies of both the classical and the modern school.[255] More recently, Naucke[256] (to whom Zaffaroni refers first and foremost) in particular has shown that the classical and modern schools were "complementary, vicarious forms of policy that demanded social security and stability through the reduction of crime",[257] and that both were ultimately concerned with "combatting crime effectively",[258] especially in regard to "dangerous individuals".[259] Accordingly, both schools present purpose-oriented arguments —"purposive retribution" ("zweckmäßige Vergeltung") versus "purposive

253 See ch I 1. including fn 14.

254 Zaffaroni (2017), p 137 ff; previously he was less clear, Zaffaroni, in Zaffaroni (2011), p 45, 46–7 (where he assumes the same "practical consequences" [referring to Muñoz Conde and Marxen], but rejects continuity in a narrower sense ["demasiado duro", "beneficio de la duda" in favour of Binding and Liszt]).

255 See ch I 2. including fn 29 and main text above. Also *cf* Frommel (1987), p 104 ff (104: "considerable doubts concerning the established picture of a contrast between absolute and relative grounds for punishment" ["erhebliche Zweifel am gängigen Bild eines Gegensatzes von absoluter und relativer Strafbegründung"]; 113: "covertly relative theory" ["verdeckt-relative Theorie"] of the classical school); Guzmán Dalbora, *RDPC* VII (2017), 231.

256 Naucke, *FS Hassemer* (2010), p 559 (including further references in fn 4).

257 Naucke, *FS Hassemer* (2010), p 563 ("sich ergänzende, vikariierende Politikformen der unbestrittenen Forderung nach gesellschaftlicher Sicherheit und Stabilität durch Verbrechensminderung").

258 Naucke, *FS Hassemer* (2010), p 564 ("effektive Verbrechensbekämpfung"); on Liszt, also *cf* Dölling, in: Dreier/Sellert (1989), p 194, 223 ("instrument for the effective protection of society" ["Instrument eines effektiven Gesellschaftsschutzes"]). This went hand in hand with a devaluation of the principle of legality, *cf* Naucke, in: Institut für Zeitgeschichte (1981), p 71, 98; concurring Frommel (1987), p 73–4.

259 Naucke, *FS Hassemer* (2010), p 563 ("Both schools take for granted that dangerous individuals must be combatted vigorously and harshly" ["Daß gegen die Gefährlichen mit Stärke und Härte gekämpft werden muß, ist beiden Schulen selbstverständlich"]).

prevention" ("zweckmäßige Prävention")[260]—and neglect both the constitutional aspects of criminal law and its punishment-limiting side.[261]

Zaffaroni is also right that Binding's concept of norms in particular—according to which norms, as emanations of state authority, must be followed unconditionally[262]—encouraged an authoritarian understanding of the state. Ultimately, it also fostered the idea of a *Führerbefehl* (an order from the Führer that is equal to the law)[263] if this order is seen as the expression of supreme state authority in line with the abovementioned

---

260 Naucke, *FS Hassemer* (2010), p 560 ff (as purpose-*free* retribution in a Kantian sense had already lost support in the 19th century, p 516). *Cf* Merkel (1899), p 687, 703 (according to whom the "idea of retribution includes rather than excludes purposive relations" ["Vergeltungsgedanke Zweckbeziehungen nicht aus-, sondern einschließt"]). Also *cf* Frommel (1987), p 107 ff ("prevention through retribution" ["Prävention durch Vergeltung"]).

261 For more detail, *cf* Naucke, *FS Hassemer* (2010), p 564 ff (564: as a consequence of the *Schulenstreit*, "the constitutional law theory of the constant limitation of criminal law is overwhelmed by the technical theory of purposes of punishment" ["Überwältigung der staatsrechtlichen Theorie einer ständigen Begrenzung des Strafrechts durch die technische Theorie der Strafzwecke"]; critically also Vormbaum (2015), p 120, 133 (from a liberal point of view, "by no stretch of the imagination" can either of the main representatives "be termed 'modern'") [quoted from English translation]. On correspondences and differences between Binding and Liszt, also *cf* Frommel (1987), p 61 ff, 113–4.

262 *Cf* eg Binding (1885), p 183 ff ("duty of obedience" ["Pflicht zum Gehorsam"] towards the norm [183], "recognition of the authorities' power to command" ["Anerkennung einer obrigkeitlichen Befehlsgewalt"], so that "the binding order" ["der bindende Befehl"] is "the will of authority" ["obrigkeitlicher Wille"] "everywhere" ["ueberall", 186]); id, (1905), p 424, 437 (emphasising the idea of loyalty in treason and high treason, although here the state and constitution in question need to exist "rightfully" ["zu Recht"]); id, (1913), p 226 ff (punishment to uphold the "authority of the violated law" ["Autorität des verletzten Gesetzes", 226], to enforce the perpetrator's "duty of obedience" ["Gehorsamspflicht"] and the state's "right to obedience" ["Gehorsamsrecht", 227], as a state reaction by "forcibly subjecting [the delinquent] to its power or authority" ["zwangsweise Unterwerfung unter seine Macht oder Herrlichkeit"] [228]; the state as the sole "subject of criminal law" ["Subjekt des Strafrechts"], the "guilty party" ["Schuldige"] as its sole "object" ["Objekt", 229]). Critically on Binding's authoritarian understanding of the state also Vormbaum (2015), p 132, 133 arguing that criminal norms address those applying the law (judges), while only the (unwritten) prohibitions (conduct norms) address the perpetrators (citizens) (ibid., p 64, 132). See also Murmann (2005), p 90 (emphasising the "duty of obedience" ["Pflicht zum Gehorsam"] towards the norm); however, also *cf* Hilliger (2018), p 159 ff, according to whom Binding understood criminal laws as simple "commands by the law command" ("Gesetzesbefehl") without an addressee.

263 On the *Führerbefehl* as a binding legal basis, *cf* eg Freisler, *DJ* 97 (1935), 1251 (law as the "noblest form of the *Führerbefehl* ["vornehmste Form des Führerbefehls"]) and Dahm, in: id et al (1935), p 101 (law as an "expression...of the *Führerbefehl*" ["Ausdruck...des Führerbefehls"]); among the secondary sources, in greater detail Marxen (1975), p 202 ff, 212 ff; Werle (1989), p 578–9, 583 ff, 602, 681 ff (688), 715, 720 (the will/order of the Führer is law, therefore instead of being bound to the law, citizens are bound to the Führer [688]); critically on the contents of the law being determined by the *Führerbefehl*, Vogel (2004), p 67.

Führer principle.[264] Thus Binding was both appropriated by NS authors[265] and criticised by postwar authors[266]—independently of his book on the "extermination of life unworthy of existence",[267] which was published

264 *Cf* ch II 1. including fn 164 and main text above.

265 Rauch (1936), p 14-5 ("Binding's conservative and authoritarian stance is most clearly evident in his norm concept" ["Bindings konservativ-autoritäre Haltung zeigt sich in eindringlichster Form in seinem Normbegriff"], the "emphasis of state power" ["Betonung der staatlichen Macht"] was "the most important thing" ["das Wichtigste"] for Binding concerning the "relation in criminal law" ["Strafrechtsverhältnis"] between the individual and the state, "crime" ["Verbrechen"] as "a refusal to obey" ["Gehorsamsverweigerung"] the state; "more than a merely authoritarian understanding of the state...the strong emphasis on the idea of disobedience" means that "the problem of crime and punishment" becomes "completely interwoven with ethical values" ["mehr als nur autoritäre Staatsauffassung...mit der starken Betonung des Gedankens des Ungehorsams", "das ganze Verbrechens- und Strafproblem mit ethischen Wertungen durchsetzt"]), 36–7 (emphasising Binding's battle against the principle of legality, especially the prohibition of analogy); Dahm (1935b), p 15 ("Binding and the classical school are alive particularly in fascist criminal law" ["Binding und die klassische Schule sind gerade im faschistischen Strafrecht lebendig"]. However, Schaffstein (1934), 8–9 presents a more differentiated view (on the one hand an "authoritarian element of the state" ["autoritäre[s] Staatselement"], on the other hand a "need for legal certainty" ["Bedürfnis nach Rechtssicherheit"]); see also Welzel, *DRWis* 3 (1938), 116–7 ("idea of the power state" ["Machtstaatsgedanke"] as borrowed from liberal historians and thus an "authoritarian side to the norm concept" ["autoritäre Seite des Normbegriffs"] and punishment as "upholding state power and authority, the state asserting itself towards the law-breaker" ["Bewährung staatlicher Macht und Herrlichkeit, der Selbstbehauptung des Staates gegenüber dem Rechtsbrecher"]; on the other hand, however, the intrinsic association with the rule of law in the guarantee aspect of the norm ["wesensmäßige Verknüpfung mit dem Rechtstaat in der garantierenden Seite der Norm"]). Also *cf* the co-opting of Binding's theory by Schwinge/Zimmerl (1937), p 28 ff ("exaggeration and simplification" ["Übersteigerung und Vergröberung", 28], "blind battle against the 'abstract concepts of the General Part'" ["blinder Kampf gegen die 'abstrakten Begriffe des AT'", 29]). On the appropriation of Binding, also *cf* Marxen (1975), p 38 ff (yet giving an overly condensed account of Welzel, *DRWis* 3 [1938], 116–7).

266 *Cf* eg Marxen (1975), p 37 ff ("understanding of the norm as an order that binds absolutely" ["Verständnis von der Norm als einem absolut bindenden Befehl", 39], "violation of the duty of loyalty towards the state" ["Verletzung der Treuepflicht gegenüber dem Staat", 40] as the core of crimes against the state).

267 Binding/Hoche (1920). This text is generally regarded as the intellectual precursor of the NS euthanasia policy (Naucke, in: Binding/Hoche (1920), p XXVIII–XXIX [establishing under administrative law an "administration of killing" (Tötungsverwaltung") to "approve killings" ("Freigabe von Tötungen") and "euthanasia" ("Euthanasie")]; Schumann (2006), p 19 ff [referring to Binding "as the intellectual trailblazer of the euthanasia projects" ["als geistigen Wegbereiter der Euthanasieaktionen", p 21-2]; Zaffaroni, in Zaffaroni, (2009b), p 7 ff [who is reluctant to posthumously condemn the authors of this text on the basis of its publication in Spanish (p 7), but emphasises Binding's historical responsibility ("la historía no se lo perdonó", p 12] and unequivocally criticises the book's content (p 14 ff), among other things as a "triste producto intelectual" that paved the way for the genocide (p 41)]). This text was also the subject-matter of the "prosecution case" in the Nuremberg Doctors' Trial (thereto Priemel [2016], p 252). In the spring of 2010, Binding's status as an honorary citizen of the city of Leipzig was rescinded because of it (Vormbaum [2015], p 133 including fn 11). We should take

posthumously in 1920 and whose relation to his theory of norms is disputed in any case.[268] As far as the—certainly controversial[269]—Liszt is concerned, his call within the second track of his purely protection- and secu-

---

into consideration, however, that the text was a product of its time in that from 1880 onwards, the discourse in the natural sciences and the philosophy of law (under the influence of social Darwinism) advocated removing the taboo on the protection of "sick" life (Hammon [2011], p 2–3 and *passim* including further references; thereto, especially on the euthanasia debate before Binding/Hoche, also Große-Vehne [2005], p 11 ff [on "killing upon request" ("Tötung auf Verlangen") in German Particular Law], 37 ff [on the euthanasia debate since 1870]; Hilliger [2018], p 283 ff, 301 ff; also see the references in ch II 1. including fn 107–108 above). According to Schmitt, *FS Forsthoff*, 1967, p 37 (61), Binding/Hoche "pondered how to prevent the abuse of their suggestions in a manner that was downright touching" ("in einer geradezu rührenden Weise darüber nachgedacht, wie man einen Mißbrauch ihrer Vorschläge...verhindern könnte"), which is why it is "dastardly" ("niederträchtig") to apportion them "any [!] blame or co-responsibility" ("irgendeine Schuld oder Mitverantwortung") for NS practice. Thus also Hilliger (2018), albeit admitting that the text contributed to the recognition of the notions of "life unworthy of existence" ("lebensunwerten Lebens") and "will to life" ("Lebenswille") (p 382), argues (p 392 ff, 400)—based on a contextualisation of the text within 19th-century scientific-biologistic debate (p 283 ff, 293 ff)—that it merely served "as providing stimuli, with no novel content" ("als Impulsgeber ohne inhaltliche Neuheiten", p 392), which had a significant effect only because of the "scholarly authority of its authors" ("wissenschaftlichen Autorität ihrer Verfasser", p 394, 400); no "continuity" ("Kontinuität") to the NS killing programme can be "historically proven" ("historisch", "belegen", p 395–6, 400–1).

268 Frommel (1987), p 75–6 gives a differentiated account (it is "unfair to measure Binding against this late work" ["ungerecht, Binding an dieser Altersschrift zu messen"], fiction of strict juristic treatment, "tendency towards covert criminal policy using doctrinal means" ["Neigung zu verdeckter Kriminalpolitik mit dogmatischen Mitteln"]); Naucke, in: Binding/Hoche (1920), p XXIII ff establishes a link (punishability of killing upon request as violating a primary norm; "the aim of the norm-theoretical undertaking" ["Absicht des normtheoretischen Unternehmens"] is "to get rid of criminal law" ["das Strafrecht loszuwerden"] in order to render "state killing" ["staatliche Töten"] easier [p XXIX]); on Naucke, also *cf* Zaffaroni (2017), p 139 including fn 276, according to whom Naucke denies a contradiction with Binding's normativism and stresses his distinction between law and norm; explicitly against Naucke's hypothesis that Binding justified killing under valid law, Hilliger (2018), p 325–6, 328 ff (357), 383 ff, 387 ff, 399–400, according to whom Binding merely (*de lege ferenda*) made a legal policy demand and there is thus no contradiction to his theory of norms.

269 Frommel (1987), p 85 ff is instructive (distinguishing between a liberal side focused upon helping through special prevention and an authoritarian "combatting" ["Kampf"] side; "contrast between his authoritarian rhetoric and his effect, which was to all intents and purposes a liberal one" ["Kontrast zwischen seiner autoritären Rhetorik und seiner faktisch liberalen Wirkung"]). Exner in particular took up this "combatting side", *cf* eg id, *ZStW* 53 (1934), 629 (according to whom Liszt "called for effective legal means of combatting dispositional criminality" ["wirksame gesetzliche Kampfmittel gegen das dispositionelle Verbrechertum gefordert"] 51 years previously); id (1939), p 261 (natural criminals as "enemies of society" ["Gesellschaftsfeinde"]), 358 ("measures of racial hygiene" ["rassehygienische Maßnahmen"] required for "incorrigible natural criminals" ["unverbesserlichen Zustandsverbrecher"], as this constitutes "predispositional criminality" ["anlagemäßiges Verbrechertum"]); on Exner including further references Frommel (1989), p 85 ff, 101–2; also ch II 1. including fn 108 and 111–112

rity-focused criminal law ("Marburger Programm")[270] to "neutralise" incorrigible criminals not only intellectually blazed a trail[271] for the NS (criminal law of the will)[272] doctrine of perpetrator types ("*Täterstrafrecht*"),[273] but also at least laid the ground for later NS legislation on the neutralisation of "*Volksschädlinge*" (elements harmful to the nation, literally "vermin of the people") through the Habitual Offenders Act[274] and the *Volksschädlingsverordnung*[275] or "*Volksschädling* Decree".[276]

---

above. Jiménez de Asúa (1947), p 92 is not critical enough in this regard. Also, according to Wetzell (2000), p 213 ff, Exner was not a professed Nazi and espoused a differentiated predisposition/environment approach; for a more critical assessment Ambos, in Dessecker et al (2019), p ##.

270 Liszt, *ZStW* 3 (1883), 1, 34 ff (reforming the criminals capable and in need of reform, deterring the criminals who do not need reform, and neutralising the criminals who are incapable of reform [36]).

271 Cf eg Marxen (1975), p 160 ff (who does, however, accurately point out the liberal orientation of Liszt's purposive punishment); Marxen, in: Reifner (1984), p 82–3 (accurately pointing out, however, that Liszt referred only to sentencing and the execution of sentences; more critically Marxen, *KritV* 73 (1990), 292–3 (Liszt's focus on the perpetrator as a precursor of *Willensstrafrecht*); a differentiated counterargument is presented by Hartl (2000), p 58 (emphasising the modern school's orientation towards special prevention and reference to the elements of the *actus reus*, which Marxen, 1975, p 160 ff also recognises, however); on juvenile criminal law in this regard Höffler (2017), p 62 ff (which is necessarily—also—perpetrator-focused, as oriented towards special prevention).

272 Thereto ch II 3. including fn 230 ff and main text above.

273 On the *Täterstrafrecht* or agent-focused criminal law, Hartl (2000), p 116–7 (distinguishing between "general" and "individual" *Täterstrafrecht*, with the former referring to the abstract and normative perpetrator types based upon the criminal law of the will and the latter to the concrete/individual criminological type of perpetrator [p 118 ff]; for more detail on the abstract types of perpetrator—which arise from the supposed "nature" of the act—ch V 5. including fn 644 ff and main text and ch VI 1. including fn 698 ff and main text below. On the embedding of the agent-focused criminal law (*Täterstrafrecht*) in police combatting of crime, see Werle (1989), p 708 ff.

274 Law against Dangerous Habitual Offenders and on Measures of Reform and Incapacitation, 24 November 1933, RGBl I 1933 995. Art. 1 sets out fiercer punishments for habitual offenders, Art. 2 details measures of reform and incapacitation. On this law, also *cf* Cavaleiro de Ferreira (1938), p 79 ff; Schmidt (1965), p 430 ff; Werle (1989), p 86 ff; Arnedo, in Zaffaroni (2017), p 59–60; for a positive account Hartung (1971), p 99 ff; from the perspective of the criminal law of the will Hartl (2000), p 233–4; drawing a comparison with the New York "Baumes Law" Hoefer, *JCL&Crim* 35 (1945), 389; on the US influence also Whitman (2017), p 159.

275 Decree against Elements Harmful to the Nation of 5 September 1939, RGBl I 1939 1679; thereto also Werle (1989), p 233 ff; Hartl (2000), p 309 ff; Vormbaum (2015), p 198 ff.

276 Liszt, *ZStW* 3 (1883), 36 ff referred to "habitual criminality" ("Gewohnheitsverbrechertum"), which he saw as present primarily in incorrigible criminals, as a "sick limb" ("krankes Glied") of the organism, as a "cancerous damage" ("Krebsschaden") eating its way "ever deeper into our social life" ("sich immer tiefer in unser soziales Leben", 36). Eb. Schmidt states that the Habitual Offenders Act fulfils "Liszt's old call to intensify the fight against habitual criminality" ("Liszts alte Forderung nach der Intensivierung

In spite of all these continuities, however, we should not overlook that the **anti-liberal and anti-individualistic** National Socialist criminal law discourse combatted the liberal approaches of both schools, regarding them as equally representative "offshoots of the same root",[277] namely of the individualist, positivist liberalism it sought to overcome.[278] National Socialism—in line with the radicalisation theory mentioned in chapter I (section 2)—thus exacerbated the state-authoritarian positions of Binding, Liszt and their contemporaries through its biologistic, *völkisch* brand of racism, brutalising criminal law practice in ways that these authors could not have conceived and that were impossible to foresee. Liberal Enlightenment thinking became the enemy, needing to be overcome in the field of criminal law, too;[279] in so doing, the anti-liberal movement made no effort to present liberalism in a differentiated light, but rather consciously created a distorted picture (straw man technique) to let its own position "shine

des Kampfes gegen das Gewohnheits-Verbrechertum", Schmidt, *MschrKrim* 33 [1942], 205, 222), which is why it does not represent "a specifically National Socialist statement on sentencing" (Schmidt [1965], p 431). Also cf (mainly critically) Marxen (1975), p 162–3; Frommel (1987), p 87 ff; Schreiber, in: Dreier/Sellert (1989), p 167–8 (not a "specifically National Socialist innovation" ["spezifisch nationalsozialistische Neuerung"]); Werle (1989), p 86 ff; Kubink (2002), p 94 ("predecessor...of biological cleansing and 'special treatment'" ["Vorläufer…der biologischen Säuberung und 'Sonderbehandlung'"]), 249 ("use of criminal law that is scarcely bound by the law any more" ["rechtlich kaum mehr gebundene Verwendung des Strafrechts"] as a "radical Lisztian line" ["radikale Liszt-Linie"]; Vormbaum (2015), p 118 ff (121-2), 134, 182, 188.

277 Schaffstein, *DStR* 81 (1935), 97, 99 ("Schößlinge derselben Wurzel"); also *cf* Wolf (1932), p 12 (springing "from the same ideological roots" ["aus den gleichen geistigen Wurzelgründen"]); also id, (1933), p 23 ("difference between brothers of the same tribe" ["Verschiedenheit von Brüdern gleicher Stammesart"]); Welzel, *DRWis* 3 (1938), 113, 119 (building upon a "shared methodological foundation" ["gemeinsamen methodologischen Boden"]); similarly critically on "Binding and Liszt's construction of the 'relation of criminal law'" ["Binding-Lisztsche Konstruktion des 'Strafrechtsverhältnisses'"] and the concept of the "claim to punishment" ["Strafanspruchs"] that rests upon it, Schaffstein, *DJZ* 39 (1934), col 1174 ff (1179–80) (this is based upon the 19th-century "bourgeois-liberal ideology of the rule of law" ["bürgerlich-liberalen Rechtsstaatsideologie", col 1176] and is impossible to reconcile with NS criminal law, as it "limits the significance of punishment to the one-dimensional, internal 'legal relation' between state and criminal" ["Bedeutung der Bestrafung auf die eindimensionale interne 'Rechtsbeziehung' von Staat und Verbrecher beschränkt", col 1180]).

278 *Cf* eg Schaffstein (1934), p 7 ff (overcoming the positivism of the old schools), 18 (*Schulenstreit* "as a dispute between two precondition-less, unpolitical academic opinions" ["als Streit zweier voraussetzungloser und unpolitischer Lehrmeinungen"]); in greater detail Marxen (1975), p 29 ff.

279 *Cf* Henkel (1934a), p 11 ("the historical task of National Socialism will be to overcome Enlightenment thinking in all regards, including in criminal law thought" ["es wird die geschichtliche Aufgabe des Nationalsozialismus sein, das Denken der Aufklärung in allen Beziehungen, so auch im Strafrechtsdenken, zu überwinden"]). On the NS counter-Enlightenment, also *cf* Cattaneo (2001), p. 233 ff.

forth all the more brightly".[280] Ernst Forsthoff made this point bluntly in his infamous text on the "total State":

> "This text does not serve the purpose of historical insight, but political action. Accordingly, it consciously uses a summary technique focused upon highlighting the main fighting positions; and the question of whether this takes us into the realm of arbitrariness [!] will purposely be left unanswered here."
> "The bourgeois age is being dissolved...ruthlessly and with the courage to follow this dissolution through to its ultimate conclusion...Only academic pedants will be concerned that this examination is a summary one and also attacks traditional matter...nobody who recognises that today's crucial task is to mobilise the people's last reserves will join in with these exhortations to be 'objective', to 'venerate the past', the purpose of which is often clearly sabotage."[281]

Accordingly, anti-liberalism—besides the anti-individualism that followed from the over-emphasis on the *Volksgemeinschaft*[282]—formed National Socialism's main focal point.[283]

---

280 *Cf* Marxen (1975), p 25 ff (27) ("um so strahlender leuchten zu lassen") (criticising the Nazis' unhistorical, superficial and distorted account of liberalism).

281 Forsthoff (1933), p 8 ("Diese Schrift steht nicht im Dienste des historischen Erkennens, sondern der politischen Aktion. Sie bedient sich darum bewußt jenes summarischen, auf die Herausstellung der wesentlichen Kampfpositionen gerichteten Verfahrens; und die Frage, ob wirklich das Feld der Willkür betreten wird, soll hier bewußt unerörtert bleiben "), 17 ("Das bürgerliche Zeitalter wird liquidiert…mit Rücksichtlosigkeit und dem Mut zur äußersten Konsequenz…Nur akademische Pedanten werden darüber erschrecken, daß diese Auseinandersetzung summarisch erfolgt und dabei auch an traditionelles Gut Hand angelegt wird…In diesen Ermahnungen zur 'Objektivität', zur 'Ehrfurcht vor der Vergangenheit', hinter denen sich vielfach deutlich die Absicht der Sabotage verbirgt, kann sich heute niemand beteiligen,…der erkennt, daß es heute darauf ankommt, die letzten Reserven aus dem Volke herauszuholen"). For another example see Lange (1933), p IV ("Here, too, the traditional occasionally has been painted blacker than it deserves upon cool consideration; only against this background can the new be defined in clear, sharp focus" ["Auch hier ist das Überlieferte mitunter schwärzer gezeichnet, als es bei kühler Abwägung verdient; nur auf diesem Untergrunde konnte das Neue klar und scharf herausgearbeitet werden"]).

282 *Cf* ch II 1. including fn 118 above.

283 Gross (2010), position. 3165 (referring to Aurel Kolnai's 1938 study "The war against the West").

Chapter IV. National Socialist Criminal Law and Neo-Kantianism

1. *The (alleged) influence of Neo-Kantianism*

Zaffaroni dedicates an entire chapter to the influence of Neo-Kantianism on NS criminal law theory.[284] He argues that the re-normativisation of criminal law brought about by Neo-Kantianism through the teleological method constituted a response to the positivist theory of dangerousness and biologistic criminology. Beyond criminal law discourse, it furthermore expressed a reinvigoration and strengthening of culture as opposed to natural science. From a criminal law perspective, it should be recalled that Neo-Kantianism on the one hand—on a meta-level, as it were—encouraged the normativisation and ethicisation of criminal law.[285] On the other hand, on the level of criminal law doctrine, it constituted the legal-philosophical foundation for the neo-classical theory of crime,[286] including its discovery of the subjective elements of wrongfulness[287] and the development of the normative theory of guilt.[288] By the time the Nazis came to power in 1933, however, the founders of the liberal Neo-Kantian school of

284 Zaffaroni (2017), p 161 ff (ch 5).

285 On the ethicisation of the concept of guilt by early Neo-Kantian criminal law thinking around 1900 (M.E. Mayer, Graf zu Dohna) and the normativisation of the elements of the *actus reus* from 1915 onwards (Mayer, later Grünhut, Mezger, Wolf) Ziemann (2009), p 120 ff, 125 ff, 137–8.

286 Also *cf* Mittasch (1939), p 144 ff (arguing against Mayer's ethical valuation, however); Marxen, in: Rottleuthner (1983), p 56; Stuckenberg, in: Kindhäuser et al (2019), p 134 ff.

287 Mezger, *GerS* 89 (1924), 207, 259 ff; Hegler, *ZStW* 35 (1915), 19, 31 ff (subjective elements of the *actus reus*) (quoted incorrectly by Zaffaroni (2017), p 168 including fn 325); Mayer (1915), p 11–2, 185 ff (subjective elements of unlawfulness as distinct from elements of guilt).

288 Mayer (1901), p 24–5, 102 ff (guilt "as a concept of the moral order" ["als Begriff der sittlichen Ordnung", 104], "legal guilt" ["rechtliche Schuld"] as the "minimum of moral guilt" ["Minimum der sittlichen", 105], culpable action as an "activation of the will contravening a duty" ["pflichtwidrige Willensbethätigung", 106, 107], which expresses an evaluative "attribution" ["Zurechnung"], through which "the value of the act...is charged to the agent" ["der Wert der That...auf Rechnung des Thäters gestellt"], so that "attributing an act to guilt" means "to qualify the action as culpable" ["eine That zur Schuld zurechnen", "die Handlung als schuldhaft zu qualifizieren", 24–5]; Frank (1907), p 9 ff (guilt as culpability, 11); later also Wolf (1933), p 38–9 (social-ethical culpability).

legal science were all already dead, with the exception of Gustav Radbruch. Radbruch himself and further adepts of liberal Neo-Kantianism, such as Max Grünhut (1893–1964) and James Goldschmidt (1874–1940), were removed from their positions relatively quickly by the National Socialists,[289] so that NS criminal law was now able to determine the content of these Neo-Kantian values—which explains Zaffaroni's questionable and ultimately untenable proposition about the influence of Neo-Kantianism on NS criminal law theory (more thereto in section 3. below). According to Zaffaroni, while previously the values providing order and structure came from liberal Enlightenment thought, it was now NS ideology that generated the ideas behind this Neo-Kantian doctrine.[290]

Zaffaroni sees Edmund Mezger as the most important of the Neo-Kantians to be inspired by National Socialism.[291] When discussing Mezger's National Socialist orientation, Zaffaroni basically refers to the work by Spanish scholar Muñoz Conde quoted above[292] as well as to Thulfaut's critical study.[293] In a footnote he also refers to his own mentor Jiménez de Asúa, who did not consider Mezger a Nazi, but thought him a person "without sufficient personal value" ("sin valor personal suficiente");[294] at any rate, however, Jiménez de Asúa did accuse Mezger of having National Socialist leanings.[295]

As we have seen above,[296] Mezger himself emphasised the *völkisch* and racist orientation of the "new" criminal law early on,[297] identified "typical

289 *Cf* Wapler (2008), p 23.

290 Zaffaroni (2017), p 170 ff; for a similar view recently García Amado (2019), without pages; however, this author even has a more limited understanding of Neo-Kantianism than Zaffaroni, namely as value-based cultural science. His position is, as will be seen in the following, even less tenable than Zaffaroni's.

291 Zaffaroni (2017), p 171 ff; previously Zaffaroni, in Zaffaroni (2009a), p 16; in the same vein García Amado (2019). Unfortunately, he did not react to an email inquiry by this author.

292 Ch I 1. including fn 1 and main text.

293 Thulfaut (2000). Critically on Mezger also Vormbaum (2015), p 196.

294 Zaffaroni (2017), p 174 including fn 341.

295 In his study on NS criminal law mentioned in ch I 2. including fn , Jiménez de Asúa initially numbers Mezger among the line of "gloriosos dogmáticos alemanes" since Feuerbach ([1947] vol VII, p 65), but later (p 87 ff, 100 ff) provides evidence for his National Socialist orientation since 1936 (referring particularly to Mezger [1936] and id [1938]).

296 Ch II 2. including fn 201–3 and main text above.

297 Mezger (1934), p V ("people and race" ["Volk und Rasse"] as the "fundamental ideas" ["Grundgedanken"] of the "new total state" ["neue totale Staat"], "idea of the racially selective breeding of the people" ["Gedanke der rassenmäßigen Aufartung des Volkes"]), 21–2 ("irrefutable demand for measures of racial hygiene to eliminate crimi-

groups of enemies of society",[298] demanded that "elements harmful to the people and the race be eliminated",[299] and—like Freisler[300]—characterised criminal law as a "law of combat for the protection and evolution of the people".[301] According to Mezger, the particular tasks of criminal law include the juristic education of the *Volksgenossen* and the atonement of crimes according to the perpetrator's guilt with the aim of upholding law and justice.[302] Guilt itself is to be measured not only according to the act (*Tatstrafrecht*, criminal law of the act), but according to the nature and personality of the perpetrator or agent (*Täterstrafrecht*, agent-focused criminal law),[303] or more precisely according to the blameworthiness of the agent's lifestyle and life decisions (*Lebensführungs- und -entscheidungsschuld*).[304] Thus Mezger, while not renouncing the concept of guilt completely, extends it indefinitely into what preceded the criminal act—to an even greater extent than in the infamous concept of *actio libera in causa*. Ulti-

---

nal strains" ["Forderung nach rassenhygienischen Maßnahmen zur Ausrottung krimineller Stämme unabweislich"]), 203 ("people and race" ["Volk und Rasse"] as the "cornerstones" ["Grundpfeiler"] of the NS state and thus of its criminal law, "responsibility of the individual towards to the *Volksgemeinschaft* ["Verantwortlichkeit des Einzelnen gegenüber der Volksgemeinschaft"]); id (2nd ed 1942), p 238 ("Volksgemeinschaft" as a "biological-historical-political factor" ["biologisch-historisch-politische Größe"], "path of racially selective breeding" ["Weg der rassischen Aufartung"], "responsibility towards the community of the people" ["Verantwortlichkeit gegenüber Volksgemeinschaft"]); also see Mezger, *MSchKrimBio* 31 (1940), 109 ("responsibility of the individual towards the *Volksgemeinschaft*" ["Verantwortlichkeit des Einzelnen gegenüber der Volksgemeinschaft"]), 110 ("*völkisch* legal and moral order" ["völkische Rechts- und Sittenordnung"] as the foundation of National Socialist "communal ethics" ["Gemeinschaftsethik"]).

298 Mezger (1934), p 3 ("typische Gruppen von Gesellschaftsfeinden").

299 Mezger (1934), p 203; id, 1942, p 238 ("Ausscheidung volksschädlicher Bestandteile") (the reference to race is missing here, but reappears two pages on, which Wetzell [2000] p 212 including fn 100 overlooks), 240 ("eradication of those parts of the population that are harmful to the people and the race" ["Ausmerzung volks- und rasseschädlicher Teile der Bevölkerung"]), 245 ("elimination...irrespective of personal guilt" ["Ausscheidung...ohne Rücksicht auf die persönliche Schuld"]); previously Mezger, *MSchrKrimPsych* 19 (1928) 391, 393 (according to the "constitutional understanding of crime" [ie focusing upon the perpetrator's physical constitution; "konstitutionellen Verbrechensauffassung"], there are "incorrigible individuals" ["Unverbesserliche"], who need to be "eliminated from human society ["Ausscheidung aus der menschlichen Gesellschaft"]); later Mezger, *MSchKrimBio* 31 (1940), 109.

300 Ch II 3. including fn 234 and main text above.

301 Mezger (1942), p 78 ("Kampfrecht zum Schutz und zur Entfaltung des Volkes").

302 Mezger (1942), p 247. Once again, Zaffaroni fails to provide the exact source here.

303 See ch III including fn 273 above.

304 Mezger (1942), p 2, 248–9; previously Mezger, *MSchKrimBio* 31 (1940), 109. Critically in this regard Grispigni (1940), in Zaffaroni (2009a), p 42 including fn 19 *in fine*; concurring Zaffaroni, in Zaffaroni, (2009a), p 17 (not applicable to juveniles, merely replacing dangerousness).

mately, it is thus the judge's responsibility to evaluate the perpetrator's lifestyle as expressed in his act in the light of *völkisch* ideology.[305] As long as the judge follows National Socialist rules, he is able to define as "guilty" and exclude from the *Volksgemeinschaft* those who have led a "bad life".[306] Mezger counters the objection that perpetrators may not know that their act is wrongful with his theory of *Rechtsblindheit* or "blindness to the law", according to which those who act without intent (*"rechtsblind"*)[307] still deserve punishment as they demonstrate an attitude towards the legal order that cannot be reconciled with the healthy sentiment of the people;[308] the same should also apply for "blindness to the facts".[309] In 1950, Mezger then substituted *Rechtsfeindschaft* or "hostility to the law" for "blindness to the law".[310] The ensuing objectification of guilt as an (objective) violation of the NS order of values, which is inherent in the concept of *Rechtsblindheit*, is taken up by Mezger in his exchange with the Italian criminal law scholar Filippo Grispigni (who had fascist leanings himself).[311] Here, Mezger separates personal culpability from objective ethical judgements on particular conduct[312] and thus ultimately gives priority to the idea of

305 Zaffaroni (2017), p 179.

306 Zaffaroni (2017), p 178 (*mala vida*); in greater detail Zaffaroni, in: Gómez E. (2011).

307 As an adherent of the (later so-called) theory of intent (*"Vorsatztheorie"*), Mezger was of the opinion that a mistake regarding wrongfulness concerned intent, *cf* Mezger (1949) (reprint 2014), p 330 ff ("knowledge of the unlawful meaning of the act" ["Kenntnis von der rechtswidrigen Bedeutung der Handlung"]), albeit "no juristic evaluation of the act" ["keine juristische Beurteilung der Handlung"] in the sense of correct subsumption, 334).

308 Mezger, *FS Kohlrausch* (1944), p 180 (184: this view does not need to be anchored in law, but is based upon the "inner power of conviction as valid German law" ["inneren Überzeugungskraft als geltendes deutsches Recht"]); on exceptions based upon incompetence, which excludes punishment, id, p 184 ff. Thereto also Zaffaroni (2017), p 180.

309 Mezger, *FS Kohlrausch* (1944), p 184.

310 Mezger (1950), p 43 ff.

311 *Cf* Grispigni (1940), in Zaffaroni (2009a), p 29 ff and Grispigni (1941a), in Zaffaroni (2009a), p 51 ff as well as (on juvenile criminal law) Grispigni (1941b), in Zaffaroni (2009a), p 71 ff. In the first two texts in particular, Grispigni defends the new NS criminal law as perfecting fascist Italian criminal law (the "Codice Rocco" of 1930), focusing first and foremost on Hans Frank (*cf* in particular Grispigni, 1941a, p 69–70) as well as Gürtner and Freisler. In such a criminal law, the freedom of the will is irrelevant, as the focus is criminal law's defence ("defensa") against dangerous perpetrators ("peligrosisimo") in the sense of a "legal-social retribution" ("retribución jurídico-social") that affects the "legal status" ("status jurídico") of every citizen (Grispigni, 1941a, p 52, 55, 65–6 and *passim*). For a critical summary on Grispigni, also *cf* Muñoz Conde, *NDP* 2003A, 303 ff (emphasising the links between him and Mezger); Codino, in Zaffaroni (2009a), p 116 ff.

312 Mezger, *MSchKrimBio* 31 (1940), 109 ("'objective' ethical judgement on a certain conduct" ["'objektives' ethisches Urteil über ein bestimmtes Verhalten"] is independent of

protection (protection from dangerous perpetrators, *defence social*) referred to at the beginning of this section.[313]

Monatsschrift
für
Kriminalpsychologie
und
Strafrechtsreform

gegründet unter Mitwirkung der Herren

Dr. Alfred Kloß
Oberlandgerichtsrat a. D. in Naumburg a. d. S.

Dr. Karl von Lilienthal †
ord. Professor der Rechte in Heidelberg

Dr. Franz von Liszt †
ord. Professor der Rechte in Berlin

herausgegeben von

Prof. Dr. med., Dr. iur. h. c. Gustav Aschaffenburg
in Köln a. Rhein

und

Dr. iur. Hans von Hentig
in München

19. Jahrgang
1928

Heidelberg 1928
Carl Winters Universitätsbuchhandlung

Figure 13: Mezger's early call for the "elimination" (Ausscheidung) of "incorrigible individuals" (Unverbesserliche) from human society, 1928

the perpetrator's freedom of will). In this essay, Mezger attempted to answer Grispigni's question of how "atonement and retribution" are to be reconciled "with the contrasting aspects of race, hereditary disposition, sterilisation etc in the new German criminal law" ("im neuen deutschen Strafrecht Sühne und Vergeltung mit den gegensätzlichen Gesichtspunkten der Rasse, der Erbanlage, der Sterilisation usw", id, 106).

313 Critically in this regard (referring to Grispigni in particular) Muñoz Conde, *NDP* 2003A, 306 ("idea de peligrosidad y que no tiene otra misión que la defensa social"), 309 ("culpabilidad social"), 310 (guilt as "responsabilidad social").

In a similar vein, Kohlrausch (whom Mezger honoured in 1944, contributing a paper to his *Festschrift*) had previously declared mistakes concerning wrongfulness—which he relates to intent in line with the mentioned "*Vorsatztheorie*"—to be negligible if the attitude expressed through the act "cannot be reconciled with the healthy opinion of the people on what is lawful and unlawful".[314] At the same time, he abandoned the distinction between ethics and law and declared *völkisch* ethics to be the standards determining right action.[315] A last name worth mentioning in this context is Wilhelm Sauer, who defined unlawfulness in substantive terms, as what conflicted with "the good of the people and a healthy sense of justice" and thus also propagated NS ideology.[316]

2. *The "Marburg School of Neo-Kantianism"*

Zaffaroni's investigation of Neo-Kantianism concentrates upon Erich Schwinge and Leopold Zimmerl as representatives of the so-called "Marburg School of Neo-Kantianism".[317] However, his account remains superficial, for while Zaffaroni accurately points out that Schwinge/Zimmerl became the leading antagonists of the so-called Kiel School (thereto ch V below), he mentions their main work[318] only in a footnote and focuses upon

---

314 Kohlrausch, *ZStW* 55 (1936), 384, 390 ("der gesunden Volksanschauung über Recht und Unrecht unvereinbar"); previously Schäfer, in: Gürtner (1934), p 50 ff (with a legislative proposal at p 53); thereto also Hartl (2000), p 155 including further references; however, in favour of "taking the mistake into account in principle" ("grundsätzliche Berücksichtigung des Irrtums") Freisler, in Frank (1934), p 6. Thereto also Zaffaroni (2017), p 183–4.

315 Kohlrausch, *ZStW* 55 (1936), 390–1 (ethics to be defined heteronomously starting from the state as "ethics of the people" ["Volksethik"]); similarly Mezger, *MSchKrimBio* 31 (1940), 110 ("communal ethics" ["Gemeinschaftsethik"]).

316 Sauer (1936), p 28–9 ("Volkswohl und dem gesunden Rechtsempfinden") (based upon a three-part concept of unlawfulness requiring an act to be "harmful to the people" ["Volksschädlichkeit"], to "conflict with a norm" ["Normwidrigkeit"] and to "conflict with the culture" ["Kulturwidrigkeit"]). Thereto also Zaffaroni (2017), p 184 ff.

317 Zaffaroni (2017), p 187 ff.

318 Schwinge/Zimmerl (1937) (quoted inaccurately as a monograph by Zaffaroni [2017], p 268 and *passim*). Reply in Schaffstein, *ZStW* 57 (1938), 295 (also reprinted in Dahm/Schaffstein [1938], p 71). Much later, Schaffstein accused Schwinge and Zimmerl of having "a political tinge" ("eine politische Färbung"), claiming that he himself and Dahm had "scrupulously abstained from any political overtones" ("jeder politischen Andeutung peinlich enthalten"; Schaffstein, *JJZG* 7 [2005], 173, 188–9). This accusation is astonishing for at least two reasons. Firstly, Schaffstein himself espoused a political understanding of criminal law, see ch I 2. including fn 35 above. Secondly, political terms, including "National Socialism" and "Führer", frequently occur in Dahm and Schaffstein's works; for just one example, see Schaffstein, *ZStW* 53 (1934), 603, where

two less important individual works.[319] This is problematic not only because in his *Habilitation** thesis on teleological interpretation Schwinge follows the Baden rather than the Marburg school of Neo-Kantianism,[320] but more importantly because the main work of Schwinge/Zimmerl was already perceived as an expression of resistance to the Kiel School's fanatic National Socialism at the time of its publication, including by opponents of National Socialism,[321] and Schwinge himself was certainly an ambivalent figure.[322]

> In their main work, Schwinge and Zimmerl—based upon a historical study of the relation between criminal law and philosophy, which is well worth reading[323]—accuse the Kiel scholars first and foremost of

---

the article's title already expresses a political orientation towards National Socialism; on further examples, see ch V below.

319 Schwinge (1938); Zimmerl, *FS Gleispach* (1936), p 173.

* As already explained previously (fn 57 above) the *Habilitation* is the German post-doctoral qualification procedure and consists mainly (but not exclusively) of the Habilitation thesis (*Habilitationsschrift*).

320 Schwinge (1930), p 4 ff; thereto Stuckenberg, in: Kindhäuser et al (2019), p 135. On the two main schools see section 3 below.

321 Thus Grünhut, who was Schwinge's mentor and was removed from the Bonn Faculty because of his Jewish descent, allegedly approved of the text (Cohn, *FS Schwinge*, 1973, p 1, 3, who himself considers it "striking" ["bemerkenswert"] in its critical openness). Mittermaier, *SchwZStR* 52 (1938), 209, 211 ff was pleased, "as are many others, by the Marburg scholars' bold foray" ("mit vielen anderen über den mutigen Vorstoss der Marburger", 211), ascribing the text a moderating influence on the Kiel scholars and concurring with it for the most part. Radbruch, *SchwZStR* 53 (1939) 109–10 identified the text with the "battle against the so-called Kiel School" ("Kampf gegen die sogenannte Kieler Schule") and referred to Schwinge's subsequent work on "irrationalism" (1938) "as necessary words at the right time" ("als notwendiges Wort zu rechter Zeit"). According to Eb. Schmidt (1965), p 429 the text was felt to be liberating.

322 On the one hand, Schwinge was a member of the "Association of National Socialist German Jurists", but not a member of the NSDAP or its organisations, and was critical of NS ideology; *cf* in this regard particularly Schwinge's colleague at the Marburg Faculty, Cohn (himself a victim of National Socialism), 1973, p 1 ff (pointing out the text "Gehorsam und Verantwortung" ["Obedience and Responsibility"], where Schwinge argued for a limit to obedience towards the political leadership [p 3–4] and for whom the attacks of "extreme left-wing student circles" ["extrem links gerichteter Studentenkreise"] in the 1960s are "hard to understand" ["schwer zu verstehen", p 5]; also see Garbe (1989), p 30, 95 ("scope for contradiction" ["Raum zum Widerspruch"]), not a fanatic NS ideologue). On the other hand, Schwinge—as an academic defender of NS military justice and a practical defender of National Socialists, including members of the SS—remained a revisionist even at an advanced age (in detail Garbe [1989], p 31 ff [role as a military judge during the War], 58 ff [apologist for NS military criminal justice]; also Görtemaker/Safferling (2016), p 437 ["lobbyist making NS military justice appear harmless" ("Lobbyist für die Verharmlosung der NS-Militärjustiz")]; critically also Vogel [2004], p 34 including further references; slightly critically, albeit defending Schwinge on the whole, Spendel, *JZ* 1994, 720).

323 Schwinge/Zimmerl (1937), p 1 ff.

radically breaking with traditional German criminal law science,[324] which had risen to prominence thanks to solid individual studies using an inductive method;[325] instead, so Schwinge and Zimmerl argue, the Kiel school advocates a deductive orientation drawing on the vague concept of "*Wesensschau*", the intuition of essences, in the sense of Husserl's phenomenology—"as the only way...of orienting German criminal law science towards the idea of National Socialism"[326]—and thus "submissively making it the hostage...of a particular philosophical trend".[327] However, "philosophical speculations" and the reference to *Wesensschau* and general "deductions" give judges "stones instead of bread",[328] resulting in a "lack of rules" and "arbitrariness",[329] which is why "the unsuitability" of the phenomenological method "for solving legal-scientific tasks...is conclusively proven".[330] Instead, "a philosophical stance satiated with and matured by experience" is necessary to "reap the benefits of the grand ideas of the political leadership and introduce them into legal life".[331] Here, we can already see that Schwinge and Zimmerl differ from the Kiel scholars not in their goal —the implementation of the "National Socialist movement, which rocks everything with its force", including and indeed through the new criminal law,[332] and in this regard an embracing of criminal law

324 *Cf* especially Schwinge/Zimmerl (1937), p 110–1, where they emphasise "basic scientific rules" ("wissenschaftlichen Grundregeln") and the importance of Binding and Liszt, who need to be understood within the context of their time, instead of being "scornfully dismissed as 'liberals' and 'individualists'" ("verächtlich als 'Liberalisten' und 'Individualisten' abzutun").

325 Schwinge/Zimmerl (1937), p 9 ff.

326 Schwinge/Zimmerl (1937), p 9 ("als einzige Möglichkeit…die deutsche Strafrechtswissenschaft an der Idee des Nationalsozialismus auszurichten").

327 Schwinge/Zimmerl (1937), p 11 ("willfährige Auslieferung…an eine bestimmte philosophische Strömung").

328 Schwinge/Zimmerl (1937), p 13, 14 ("philosophischen Spekulationen", "Wesensschau", "Deduktionen", "Steine statt Brot").

329 Schwinge/Zimmerl (1937), p 55 ("Regellosigkeit", "Willkür").

330 Schwinge/Zimmerl (1937), p 15 ("die Untauglichkeit", "zur Lösung rechtswissenschaftlicher Aufgaben…zur Evidenz erwiesen ist"). Similarly *Mittermaier*, SchwZStR 52 (1938), 217, 224 ("abundantly emotional '*Wesensschau*'" ["reichlich gefühlsmäßige 'Wesensschau'"], "unclear, arbitrary emotional judicature" ["unklare willkürliche Gefühlsrechtsprechung"]).

331 Schwinge/Zimmerl (1937), p 13 ("an der Erfahrung gesättigte und an der Erfahrung gereifte philosophische Haltung", "die großen Gedanken der politischen Führung auszumünzen und in das Rechtsleben einzuführen").

332 Schwinge/Zimmerl (1937), p 109 and the following quoted passages ("der alles erschütternden Gewalt der nationalsozialistischen Bewegung"). Moreover, anti-Semitic tendencies can be found on p 51, which mentions the betrayal by the Jews.

science's political task[333]—but *only in their method* (which makes it hard to understand the work's positive reception, mentioned above).[334] Thus, it is fair to speak of a "**mock battle**" ("Scheingefecht") between the Kiel and Marburg scholars.[335] Thus Schwinge/Zimmerl also speak of the "fetters of positivism", which were however "repressed and overcome before 1933".[336] While they strongly criticise the Kiel School's espousal[337] of Schmitt's doctrine of "concrete order- and form-based thinking",[338] among other things because of Schmitt's ex-

---

333 See ch I 2. including fn 35 ff and main text above.

334 Also *cf* Wolf, *DRWis* 4 (1939), 168, 171–2 ("a process concerning legal procedure, a fight about the way of fighting, a methodological dispute" ["ein Prozeß um das Prozedieren, ein Kampf um die Kampfesweise, ein Methodenstreit", 171], but with a shared "National Socialist basic attitude and goal" ["nationalsozialistische Grundhaltung und Zielrichtung", 172]). Wolf furthermore denies a "dispute of the schools, as there is no difference between those disputing in terms of their criminal policy" ("Schulenstreit, weil gar kein kriminalpolitischer Gegensatz zwischen den Streitenden vorhanden ist", 173). Moreover, "the writings of the Kiel scholars do not contain any practical programme for a new legislative policy, a new structure for degrees of penalty, a new execution of sentences that could not also have been implemented according to the principles of the Marburg scholars" ("läßt sich kein praktisches Programm einer neuen Gesetzgebungspolitik, einer neuen Strafmaßgestaltung, eines neuen Strafvollzugs in den Schriften der Kieler entdecken, das nicht auch nach den Grundsätzen der Marburger verwirklicht werden könnte", ibid).

335 *Cf* Garbe (1989), p 28. In this sense, also *cf* as early as the 1940s Blasco y Fernández de Moreda, *Criminalia* IX (4/1943), 241 ("mismos resultados"); followed by Jiménez de Asúa (1947), p 106 ff (108). Similarly, also Marxen (1975), p 240 ff (244–46), 250–1, who gives Schwinge/Zimmerl great credit for defending legal certainty through traditional doctrine, but ultimately sees their goals as the same as far as the implementation of NS ideology is concerned. Zaffaroni, in Zaffaroni (2011), p 9, 11 ultimately takes the same view (claiming, however, that the Kiel scholars did not consider the Marburg scholars to be "sufficiently National Socialist" [p 25]). Critically however Ziemann (2009), p 132 including fn 717.

336 Schwinge/Zimmerl (1937), p 23 ("Fesseln des Positivismus", "schon vor 1933 zurückgedrängt und überwunden worden"). On National Socialism's battle against positivism, see eg ch II 2. including fn 209 ff and main text above.

337 Ch V 4. including fn 587 and main text and ch VI 5. including fn 623 below.

338 Schmitt (1934), p 8, 13, 16 ff ("konkreten Ordnungs- und Gestaltungsdenken") (distinguishing it from rule- and law-based thinking and decision-based thinking, p 8). In concrete order-based thinking (*konkretes Ordnungsdenken*), "the rule is only a part and a means of the order...the norm or rule does not create the order; rather, it only has a certain regulatory function on the basis and in the context of a given order" ("die Regel nur ein Bestandteil und ein Mittel der Ordnung…Die Norm oder Regel schafft nicht die Ordnung; sie hat vielmehr nur auf dem Boden und im Rahmen einer gegebenen Ordnung eine gewisse regulierende Funktion", ibid, p 13). By contrast, the law arising from rule- and law-based thinking "destroys the concrete order of the king or Führer" ("zerstört", "die konkrete Königs- oder Führer-Ordnung) through the "rule of law" ("Herrschaft des Gesetzes"); "the lords of the Lex subjugate the Rex" ("die Herren der Lex unterwerfen den Rex", p 15). The "legal order is bound to concrete normal

cessive "tendency towards antithetical contrasts"[339] and his attack on abstract concepts (such as the elements of the *actus reus*);[340] at the same time, however, they explicitly recognise his contribution to the development of a National Socialist criminal law science,[341] especially in view of the significance of the concrete (National Socialist) order[342]

concepts" ("Rechtsordnung ist an konkrete Normalbegriffe gebunden"), that "produce norms out of and for their own order" ("Normen aus ihrer eigenen Ordnung heraus und für ihre eigene Ordnung hervorbringen", p 23). In a nutshell, concrete order-based thinking, which is purposely vague, served to transform NS ideology into valid law through the "concrete orders" of lived reality (marriage, labour, the military etc) which have been shaped by a series of norms and rules according to the Nazi leadership's wishes; in greater detail *Rüthers* (1989), p 62 ff (75–6 including further references); also Rückert, in id (2018a), p 274–5.

339 Schwinge/Zimmerl (1937), p 21 ("Neigung zu antithetischen Gegenüberstellungen"). However, Schmitt (1934), p 11 denies such an antithetical focus of his three types of thinking and instead emphasises their "difference" ("Verschiedenheit").

340 Schwinge/Zimmerl (1937), p 17 ff, 81 ff (regarding the elements of the *actus reus* [*Tatbestand*]).

341 Schwinge/Zimmerl (1937), p 23 ff ("thus National Socialist criminal law science cannot thank him enough" ["so kann ihm die nationalsozialistische Rechtswissenschaft nicht dankbar genug…sein"]).

342 Schmitt (1934) ascribes his types of thinking to various peoples and races (p 9) and considers medieval Germanic thought already to be "concrete order-based thinking through and through" ("durch und durch konkretes Ordnungsdenken", p 10), and "concrete order- and community-based thinking" ("konkrete Ordnungs- und Gemeinschaftsdenken") has "never ceased" in Germany ("niemals aufgehört", p 42), and was "brought back to life again" ("noch einmal lebendig", p 45) by Hegel's legal and political philosophy, so that in Hegel the state becomes "the concrete order of orders, the institution of institutions" ("die konkrete Ordnung der Ordnungen, die Institution der Institutionen", p 47). In National Socialism, "concrete order-based thinking has come back to life...the legal axiom that loyalty, discipline and honour cannot be separated from the leadership has become easier to understand...and today, when the movement underpinning the state has sworn steadfast loyalty to the Führer, we are once again able to do direct justice to the legal nature of oaths of loyalty" ("das konkrete Ordnungsdenken wieder lebendig geworden…das rechtliche Axiom, daß Treue, Disziplin und Ehre von der Führung nicht abgetrennt werden dürfen, besser verständlich… Auch können wir heute, da die staatstragende Bewegung dem Führer unverbrüchliche Treue schwört, dem rechtlichen Wesen eines Treueides wieder unmittelbar gerecht werden", p 52); the state "no longer has the monopoly on the political, but is merely an organ of the movement's leader" ("hat nicht mehr das Monopol des Politischen, sondern ist nur ein Organ des Führers der Bewegung", p 66–7). This thinking has become established in legal science, replacing positivism with blanket clauses that "can be related to the interests of the entirety of the people" ("das Interesse des Volksganzen bezogen werden", p 58–9). In criminal law, "undefined" elements of crimes and "normative" characteristics of the elements of crimes have gained currency, the abstract concepts of the General Part are being pushed aside in favour of concrete elements of the *actus reus* (p 60). This is safeguarded institutionally by the estates-based (National Socialist) organisation of the (new) jurists (p 65).

that influences how all law is interpreted,[343] and the role of the judge, who "as the legislator's collaborator" is called to "render the Führer's will concrete".[344]

Wesensschau
und
konkretes Ordnungsdenken
im Strafrecht

von

E. Schwinge und L. Zimmerl
Professoren an der Universität Marburg

1937

LUDWIG RÖHRSCHEID-VERLAG BONN

Figure 14: The Marburg (more traditional) reply of 1937 to the Kiel anti-liberal and authoritarian booklet of 1933; however, it should be noted that both texts agreed on the overall goal of implementing the NS ideology

343 Schwinge/Zimmerl (1937), p 23 (according to whom "all legal-scientific concepts...are embedded in concrete 'orders' that affect their interpretation and influence their content" ["alle rechtswissenschaftlichen Begriffe in...konkreten 'Ordnungen' stehen, die auf ihre Auslegung zurückwirken und ihren Inhalt beeinflussen"]), 24 ("following the

Schwinge and Zimmerl acknowledge that the Kiel scholars bring "concrete order-based thinking"—as "the National Socialist type of thinking *par excellence*"—and phenomenology together "in an original manner",[345] but claim that they have gone too far in their battle against abstraction and their criticism of *Trennungsdenken* (thinking in the separate Kantian categories of *Sein* [being] / matter vs *Sollen* ["ought"] / value).[346] It is unnecessary to distinguish between wrongfulness and guilt,[347] nor is there any need to abolish the concept of *Rechtsgut* (protected legal interest)[348] or Beling's concept of *Tatbestand* (definitional elements of the offence),[349] nor does the law on appeal ("Revisionsrecht") need changing to create a National Socialist criminal law.[350] Rather, all of these traditional concepts can be modernised in terms of their "legal content" ("rechtsinhaltlich") and be "filled" with National Socialist content instead: wrongfulness as (NS-inspired) "harmfulness

National Socialist revolution...reshaping of the fundamental ideas of the *entire order*" ["im Gefolge der nationalsozialistischen Umwälzung...Umgestaltung der tragenden Ideen der *Gesamtordnung*"), 24–5 (observation of the "*special orders* of *völkisch* life" ["*Sonderordnungen* des völkischen Lebens", all italics in the original text]). Marxen (1975), p 238–9 sees more of a "consonance" ("Gleichklang") with Schmitt's doctrine than any "dependency" ("Abhängigkeit") upon it.

344 Schwinge/Zimmerl (1937), p 27 ("als Mitarbeiter des Gesetzgebers", "Führerwillen zu konkretisieren") (emphasising the equal status of law and judge's verdict); also ibid, p 75–6 (judge as the executor of the NS legislator in line with subjective theory, deviation only in the case of pre-NS laws).

345 Schwinge/Zimmerl (1937), p 27 ("konkretes Ordnungsdenken", "nationalsozialistischen Denktyp schlechthin", "in origineller Weise mit einander verbunden").

346 Schwinge/Zimmerl (1937), p 28 ff ("exaggeration and simplification" ["Übersteigerung und Vergröberung", 28], "blind battle against the 'abstract concepts of the General Part'" ["blinder Kampf gegen die 'abstrakten Begriffe des AT'", 29]).

347 Schwinge/Zimmerl (1937), p 33 ff (arguing especially against the Kiel School's subjectivisation, which does not serve "criminal law in the service of the *Volksgemeinschaft*" ["dem Strafrecht im Dienste der Volksgemeinschaft", p 40 ff, 41] and that also goes beyond Freisler's *Willenstrafrecht* [see ch II 3 including fn 230 ff above], as Freisler essentially links subjectivisation only to consequences for the punishability of attempt [43 ff]). Explicitly against this Schaffstein, *ZStW* 57 (1938), 300–1, who accuses Schwinge/Zimmerl of misinterpreting Freisler. The high regard in which well-recognised criminal law scholars held Freisler is quite astonishing. However, according to Schaffstein, *JJZG* 7 (2005), 187, Dahm "always kept his distance from Freisler and...often commented rather disparagingly on his vanity and empty pathos" ("Freisler gegenüber immer auf Distanz gehalten und sich...oft recht abfällig über seine Eitelkeit und sein hohles Pathos geäußert").

348 Schwinge/Zimmerl (1937), p 60 ff.

349 Schwinge/Zimmerl (1937), p 78 ff.

350 Schwinge/Zimmerl (1937), p 95 ff (especially against Siegert).

to the community" ("Gemeinschaftsschädlichkeit")[351] conflicting with the "social-ethical sentiment" of the people,[352] who are constituted as a "community of blood";[353] guilt as a will that contradicts National Socialism.[354] Taken together, wrongfulness and guilt thus represent the harm caused to the "Volksgemeinschaft" by a certain type of perpetrator;[355] a teleological concept of protected legal interests, which is to be oriented not only towards the purpose of the elements of the offence but also—in contrast to the traditional liberal understanding[356]—towards the superior purpose of the National Socialist community and its law;[357] the substantive formation or normativisation of offences

---

351 Schwinge/Zimmerl (1937), p 33-4, 40 ("the act's character as violating the interests of society" ["gesellschaftsinteressen-verletzenden Charakter der Tat", 40], 57–8 (development of "substantive unlawfulness" ["materiellen Rechtswidrigkeit"] on a NS basis; concretisation of "justice and injustice" ["Recht und Unrecht"] through the "National Socialist worldview as expressed...in the Party's programme and the speeches and writings of the Führer" ["nat.-soz. Weltanschauung, so wie sie...im Parteiprogramm und in den Reden und Schriften des Führers zum Ausdruck kommt"]).

352 Schwinge/Zimmerl (1937), p 49 (National Socialist battle against the still widespread "pure individual ethics" ["reine Individualethik"] through "social-ethical sentiment" ["sozialethisches Empfinden"]).

353 Schwinge/Zimmerl (1937), p 58 ("Blutsgemeinschaft").

354 Schwinge/Zimmerl (1937), p 58–9.

355 Schwinge/Zimmerl (1937), p 59.

356 Binding is also co-opted in this regard, as his doctrine of protected legal interests or goods (*Rechtsgüter*) was (according to Schwinge/Zimmerl) oriented towards the social value of these goods and thus could "have come from a textbook on the new NS criminal law" ("aus einem Lehrbuch des neuen nationalsoz. Strafrechts stammen", Schwinge/Zimmerl [1934], p 65).

357 Schwinge/Zimmerl (1937), p 62 ff (methodological concept of protected legal interests oriented towards the "purpose of the rules of the Criminal Code" ["Zweck der Vorschriften des StGB"] and Freisler's (!) "teleological interpretation of laws" ["teleologischer Gesetzesauslegung", 62–3], "orientation of the law towards the idea of the community and the imbuing of judicature with the spirit of National Socialism" ["Ausrichtung des Rechts am Gemeinschaftsgedanken und der Durchdringung der Rechtsprechung mit dem Geiste des Nationalsozialismus", 64], "superiority of *völkisch* communal values" ["Überlegenheit der völkischen Gemeinschaftswerte"], "spirit of the National Socialist renewal of the law" ["Geiste der nationalsoz. Rechtserneuerung", 65], "teleological" method focused on the "content of the law" ["teleologische und rechtsinhaltliche"] corresponds to "National Socialist legal thought" ["nationalsoz. Rechtsdenken"], "National Socialist concept of protected legal interests" ["nationalsoz. Rechtsgutsidee"] as expressing new legal thinking on protected legal interests [72], replacing the "individualist" ["individualistischen"] by a "socialist" ["sozialistischen"] concept of protected legal interests [73, once again referring to Freisler]; harmfulness to the community ["Gemeinschaftssschädlichkeit"] "defined by the National Socialist worldview" ["nationalsoz. Weltanschauung bestimmt", 74]). Also see Schwinge (1930) (not quoted by Zaffaroni); against the teleological methods, by contrast, Schaffstein, *FS Schmidt* (1936), p 49, 59 ff.

based on the National Socialist *Weltanschauung*;[357] and the use of a system of appeals to ensure legal certainty and coherence in the collective interest of the community.[359]

Schwinge takes up these reflections—which obviously contain more than mere "concessions to National Socialism"[360]—in his later book on "irrationalism". Here, too, he rejects as overly irrational[361] the holistic perspective and *Wesensschau* of the Kiel School, which was influenced by vitalism and the philosophy of intuition,[362] and which he sees as contrasting with the "analytical methodology of Neo-Kantianism".[363] While he counters this perspective by "postulating precise research"[364] and "permeating the law with logic"[365], which is a better fit for the German mentality—which wants "what is universally valid, fixed and clearly comprehensible"[366]— he essentially suggests a compromise between intuition and rationality when

358 Schwinge/Zimmerl (1937), p 79 (creation of offences on the basis of National Socialism), 88–9 (orientation of the content of the law towards the "wellbeing of the German Reich and the German people" ["Wohl des deutschen Reiches und des deutschen Volkes"]), 92 (determining the legal content of offences with regard to the "German people's community of blood" ["Blutsgemeinschaft des deutschen Volkes"]), 94 (use of normative elements where "the fundamental idea cannot be clearly expressed through descriptive elements" ["Grundgedanke durch deskriptive Merkmale nicht klar zum Ausdruck gebracht werden kann"], but if possible avoiding unclear and ambiguous terms such as "popular sentiment" ["Volksempfinden"] (!)).

359 Schwinge/Zimmerl (1937), p 98 ("*collectivist* character" ["*kollektivistisches* Gepräge"] of appeal [italics in the original], "predictability of law in the Third Reich" ["Berechenbarkeit des Rechts im Dritten Reich"] as in any other "cultural state" ["Kulturstaat"]), 102 (review of judicial discretion to guarantee a uniform orientation towards the "National Socialist worldview" ["nationalsoz. Weltanschauung"], 105 (review of the correct interpretation of the "healthy sentiment of the people ["gesunden Volksempfindens"]—however, this is contradictory given the warning against using the healthy sentiment of the people on p 94 above, see previous fn).

360 Played down in these words by Ziemann (2009), p 132 including fn 717 ("Konzessionen an den Nationalsozialismus").

361 Schwinge (1938), p 16 ff, 43 ff.

362 Schwinge (1938), p 3 ff.

363 Schwinge (1938), p 16 ("analytisch verfahrende[n] Methodik des Neukantianismus").

364 Schwinge (1938), p 31 ("Postulat exakter Forschung").

365 Schwinge (1938), p 38 ("logische Durchdringung des Rechts"). Even more pointedly Schwinge (1938), p 68: "Form against formlessness, analysis against intuition, conceptual-logical precision against the darkness of rationally inconceivable essentiality" ("Form gegen Ungeformtheit, Analyse gegen Schau, begrifflich-logische Bestimmtheit gegen das Dunkel der rational nicht zu fassenden Wesenshaftigkeit").

366 Schwinge (1938), p 33–4 ("Allgemeingültige, Feste und eindeutig Begreifbare") ("legal certainty" ["Rechtssicherheit"] as a "fundamental value" ["Grundwert"], referring to Göring (!)), 68 (the "German demands clarity, fixity and logical tidiness in law" ["Deutsche fordert Klarheit, Festigkeit und logische Sauberkeit im Recht"], he is "willing to accept rigour, even harshness, but he wants to have the feeling that the law measures his conduct by a standard that is safeguarded against the danger of human error

he recognises the former's role "in the progress of human insight" and sees the latter's function merely as setting boundaries to excessive irrationalism.[367] Similarly, he recognises that a "holistic perspective and precise conceptual analysis need to work hand in hand and complement one another",[368] with "the wholes" needing to be "filled with content and able to be made concrete".[369] This brings us back to the definition of legal content by NS ideology, which shows what Schwinge's real concern was,[370] namely the *implementation of NS legal thinking* through formalisation and rationalisation (he was a true Neo-Kantian in this regard) while at the same time accepting the Führer principle.[371]

Zimmerl, too, while much less influential than Schwinge, placed his theory in the service of the NS state in that he rejected the classic liberal interpretation of the principle of legality—protection from state despotism—by stating that this principle required a contrast between state and individual that could *per se* not exist in the *völkisch* NS state, in which the individual *Volksgenosse* "is only meaningful, his existence only justified as a member of the Volksgemeinschaft".[372] Furthermore, while Zimmerl also acknowledged—as the second function of the legality principle—that the judge was bound to the will of the NS legislator (and thus to the will of

---

and human arbitrariness" ["bereit, Strenge, ja selbst Härte hinzunehmen, aber er will das Gefühl haben, daß sein Verhalten vom Recht mit einem Maß gemessen wird, das gegen die Gefahr menschlichen Irrtums und menschlicher Willkür sichergestellt ist"], referring to the "*völkisch* sense of justice" ["völkische Rechtsempfinden"]).

367 Schwinge (1938), p 41–2.

368 Schwinge (1938), p 57 ("Ganzheitsbetrachtung und exakte begriffliche Analyse Hand in Hand arbeiten und einander ergänzen müssen"); also p 59 ("relation of continuous mutual dependency" ["Verhältnis durchgängiger wechselseitiger Abhängigkeit"]) and p 60 ff (where he mentions "healthy examples of such a holistic perspective" ["gesunde Beispiele einer solchen ganzheitlichen Betrachtungsweise"] in German legal science and then cites "counter-examples" ["Gegenbeispiele"]).

369 Schwinge (1938), p 64 ("die Ganzheiten", "inhaltserfüllt und konkretisierbar").

370 Wolf, *DRWis* 4 (1939), 168 sees the main accomplishment of Schwinge's text as having emphasised "the fundamental side" of the dispute with the Kiel scholars that is "rooted in the history of thought" ("die grundsätzliche, geistesgeschichtliche Seite", 170) and the "philosophical, scientific-theoretical" ("philosophisch, wissenschaftstheoretische") nature of the "matter" ("Angelegenheit", 173).

371 Accurately in this regard Zaffaroni (2017), p 188 ("darle racionalidad al nazismo"), 193 ("irracionalismo en la base de la decisión politíca", "conceptualización racional").

372 Zimmerl, *FS Gleispach* (1936), p 173 ("nur als Glied der Volksgemeinschaft Sinn und Daseinsberechtigung erhält") ("National Socialism will never be able to recognise a natural contrast between the *Volksgemeinschaft* organised in the state and the individual *Volksgenosse*" ["Einen naturgegebenen Gegensatz zwischen der im Staat organisierten Volksgemeinschaft und dem einzelnen Volksgenossen…kann der Nationalsozialismus niemals anerkennen"]). Thereto Zaffaroni (2017), p 194–5.

the Führer),[373] he wanted to see this as setting legislative boundaries to overly punitive judges;[374] other than that, he tried to limit "the healthy sentiment of the people",[375] which he felt to be problematic,[376] in such as way that it should be subordinate to criminal liability according to the "fundamental idea of a criminal law".[377] Zaffaroni fails to mention these attempts at limitation, which are certainly oriented towards the rule of law.

3. *Neo-Kantianism—a forerunner of National Socialist criminal law?*

Attentive readers will have noticed the implicit criticism of the link that Zaffaroni constructs between Neo-Kantianism and NS criminal law. At a later point in his book,[378] Zaffaroni brands "the" (!) Neo-Kantians as mere technocrats loyal to the regime (in contrast to the genuine Nazis of the

---

373 Zimmerl, *FS Gleispach* (1936), p 173–4 (primacy of the legislator due to "idea of leadership" ["Führergedanken"], legislator as the "supreme leader" ["Oberführer"]).

374 Zimmerl, *FS Gleispach* (1936), p 174 ("It can...be of the greatest significance that the judge does not arbitrarily or over-zealously punish an act that the legislator...did not wish to be punishable" ["Es kann…von größter Bedeutung sein, daß der Richter nicht willkürlich oder aus Übereifer eine Tat bestraft, die der Gesetzgeber…straflos lassen wollte"]).

375 Zimmerl, *FS Gleispach* (1936), p 175 ("fiction of a clearly identifiable popular sentiment that also judges difficult individual questions consistently" ["Fiktion eines klar erkennbaren, auch die schwierigen Einzelfragen einheitlich beurteilenden gefundenen Volksempfindens"].

376 Zimmerl, *FS Gleispach* (1936), p 175–6: no "loosening of the binding of the judge to the law" ("Lösung der Bindung des Richters an das Gesetz"), as the fundamental idea of the criminal law forms the first and superordinate condition of criminal liability; healthy sentiment of people is not a "second source of the law" ("zweite Rechtsquelle"), as "this opinion would only be tenable if the people's healthy sense of justice were in itself able to justify liability" ("diese Meinung wäre nur haltbar, wenn das gesunde Rechtsempfinden des Volkes für sich allein imstande wäre, die Strafbarkeit… zu begründen"). This conflicted with the National Socialist view, *cf* ch II 1. including fn 117 above.

377 This was the (alternative) first condition of criminal liability according to the altered § 2 StGB (RGBl I 1935 839), fn 181 above.

378 Zaffaroni (2017), p 232 (drawing a distinction to the staunch Nazi Dahm: "los neokantianos la asumían solo como *tecnócratas al servicio del régimen que fuese*" [italics in the original text]). Zaffaroni considers Dahm's criticism of Neo-Kantianism to be justified in principle (Zaffaroni (2017), p 235 ff ["críticas en general coherentes", 237]), but at the same time accuses Dahm of only wanting to destroy the Neo-Kantian theory of crime so as to establish the NS unified concept of the perpetrator on its ruins and legitimate the terrible crimes of the NS state (ibid, p 237). While Dahm proves himself to be an "intelligent dogmatist" by uncovering the internal contradictions of the Neo-Kantian model of crime, the sole purpose of this endeavour was to establish the NS doctrine of crime (ibid, p 238).

Kiel School), revealing an incomprehensible antagonism to the whole Neo-Kantian movement that blithely ignores—possibly due to its selective reception in Latin America—the "multifariousness"[379] of what Neo-Kantianism actually encompasses.[380] Zaffaroni classes certain thinkers as (juristic) Neo-Kantians without even defining what this term means.[381] Without a conceptual explanation, however, it is impossible to prove a particular author's affinity to Neo-Kantianism; at best, we can point out teacher-student relations, but even categorising a teacher as a Neo-Kantian requires the concept of Neo-Kantianism to be defined.[382]

Neo-Kantianism is "not a self-contained school",[383] but a "political movement with many diverse branches"[384] that existed since the late 19th century, bringing together many very different (individualist and collectivist)[385] lines of thought.[386] The common denominator of all these lines was their attempt to respond to the scientistic, materialistic worldview of the 19th century.[387] The transition from materialism to (Neo-Kantian) idealism took place through mediating approaches that (initially) did not re-

---

379 Wiegand (2014), p 93 ("Mannigfaltigkeit").

380 *Cf* Guzmán Dalbora, *RDPC* VII (2017), 231, according to whom translations have familiarised Hispanic America only with the "liberal mode" ("modalidad liberal") of criminal law Neo-Kantianism.

381 On this widespread error Wapler (2008), p 41.

382 On the criteria mentioned here (teacher/student relationship and affinity with Neo-Kantianism in terms of content), *cf* Wapler (2008), p 148.

383 *Cf* eg Holzhey, in: Ritter (1984), col 749, quoting F. Paulsens ("not a self-contained school, but the endeavour to subject the concepts we operate with to epistemological review" ["keine abgeschlossene Schule, sondern das Bestreben, diejenigen Begriffe, mit welchen wir operieren, einer erkenntnistheoretischen Prüfung zu unterwerfen"]); Ziemann (2009), p 23 ("not a self-contained form" ["keine geschlossene Gestalt"]).

384 Wapler (2008), p 29 ("vielfältig verzweigte politische Bewegung") ("collective designation" ["Sammelbezeichnung"]).

385 Emphasised by Wapler (2008), p 18 ff, 213 ff, for whom the different individualist or collectivist understandings of the value of law were crucial in determining the scholars' legal-philosophical and methodological orientation (more towards the individual or towards the community), but she also stresses the multiplicity of the various individual understandings.

386 Thereto including further references Holzhey, in: Ritter/Gründer (1984), col 747 ff (depicting the various strands existing since around 1875, which differ both in terms of content and geography and according to L.W. Beck had "little in common" [cited in ibid, 750]); also Österreich (1951), p 416 ff (distinguishing between seven "lines of Neo-Criticism" ["Richtungen im Neukritizismus", 417]).

387 Thereto instructively Wiegand (2014), p 41 ff; also Lepsius (1994), p 304 (compensating the deficits of the natural science method); Murmann (2005), p 104–5 ("turn against natural-scientific thought" ["Wendung gegen das naturwissenschaftliche Denken"], "independence of the humanities from the natural sciences" ["Selbständigkeit der Geisteswissenschaften gegenüber den Naturwissenschaften"]); Stuckenberg, in: Kindhäuser et al (2019), p 125.

ject the reductionist, scientistic worldview wholesale, but instead aimed to complement it.[388] Around the turn of the century, two main strands emerged:[389] the Marburg (logicist) line and the Baden or southwest German (value-theoretical and criticist) line.[390] Their most important representatives[391] are Cohen, Natorp and (with a legal-philosophical focus) Stammler on the one hand and Windelband, Rickert, Lask and (with a legal-philosophical focus) Radbruch[392] and Kelsen on the other hand.[393] However, we would need to investigate each individual author's personal relation to National Socialism and whether (and if so, how) their theory facilitated or served National Socialism. Other authors, such as Mezger[394] and Schwinge/Zimmerl, all three mentioned by Zaffaroni, were influenced by Neo-Kantianism—something that probably applies to all authors in the Humanities, given Neo-Kantianism's importance in the early 20th century, and thus is hardly significant—but were certainly not important

388 *Cf* Wiegand (2014), p 47 ff (going into detail on R.H. Lotze and F.A. Lange in particular).

389 Zaffaroni (2017) only mentions these in passing on p 166.

390 Holzhey, in: Ritter/Gründer (1984), col 750–1 (late 19th and early 20th century); also see Wapler (2008), p 29 ff, 38 ff; Lepsius (1994), p 305; Stuckenberg, in: Kindhäuser et al (2019), p 126–7. On the Marburg line, Müller (1994), p 1 ff, who questions the existence of a unified legal philosophy in Marburg and thus a "school" ("Schule") in the narrower sense (ibid, p 8) and prefers to speak of a "legal-philosophical working group" ("rechtsphilosophische Arbeitsgemeinschaft", p 6) whose existence can, however, "be regarded to have failed" ("als gescheitert anzusehen war", p 6) by "1913 at the latest" ("spätestens 1913", p 6) because of the unsolvable "conflict between natural law doctrines and legal-positivist points of view" ("Widerstreit von Naturrechtsdoktrinen und rechtspositivistischen Auffassungen", p 3). In detail on the southwest German line, Wapler (2008), p 16–7 ("value-theoretical line of tradition" ["werttheoretische Traditionslinie"], 40–1 (emphasising its diversity) and *passim*, distinguishing between the philosophical concept of value (p 29 ff) and—building upon this concept—the juristic concept of value (p 147 ff) and showing that transitions to legal philosophy (collectivism, teleological conceptualisation) are only to be found in Lask's case (p 144 ff, 151–2); distinguishing between philosophical and juristic Neo-Kantianism also Lepsius (1994), p 304 ff, 318 ff; on Neo-Kantianism in criminal law, see especially Ziemann (2009), p 25 ff.; also Stuckenberg, in: Kindhäuser et al (2019), p 132 ff.

391 Wapler (2008), p 16–7, 29, 38, 39–40; Lepsius (1994), p 305; Dreier/Paulson (1999), p 236–7.

392 On Radbruch in detail Wiegand (2014), p 103 ff; also Kaufmann/von der Pfordten, in: Hassemer et al (2016), p 80 ff; Mahlmann (2017), p 179 ff.

393 On Neo-Kantianism's influence on Kelsen's pure theory of law, *cf* Paulson, in: Alexy et al (2002), p 13 ff; on Kelsen's pure law Neo-Kantianism Lepsius (1994), p 324 ff.

394 Critically in this regard even Muñoz-Conde, Prólogo, in Zaffaroni (2017), p 20 ("un tanto exageradamente"). Ziemann only refers to Mezger in passing in this regard (eg p 123 including fn 661) and explicitly does not number him among the Neo-Kantian criminal law scholars (p 126 including fn 678); concurring Stuckenberg, in: Kindhäuser et al (2019), p 132 ff (mentioning Mezger only in passing as an antagonist of Welzel with regard to the latter's ontological approach).

representatives of this line of thought (Mezger, who was (more) important as a criminal law scholar, even less so than Schwinge). Categorising authors in this manner is hard not least because Neo-Kantianism in criminal law[395]—just like juristic Neo-Kantianism in general—had no coherent, self-contained theory.[396]

The **core content** of (juristic) Neo-Kantianism is not easily defined.[397] The connection to Kant's philosophy is more complicated than the name "Neo-*Kantianism*" would seem to suggest, as the movement was concerned not (only) with a "return to Kant",[398] but with a neo-idealist development of his epistemology that had strong Hegelian elements.[399] Thus Windelband and Rickert, for example, construct a collectivist understanding of law and the state in which not much remains of Kant's individualist intent with its safeguarding of liberty, and in which the influence of Fichte and Hegel is clearly evident.[400] On the other hand, efforts to define the "*a priori* fundamental concepts of law"[401] through the subject's active role in the

---

395 Ziemann (2009), p 119 ff distinguishes between three main phases: (i) the beginnings of Neo-Kantian criminal law thought around 1900, (ii) its popularisation in the 1920s and (iii) its decline in the 1930s dispute over methods and orientation.

396 Ziemann (2009), p 103–4, 106 ff at least includes Schwinge among the main representatives of Neo-Kantianism in criminal law alongside M.E. Mayer, E. Wolf and Grünhut (in greater detail Ziemann [2009], p 117 ff, references in fn 529), but emphasises the difficulty of categorisation as southwest German Neo-Kantianism did not produce a "self-contained system of criminal law" ["geschlossenes Strafrechtssystem", ibid, p 103). Stuckenberg, in: Kindhäuser et al (2019), p 135 includes Honig in this list.

397 Wapler (2008), p 23 ("extraordinarily unclear" ["außerordentlich unklar"]).

398 As was still claimed by Lange, the founder of Marburg Neo-Kantianism, Lange (1915), p 3 ("go back to Kant" ["auf Kant zurückgehen"]). References to earlier Neo-Kantians (Liebmanns etc) in Österreich (1951) IV, p 418; also Stuckenberg, in: Kindhäuser et al (2019), p 125.

399 Wapler (2008), p 31–2 (reference to Kantian epistemology in the first Neo-Kantian works of the mid-19th century), 33 ff (neo-idealist development of Kant's epistemology); on the "epistemological divergences" ("erkenntnistheoretischen Divergenzen") between Kant and the so-called Marburg school, *cf* Müller (1994), p 11 including fn 18. Also *cf* von der Pfordten, *JZ* 2010, 1022 ff, who not only sees "little" ("wenig") of Kantianism in Neo-Kantianism (Neo-Kantianism develops and changes Kantianism, but "has little to do with Kantianism in the proper sense" ["richtig verstanden, wenig…zu tun hat", 1022]; turn towards Neo-Hegelianism in the early 20th century [1023]; while methodological dualism is "genuinely southwest German Neo-Kantian" ["genuin südwestdeutsch neukantianisch"], it is actually "very un-Kantian" ["sehr unkantisch", 1024]), but also is unable to find the core elements of Radbruch's legal philosophy—law must be focused upon the idea of the law, that is, justice—in Kant or the Heidelberg Neo-Kantians (1025); also *cf* von der Pfordten (2004), p 333–379, where he traces Radbruch's idea of the law back to Hegel and thus declares Radbruch's Neo-Kantianism to be Neo-Hegelianism. See also more recently Paulson, *JZ* 2018, 1064.

400 Wapler (2008), p 25.

401 Braun (2001), p 6 ("apriorischen Grundbegriffe des Rechts").

process of gaining knowledge[402] and an *a priori* conceptualisation that "creates" its object ("gegenstandserzeugend"),[403] reveal a closeness to Kant's epistemology.[404] From a methodological perspective, Neo-Kantianism thus represents a *scientific epistemology*[405] that in its juristic variety becomes an *epistemology of law*.[406] Another key shared trait of Neo-Kantian thought is its *methodological dualism*, that is, its differentiation between reality (matter, being or *Sein*) and value (form, "ought" or *Sollen*).[407] Thus the concept of value is understood in formal terms by southwest German Neo-Kantianism (which has a value-theoretical orientation),[408] but otherwise—in line with the abovementioned individualist and collectivist tendencies[409] and the difference between value absolutism and value relativism—is not used consistently;[410] in juristic southwest German Neo-Kantianism, particularly

402 Wapler (2008), p 44, 173.

403 Lepsius (1994), p 333 ("understanding of reality that is only produced through the method itself" ["Wirklichkeitsverständnis, das durch die Methode erst erzeugt wird"]); for a differentiated discussion of the concept of the object, Wapler (2008), p 45–6, 156–7; on National Socialist conceptualisation, which abolishes the object, see the following section (4.) including fn 467.

404 Explicitly tracing Neo-Kantianism back to Kant, Ziemann (2009), p 33 ff, especially his *a priori* form of knowledge (p 36 ff); also see Mittasch (1939), p 126 ("knowledge of what is theoretically correct" ["Erkenntnis des theoretischen Richtigen"] as the goal of legal science); Murmann (2005), p 104 ("harking back to Kant's epistemological approach" ["Rückbesinnung auf den erkenntnistheoretischen Ansatz Kants"]).

405 Österreich (1951), p 416 ("emphasis on the significance of thinking for knowledge" ["Betonung der Bedeutung des Denkens für die Erkenntnis"]).

406 Wiegand (2014), p 90–1 ("meta-theory of knowledge" ["Metatheorie der Erkenntnis"]); Lepsius (1994), p 335 including fn 108; Wapler (2008), p 148; Ziemann (2009), p 32 ff (epistemology as a method); also Braun (2001), p 6.

407 Wapler (2008), p 37–8, 42–3, 155–6; Lepsius (1994), p 333; Dreier/Paulson (1999), p 13, 237; von der Pfordten, *JZ* 2010, 1024, 1026; for an instructive illustration, see Kaufmann/von der Pfordten, p 82; differentiating, Ziemann (2009), p 105–6; on the origin of the contrast beween *Sein* and *Sollen* in Kant, Loos (1970), p 36 ff. – By adding the further category of law as a "cultural phenomenon" ("Kulturerscheinung"), Radbruch himself turned this into a methodological trialism and converted his legal philosophy into a "cultural philosophy of law" ("Kulturphilosophie des Rechts") (*cf* Dreier/Paulson (1999), p 6 including fn 2, 25; p 237–8; Wapler (2008), 155, 194–5, 201–2).

408 Wapler (2008), p 43, 157.

409 Fn 386 above.

410 Wapler (2008), p 26–7 (eg it is controversial whether the individual human being or the community should be seen as the law's highest purpose), 31 (absolutist understanding of value in Windelband, Rickert and Lask vs a relativist understanding in the legal-philosophical Neo-Kantians, especially Radbruch, see next fn), 41 ff (value theory of southwest German Neo-Kantianism between metaphysics and relativism); also Ziemann (2009), p 71 ff (objective and absolute claims by valuations that really are subjective and relative); for a differentiated account on Windelband and Rickert concerning the *Sein–Sollen* dichotomy, Loos (1970), p 39 ff; see generally Braun (2001), p 6 (recognition of a value relation and justice as the goal of the law).

in Radbruch's theory, value-relative positions became dominant.[411] The valuations of the active subject become values independent of said subject, giving rise to the distinction between valuations (which are made individually) and values (which are accessible through scientific insight).[412] Value philosophy (*Wertphilosophie*)[413] takes on a legitimating function,[414] leading to a denial of the scientific facticity of law.[415] Finally, Neo-Kantianism is a *cultural philosophy* in that culture forms the (normative) antithesis to nature and creates the value relation of Neo-Kantianism ("value-relational cultural science" or "wertbeziehende Kulturwissenschaft").[416] This value relation also defined Neo-Kantian criminal law theory, which was concerned with supplanting positivist-naturalist criminal law thinking with value- and purpose-oriented (teleological) criminal law thinking,[417] which continues to play a dominant role to this very day in the form of the instrumentally rational ("*zweckrational*") or functional criminal law system.[418]

---

411 Wapler (2008), p 160–1 (Radbruch, Kelsen as representatives of a strict value relativism as opposed to the overwhelming majority of the legal philosophers influenced by Windelband's and Rickert's theory of absolute value, such as Stammler and M.E. Mayer); on Radbruch in this regard also Ziemann (2009), p 86 including further references; on Jellinek's value relativism, Wapler (2008), p 165 ff.

412 Wapler (2008), p 47–8; also Wiegand (2014), p 224.

413 On the "value science" ("Wertwissenschaft") of southwest German Neo-Kantianism, Ziemann (2009), p 82 ff.

414 In detail Ziemann (2009), p 70 ff; on value-related (and reality-related) criminal law conceptualisation, Mittasch (1939), p 3–4.

415 *Cf* Wolf (1933), p 27 (rediscovery of law "as a value...and...not just as a fact" ["als einen Wert...und...nicht bloß als Faktum"]); on (Rickert's) Neo-Kantianism as a complementary theory to positivism (empirism) Welzel (1962), p 190 (quoting Jaensch); Loos (1970), p 4.

416 *Cf* Mittasch (1939), p 3, 18–9, 22–3 (value relation as expressing the "specifically cultural-scientific character of legal science" ["spezifisch kulturwissenschaftliche Charakter der Rechtswissenschaft", 3]; Ziemann (2009), p 56 ff (culture as both a guideline and a purpose). Lask transfers the "value-relational cultural science" ("wertbeziehende Kulturwissenschaft") to law (ibid, p 63 ff), and it also plays an important role in Radbruch (methodological trialism, see fn 408 above; ibid, p 65 ff, 101–2). On value-relational, cultural-scientific thinking within the context of the theory of protected legal interests, Amelung, in: Alexy (2002), p 363, 365 ff.; on the ensuing distinction between natural and cultural science Stuckenberg, in: Kindhäuser et al (2019), p 128–9.

417 Going back to Liszt, *cf* Mittasch (1939), p 20 ff, 84 ff; also Ziemann (2009), p 143.

418 Summarising including further references Roxin (2006) § 7 mn 26 ff; Jakobs (1993), p VII–VIII ("(re-)normativisation of concepts" ["(Re-)Normativierung der Begriffe"]), 5–6 (defining the content of criminal law concepts of the remit of criminal law, especially the general preventive affirmation of norms); also Schünemann, in: id (1984), p 45 ff (Roxin's ascription of the tiers in the structure of crime to individual guiding values as a "fruitful development of Neo-Kantianism, which had petered out in value relativism" ["fruchtbare Fortentwicklung des im Wertrelativismus versandeten Neukantianismus", 47], "instrumentally rational system thinking" ["zweckrationale Systemdenken"] as a

As far as the aforementioned[419] Schwinge is concerned, as a student and protégé of the Neo-Kantian criminal law scholar Max Grünhut[420] (who was removed from his position by the Nazis, as mentioned above), he was originally influenced by (Baden) Neo-Kantianism, as per his teleological conceptualisation developed in his *Habilitation* thesis of 1930.[421] In his 1934 co-publication with Zimmerl[422] at the latest, however, Schwinge turned towards Schmitt's concrete order-based thinking,[423] infused his concept of legal interests with National Socialist ideology,[424] and rejected Neo-Kantian methodological dualism.[425] In this regard, his work, in substance, was in agreement with the Kiel School (which he actually fought against), and not only as far as their antagonism to Neo-Kantianism was concerned,[426] but also in regard to their "undoubtedly clear National Socialist attitude",[427] which is why it is certainly possible to speak of a (methodological) "mock fight" between Schwinge and the Kiel scholars.[428] The reason that Neo-Kantianism declined in the 1930s at the same time as the NS movement gained in strength was not, as Zaffaroni implies, its merging with National Socialism, but, quite to the contrary, its ideological

---

"development of Neo-Kantianism" ["Fortentwicklung des Neukantianismus", 51]; "remarkable renaissance" ["frappierende Renaissance"] of the Neo-Kantian Lask's conceptualisation theory by Jakobs [54]); also see Stuckenberg, in: Kindhäuser et al (2019), p 146 (current functional approaches without Neo-Kantianism "hardly conceivable").

419 Section 2. including fn 323 and main text above.

420 On his Neo-Kantian bent, Ziemann (2009), p 115 ff.

421 *Cf* Cohn (1973), p 2 (influence of Windelband and Rickert); Wapler (2008), p 151–2, 211 (Lask's influence); Stuckenberg, in: Kindhäuser et al (2019), p 135; on Schwinge's teleological concept of legal interests, Amelung (1972), p 133–4, 134 ff (critically).

422 Section 2. including fn 324 ff and main text above.

423 Section 2. including fn 342 and main text above.

424 Section 2. including fn 358 and main text above. Critically also Amelung (1972), p 139, 229.

425 Schwinge/Zimmerl (1937), p 47 towards the end, 58 (in favour of an equivalence of law and ethics, "not opposites" ["keine Gegensätze"]); however, also see ibid, p 50 (against complete equivalence). On Schwinge, also see Wapler (2008), p 254.

426 Eg Schaffstein, *ZStW* 56 (1937), 105 ("most recent developments characterised by a rejection of" the value philosophy of the southwest German school ["neueste Entwicklung im Zeichen der Abkehr von"]), 106 ("from Neo-Kantianism to a theory of conceptualisation influenced partly by phenomenology, partly by Hegelianism" ["vom Neukantianismus zu einer teils phänomenologisch, teil hegelianisch beeinflußten Begriffsbildungslehre"], neo-Kantian doctrine with teleological conceptualisation, abstract theory of elements of crimes, substantive unlawfulness and normative guilt as a "transitional stage that has already been outgrown" ["bereits überwundenes Durchgangsstadium"]).

427 Wolf, *DRWis* 4 (1939), 172 ("unzweifelhaft klaren nationalsozialistischen Grundhaltung").

428 Garbe (1989), p 28 ("Scheingefecht"); see section 2. including fn 335 above.

neutrality and liberal tendency,[429] for which there was no longer any space in these times of *völkisch*, racist prepotency.

As far as *teleological conceptualisation* is concerned, it was famously advocated not only by Neo-Kantians with National Socialist leanings, but also before this by some of the (Jewish) victims (Grünhut,[430] Honig[431]) of National Socialist persecution.[432] This is hardly surprising, for teleological conceptualisation is nothing other than the consequence of the Neo-Kantian, value-related pre- and re-formation of the concepts of criminal law.[433] It exists as such to this day within the instrumentally rational or functional system of criminal law,[434] and is a recognised method of interpretation.[435] As to the "Marburg School", in our context mainly represented by Schwinge, it must not be overlooked that of its abovementioned main representatives, only Stammler was co-opted by the National Socialists,[436] while Cohen was discriminated against because of his Jewish descent;[437] furthermore, whether Stammler really belonged to the school is disputed, not least because of the differences between him and Cohen.[438] Finally, as

429 Ziemann (2009), p 130 ff (130); Stuckenberg, in: Kindhäuser et al (2019), p 145.

430 On Grünhut in this regard, including further references, Ziemann (2009), p 116–7.

431 *Cf* Honig (1919). On Honig in this regard, also see Ziemann (2009), p 118 including fn 625 ("the real founder of 'teleological conceptualisation'" ["der eigentliche Begründer der 'teleologischen Begriffsbildung'"); on his concept of protected legal interests, Amelung (1972), p 130 ff, 134 ff (critically).

432 On Stammler's teleological perspective, Ziemann (2009), p 101.

433 Thereto Mittasch (1939), p 30–1; Ziemann (2009), p 135 ff.; Stuckenberg, in: Kindhäuser et al (2019), p 129 ff (146).

434 Fn 419 above.

435 *Cf* eg Zippelius (2012), § 10 II.

436 *Cf* Müller (1994), p 9–10 including further references.

437 *Cf* eg Riecke (1935), p 11 ff, for whom the distance between (Marburg) Neo-Kantianism and NS racism is already proven by the fact that Cohen, as "this line's main representative" ("Hauptvertreter dieser Richtung"), is a Jew and pursues "a philosophy in his system of classification" ("in seiner Systematik eine Philosophie") "that derives from the basic Jewish psychological attitude and that he himself proclaims to be the culmination of intellectual life in his ethics" ("die aus der psychologischen Grundhaltung des Judentums stammt und von ihm selbst in seiner Ethik als Höhepunkt des geistigen Lebens proklamiert wird", ibid, p 11). In actual fact, Cohen's epistemology—being as "the being of thinking" ("das Sein des Denkens")—cannot be reconciled with NS racism because this "being of thinking" cannot be seen as exhaustive, and value and real life need to be added to it (thereto ibid p 13–4).

438 *Cf* Müller (1994), p 3 ("belonging to the school...negated" ["Schulzugehörigkeit... verneint"]), 8 ff ("supposed rejection" ["vermeintliche Abkehr"]) including further references.

regards the left-wing, liberal[439] Neo-Kantian legal philosophers,[440] it is to be noted that most of them were the losers and victims of the NS takeover,[441] while other Neo-Kantians came to terms with the Nazi regime or even actively supported it.[442] This latter group included Dahm (a student of Radbruch) as well as Erik Wolf (a student of Lask);[443] we will return to them in chapters V and VI. All in all, the accusations that Zaffaroni levels at Neo-Kantianism are far too sweeping; the necessary in-depth investigation of the authors he mentions (or of other "Neo-Kantian" authors) in regard to their possible contributions to National Socialism is lacking.

4. *Collectivism and material theories of value—forerunners of National Socialist criminal law?*

In actual fact, matters are far more complicated. While the absolutist understanding of value and the collectivist approach of the southwest German school can be seen to have a certain affinity to totalitarian ideologies[444] (especially as Rickert, one of its most important exponents, turned to National Socialism[445]), we cannot deduce a linear development from

---

439 Lepsius (1994), p 305–6 emphasises the affinity to democratic socialism, especially in the case of the Marburg line.

440 Zaffaroni (2017), p 169, only mentions Radbruch, M.E. Mayer, Grünhut, Freudenthal, Goldschmidt and H. von Weber in passing, but not Kelsen, for example.

441 Ziemann (2009), p 131 mentions Grünhut, Radbruch and Honig as criminal law Neo-Kantians in this regard.

442 Ziemann (2009), p 132 mentions E. Wolf, Schwinge and Mezger as criminal law Neo-Kantians in this regard (although he does not count Mezger as a Neo-Kantian, see fn 395 above).

443 According to Amelung, in: Alexy (2002), p 369, Wolf was the "'shooting star' of Neo-Kantian criminal law" ("'shooting star' der neukantianischen Strafrechtswissenschaft").

444 *Cf* eg on the *völkisch* "idea of the state" ("Staatsidee") as the final goal of the value-relational concept of criminal law Mittasch (1939), p 4, 25–6, whose views incidentally are firmly based upon NS law (see eg his reference to "Jew" as a descriptive term in the Nuremberg "Blood Protection Law" [p 50] and his approval of Nazi reformatory efforts [p 100]); Riecke (1935), p 11 even sees the southwest German school, in contrast to Marburg Neo-Kantianism, as "readily" comparable "with the problem of the idea of race" ("ohne weiteres mit der Problematik des Rassegedankens"), as it is defined "by irrational elements of being" ("durch irrationale Seinselemente"); critically also Cattaneo (2001), p 222, 225 (Neo-Kantian value-based understanding of protected legal interests ["Rechtsgüter"] as a rejection of the liberal understanding of protected legal interests). On the closeness of Radbruch's transpersonalism (1932, p 54 ff [Dreier/Paulson (1999), p 58 ff]) to NS ideology, see Wiegand (2014), p 187 ff; critically Wapler (2008), p 229–30. At any rate, Radbruch's value-relativism/-pluralism (fn 447 below) and his concept of the idea of the law (fn 448 below) speak against totalitarian tendencies.

445 Wapler (2008), p 32, 140 ff.

Neo-Kantianism to the NS regime from this, for two reasons. Firstly, the way that value is understood does not predetermine the *content of the values* propagated, and many representatives of juristic Neo-Kantianism rejected value absolutism/collectivism. Thus Radbruch in particular on the one hand advocated value relativism and value pluralism,[446] and on the other hand declared justice as the expression of the idea of the law to be the law's highest purpose.[447] Secondly, the *basic (methodological) assumptions* of Neo-Kantianism, particularly methodological dualism, cannot be reconciled with National Socialism.[448] Thus Radbruch already noted in 1933 that the National Socialists regarded the distinction between law and morals as "a mere liberal prejudice".[449] Lepsius stated in 1994 that Neo-Kantianism "cannot be made responsible for the emergence of National Socialism",[450] for anyone "who was a Kantian could not become a National Socialist".[451] While this is something of an overstatement in that important Neo-Kantians (such as Rickert and Stammler) did embrace National Socialism, which shows that more is needed than a certain methodological commitment,[452] nevertheless, the basic claim that the fundamental assumptions of

---

446 In the preface to his Legal Philosophy (1932, p VI [cited from Dreier/Paulson, 1999, p 3–4]), Radbruch already emphasised the need to adhere to rationalism and relativism ("as the intellectual precondition of democracy" ["als gedankliche Voraussetzung der Demokratie"]) against the rise of irrationalism; on relativism in greater detail ibid, p 10 ff [17 ff].

447 Radbruch (1932), p 30 [cited from Dreier/Paulson, 1999, p 34] ("The idea of the law can be none other than justice" ["Die Idee des Rechts kann nun keine andere sein als die Gerechtigkeit"]), 32 [37] ("law is the reality whose meaning is to serve justice" ["Recht ist die Wirklichkeit, die den Sinn hat, der Gerechtigkeit zu dienen"]), with "justice in this sense" meaning "equality" ("Gerechtigkeit in solchem Sinne Gleichheit", p 30 [35]); the idea of the law is to be understood as a triad of justice, purposiveness and legal certainty (§§ 7–10); thereto also Dreier/Paulson (1999), p 239; with regard to Kantorowicz Paulson, *JZ* 2018, 1067.

448 NS authors explicitly rejected methodological dualism and *Trennungsdenken*, calling for ethicisation instead, *cf* ch II 2. including fn 193 above and ch V 3. including fn 557 below. However, there was a continuity with earlier perspectives in this regard, too, see eg Liszt, *ZStW* 27 (1907), 91 (in favour of a "synthesis between what is and what ought to be" ["Synthese zwischem dem Seienden und dem Seinsollenden"] as the core of a "normative science" ["normativen Wissenschaft"], against Neo-Kantians as diverse as Windelband, Rickert, Radbruch and Stammler).

449 Radbruch (1933/1957), p 74 ("ein bloßes liberalistisches Vorurteil").

450 Lepsius (1994), p 304 ("für die Entstehung des Nationalsozialismus nicht verantwortlich gemacht werden kann").

451 Thus Lepsius (1994), p 341 ("Kantianer war, konnte nicht Nationalsozialist werden").

452 On Rickert in this regard Wapler (2008), 258, who deduces from this (among other things) that "a particular epistemological view...obviously" does not provide "immunity against totalitarian ideology" ("bestimmte erkenntnistheoretische Auffassung…offenkundig noch keine Immunität gegen totalitäres Gedankengut"); on further counterexamples, von der Pfordten, *ARSP* 82 (1996), 593.

Neo-Kantianism—value relativism and methodological dualism—are irreconcilable with National Socialism is correct.[453] From a NS perspective, the original (relativist) Neo-Kantian normativisation had become bogged down in the positivism of existing values, which is why it needed to be transcended and an (absolutist) orientation towards the new National Socialist valuations embraced.[454] And indeed, Schwinge's National Socialist turn from an originally Neo-Kantian position on the one hand and Radbruch's consistent opposition to National Socialism on the other hand confirm the assumption that a value-relativist, ideologically neutral position (as always adopted by Radbruch)[455] has a greater affinity with democracy and is more hostile to dictatorship than a value-absolutist, ethicising position (as adopted by Schwinge).[456]

---

453 *Cf* in this regard Lepsius's study (1994, p 335 ff [341]) on Laun's concept of the *Volk*, which, while it did not differ from the NS *Volk* concept in terms of its content and function, still adhered to methodological dualism and thus did not adopt the NS being-focused understanding of reality with its consequence of a conceptualisation that abolished contrasts and antitheses ("gegensatzaufhebende Begriffsbildung"). Concurring with Lepsius in principle in this regard, Wapler (2008), p 258; von der Pfordten, *ARSP* 82 (1996), 593. *Cf* on Marburg Neo-Kantianism Müller (1994), p 9, who points out that the NS aversion "to thinking in the critical spirit of Kant" ("gegen das Denken im kritischen Geiste Kants") led "the National Socialists to ostracise" the Marburg scholars as a whole ("von den Nationalsozialisten geächtet wurden"). On anti-liberal thinking's antagonism to southwest German Neo-Kantianism because of the latter's apolitical relativism, Marxen (1975), p 170–1.

454 For a basic account, *cf* Schaffstein (1934), p 11 ff (critically on the value-related, teleological method of southwest German Neo-Kantianism [11], whose "ethical relativism" ["ethischen Relativismus"] made it impossible to advance to the "correct values" ["richtigen Werten", 12] and which had failed to produce "a real and conscious political valuation" ["eine echte und bewußte politische Wertung", 13]; instead, Schaffstein calls for an orientation towards the new *völkisch* and racist valuations of the totalitarian NS state and the Führer principle [18 ff, 23 ff]).

455 A fact unaltered by the critical and differentiated appraisal ("relativisation" ["Relativierung"]) of the 1922 "Radbruch Draft" for a German General Criminal Code in Goltsche (2010), p 367 ff (396) (see critically also Vormbaum (2011), p 17 ff). While this appraisal's criticism is certainly accurate, especially concerning the Draft's (Lisztian) subjectivisation in line with agent-focused criminal law, its tendencies towards the criminal law of the will and its particularly harsh treatment of so-called habitual offenders (Goltsche [2010], p 370 ff, 385, 391, 395–6), these aspects are due both to the influence of Radbruch's teacher Liszt and to pragmatic factors (also *cf* ibid, p 7–8, 387 ff), which do not change the fact that Radbruch's position was value-relativist, ideologically neutral and thus fundamentally liberal.

456 As is well known, Welzel took a different view and criticised Radbruch's relativism precisely because it "inevitably" ("zwangsläufig") leads to "the surrendering of the law to power" ("zur Auslieferung des Rechts an die Macht", Welzel, 1962, p 188, 252).

Against this background it is necessary to make a distinction[457]—omitted by those who link Neo-Kantianism to NS criminal law[458]—between the (originally) formal, epistemologically oriented Neo-Kantianism and the material, phenomenologically oriented *theories of value and being* by scholars such as Max Scheler[459] and Nicolai Hartmann,[460] which emerged from Neo-Kantianism[461] and became dominant in the 1930s.[462] It is certainly possible to see these theories as the legal-philosophical starting point or foundation of National Socialism,[463] as they combatted Neo-Kantian formalism and its ideological neutrality.[464] Instead, they advocated the (National Socialist) merging of *Sein* (being) and *Sollen* (ought)—leading *Sollen* to become imbued with or oriented towards reality (the "concrete

457 Schmitt, *FS Forsthoff*, 1967, p 37 (44, 49) also emphasises this distinction; similarly Wiegand (2014), p 79–80 (southwest German Neo-Kantianism "not a value *ethics*" ["keine Wert*ethik*"] ["inadmissible ethicisation" ("unzulässige Ethisierung")], but "a philosophy of *theoretical validity*" ["eine Philosophie der *theoretischen Geltung*", italics in the original text]); in regard to the basic position of (Scandinavian) Neo-Kantianism, which was critical of metaphysics (albeit only referring to Hageström), Lindner (2017), p 29.

458 Neither Zaffaroni (2017) nor García Amado (2019) make this distinction. The latter cites Ferrajoli (1995), p 186, where this autor puts both theories on an equal footing, referring to "sugerencias neokantianas y de la filosofía de los valores" (in the edition of 2005, cited here, the quote is on p. 486).

459 Scheler (1916); Scheler (1919).

460 Hartmann (1926).

461 Amelung (1972), p 226 and *passim* speaks of post-Neo-Kantian theories in this regard, or of theories "that took over from Neo-Kantianism" ("den Neukantianismus ablösten", p 224); Wapler (2008), p 24, 27, 243 speaks of a turn towards or transitions to material theories of being; similarly Paulson, *JZ* 2018, 1064; Stuckenberg, in: Kindhäuser et al (2019), p 145 (displaced by theories of value).

462 Wapler (2008), p 162.

463 On the value theories' NS tendencies, eg Amelung (1972), p 141 ("hypostasisation of the value judgement that constitutes interests" ["Hypostasierung des güterkonstituierenden Werturteils"]), 224 (more dangerous for democracy than "Neo-Kantian relativism" ["der neukantianische Relativismus"]), 226 ff (shared "battle against the naturalist and (formal) liberal dogma of crime as a causal violation of protected legal interests" ["Kampf gegen das naturalistische und (formal-)liberale Dogma vom Verbrechen als kausaler Rechtsgutsverletzung", 226], legitimated "by *völkisch* cultural values" ["an völkischen Kulturwerten", 227]); Wapler (2008), p 243 ff; also Frommel, *JZ* 2016, 913 (facilitation of National Socialism, but no proof); on the irrationalism of vitalism (Bergson, Nietzsche, Dilthey) as the precondition of anti-liberal criminal law, Marxen (1975), p 18, 47 ff. – Also see the dispute concerning the phenomenological foundations of the Kiel theories in Schwinge/Zimmerl (1937), section 2. including fn 327 ff and main text above; against this Dahm *ZStW* 57 (1938) 225, 285, and ch V 2. including fn 549 ff and main text below.

464 *Cf* Ziemann (2009) p 133 ("criticism of Neo-Kantian formalism and...turn towards ontologically given material" ["Kritik am neukantianischen Formalismus und...Hinwendung zu einem ontologisch vorgegebenen Material"], referring to Welzel); also Marxen (1975), p 55, 170–1 ("feeble relativism" ["schwächliche Relativismus"] of Neo-Kantianism).

orders" of the people and their way of life)[465] and resulting in a conceptualisation that abolishes contrasts and antitheses ("gegensatzaufhebende Begriffsbildung")[466]—as well as the ethicisation and metaphysical intellectualisation of (criminal) law.[467] Their irrationalism was opposed by none other than Schwinge[468] (controversially styled as the main representative of National Socialist Neo-Kantianism by Zaffaroni).

Nevertheless, it is fair to say that southwest German Neo-Kantianism's *absolutist-collectivist* concept of value already contained the seeds of the material theories of value,[469] and that collectivism, as the main foundation of these theories, facilitates totalitarian tendencies such as those of National Socialism, for a collectivist approach implies precisely that conflicts between the individual and the collective will be resolved on the higher level of the collective to the individual's disadvantage.[470] On the other hand, the transition from the Neo-Kantian concept of value to the material theories of value and from these to National Socialism was by no means inevitable

---

465 Wapler (2008), p 243; on National Socialism's battle against methodological dualism, also ibid, p 32, 249–50, 258.

466 Lepsius (1994), p 146 ff and *passim* (dialectical abolition of the natural and intellectual elements of a concept, of being and ought, reality and value on a higher conceptual level as well as of real contrasts such as that between individual and people on a higher real level, for example the will of the Führer as an expression of the will of the people [E.R. Huber], so that the concepts appear "as the embodiment of a valid reality" ["als Verkörperung einer werthaften Wirklichkeit", 149, 153], so that normative "validity" ["Werthaftigkeit"] becomes real validity as the new reality [153–4]).

467 On the transformation of the content of the (originally formal) concept of value in this regard, Ziemann (2009), p 138 ff ("transformation of the value-relational, formal...into a value-implementing, material concept of value" ["Transformation des wertbeziehend-formalen...zu einem wertverwirklichend-materialen Wertbegriff", 141]); also Vogel (2004), p 72 (cultural goods become socially and ethically charged in value-relational thinking). However, also see Cattaneo (2001), p 237–8, who sees Hartmann's understanding of ethics as a stark contrast to that of National Socialism.

468 Section 2. including fn 324 ff and main text, 363 ff and main text above. Critically also Mittasch (1939), p 17–8.

469 Also see Wapler (2008), p 245 ("transition to material theories of being already set up in southwest German Neo-Kantianism" ["Übergang zu materialen Seinsphilosphien im südwestdeutschen Neukantianismus bereits vorbereitet"]), who in the following (p 246 ff) presents "striking examples" ("markante Beispiele") of this transition, namely the turn towards Neo-Hegelianism in Erich Kaufmann and Binder, and Sauer's theory of monads of value (*Wertmonaden*). Here, we can also mention Erik Wolf, who in 1933 established the new criminal law system's "view of value and reality" ("Wert- und Wirklichkeitsbetrachtung") based upon southwest German Neo-Kantianism among other things, referring seamlessly to Husserl and Heidegger's phenomenology, through which the Neo-Kantian "realisation" of law's independence from the natural sciences "beyond methodology" ("Einsicht über das Methodologische hinaus") became established (Wolf [1933], p 27–8, 32; on this text, see ch VI 1. including fn 704 ff and main text below).

470 Also *cf* Wapler (2008), p 259.

or linear.[471] Countless examples prove this, not least the Neo-Kantian thinkers persecuted because of their Jewish origins,[472] but above all the abovementioned methodological difference between these theories and (juristic) Neo-Kantianism, especially in its value-relativist, value-pluralist form (Radbruch), which is diametrically opposed to the authoritarian absolutising of particular values or a particular ideology.[473]

The classic criticism of grounding the law on value[474] targets the purely intuitive justification of values, as this justification is impossible to understand intersubjectively and ultimately leads to an irrational "*tyranny of values*"[475] over the law.[476] More recently, this critique has manifested as criticism of a metaphysical legal science that puts the case for ideologically charged, substance-ontological truths or judgements on what is right.[477] As such, this criticism is directed also and above all against material theories of value. However, we should not overlook that the significance of values

471 Also *cf* Wapler (2008), p 249 ("not inevitable" ["nicht zwangsläufig"], but "turn to National Socialism...certainly stands to reason...from the perspective of a national-conservative collectivism" ["Wendung zum Nationalsozialismus...aus der Sicht eines nationalkonservativen Kollektivismus...durchaus naheliegend"]).

472 Wapler (2008), p 249 mentions the Neo-Hegelian Erich Kaufmann in this regard. In other cases, such as Binder and Sauer, their support for National Socialism was not unreserved; eg Binder maintained that the individual must be respected, *cf* Wapler (2008), p 250 ff; critically on Sauer, however, Jiménez de Asúa (1947), p 92 ff. On the other hand, the Kiel scholars, including Dahm (who had been a disciple of Radbruch!), rejected Neo-Kantianism in general and teleological conceptualisation in particular, *cf* section 3. including fn 427 above and Wapler (2008), p 253–4.

473 The flipside of relativism is its lack of a human rights/fundamental rights limitation of "flawed law" ("unrichtiges Recht"), which famously led to Radbruch's natural law "turn", thereto fn 499 ff and main text below.

474 Bockenförde, in: Dreier (1990), p 33 ff.

475 This expression was coined by Hartmann (1926), p 524 ("Tyrannei der Werte"). However, it was turned against the theorists of value by their critics, *cf* eg Schmitt, *FS Forsthoff* (1967), p 59.

476 *Cf* Bockenförde, in: Dreier (1990), p 41 ff (value-based thinking lacks "a rational foundation structured around discursive mediation" ["eine rationale, auf diskursive Vermittlung angelegte Grundlage"] and thus opens "the floodgates to the methodologically uncontrollable subjective opinions and views of judges and legal scholars as well as to the dominant current values and valuations of society" ["die Schleuse für das Einströmen methodisch nicht kontrollierbarer subjektiver Meinungen und Anschauungen der Richter und Rechtslehrer sowie der vorherrschenden zeitigen Tageswerte und -wertungen der Gesellschaft", p 41]; thus eg Mittasch (1939), p 32–3 ("value-relational legal science is not only rational, but also 'emotional-casuistic'", as "values and their relative validity...cannot be wholly grasped rationally" ["wertbeziehende Rechtswissenschaft nicht nur verstandesmäßig, sondern zugleich auch 'gefühlsmäßig-kasuistisch'...Werte und ihre relative Geltung...nicht bis ins letzte rational erfaßbar"]).

477 Lindner (2017), p 4 ff, 181 (metaphysical temptation as the assertion of extra-legal ideas of value, morals and justice through organised power structures, for example during the NS period, which is why metaphysical self-restraint is necessary).

and valuations for any legal order is undeniable and indeed unavoidable.[478] Essentially we are dealing with a methodological criticism that can be countered by disclosing and explaining the foundations on which the respective valuation is based;[479] in a democratic state under the rule of law, these foundations arise from the state's liberal constitution, which is rendered concrete through case law (constitutionalised criminal law!). The criticism directed against material theories of value thus does not apply to rational, intersubjectively and discursively mediated and constitutionally anchored value foundations.[480] It is certainly ironic that precisely Carl Schmitt[481] and Ernst Forsthoff[482] styled themselves and are cited as critics of the grounding of law on value,[483] given that these authors were co-responsible for the National Socialist tyranny and absolutisation of values, validating this tyranny and absolutisation in their legal theory.[484]

However, rejecting any grounding of the law in value *a limine* because of the National Socialist "tyranny of values"[485] would mean throwing the baby out with the bath water.[486] The abovementioned (pluralist) values of the liberal constitutional state, for example—in particular human dignity,

---

478 As stated accurately by Starck, in: Dreier (1990), p 47 ff.

479 *Cf* eg Starck, in: Dreier (1990), p 51 ff, who suggests inter-subjective recognition from an empirical-historical and legal comparative perspective as well as fundamental anthropological assumptions as criteria of rightness.

480 Also *cf* Starck, in: Dreier (1990), p 49.

481 Schmitt, *FS Forsthoff* (1967), p 37 ff (49, 59 ff). However, Schmitt remains silent on his own role; while he establishes a link to the National Socialist, racist absolutisation of the German people as the "highest value" ("Höchstwert", Hitler), he does so as if none of this concerned himself (p 42).

482 Forsthoff, *Festgabe Schmitt* (1968), p 185 (190, 209–10), who warns against the easy "up-, re- and de-valuation" ("Auf-, Um- und Abwertung") of values and thus against understanding fundamental rights as such ("If National Socialism had encountered fundamental rights in the form of values in 1933, it would not have needed to abolish them" ["Hätte der Nationalsozialismus 1933 die Grundrechte als Werte vorgefunden, dann hätte er sie nicht abzuschaffen brauchen", p 190]), rejecting the "material charging of the law" ("materiale Aufladung des Rechts", p 209) for this precise reason (pointing out the "de- and re-valuations" ["Ab- und Umwertungen"] of the century [ibid]); arguing against Forsthoff Starck, in: Dreier (1990), p 50.

483 Thus in Bockenförde, in: Dreier (1990), p 34, 46.

484 Accurately in this regard Robbers, in: Dreier (1990), p 162, 167–8 (pointing out Schmitt's absolutising of individual values and his friend-foe thinking).

485 Schmitt, *FS Forsthoff* (1967), p 37 ff.

486 Similarly Starck, in: Dreier (1990), p 50 ("The fact that the valuations which formed the foundation of the NS regime ultimately proved to be contemptuous of human life, as everyone can see, does not mean that we have to fundamentally criticise all valuations as foundations of the law" ["Weil sich die Wertungen, die Grundlagen des nationalsozialistischen Regimes waren, letztes Endes für jedermann erkennbar, als menschenverachtend herausgestellt haben, müssen wir nicht zur Fundamentalkritik aller Wertungen als Grundlagen des Rechts schreiten"]).

justice and substantive equality—certainly constitute a normative programme that is able to counter totalitarian tendencies antagonistic towards human rights.[487] A programme such as this is a necessary complement to positivism, for while it was not—contrary to a well-known myth circulated by former and new Nazis in the postwar period[488]—positivism alone that rendered German jurists defenceless against NS injustice. This so-called **positivism or defencelessness thesis** of Radbruch's[489] is in fact a positivism **myth**, for National Socialism itself, as already shown above,[490] combatted positivism because of its restrictive effect, enlisting first and foremost the judges as operators of a "natural law thinking" perverted by racism and *völkisch* ideology;[491] the law was only to be strictly binding for NS legislation, especially the *Führerbefehl*.[492] Thus it is well recognised today that the German jurists' compliance with National Socialism arose from the combination of "a perverted legal positivism...and a perverted 'natural law thinking'".[493] Notwithstanding, in the postwar period many jurists (with NS leanings) retrospectively styled their battle against the

487 On the corresponding human-rights-focused value-based orientation of comparative law, see Ambos, *RW* 8 (2017), 247, 271–2 (English version in 24 *UCLA J. Int'l L & For. Aff.* (forthcoming 2020)).

488 On eg Schwinge, see Garbe [1989], p 76 including further references; also see Welzel, *FS Niedermeyer* (1953), p 279–8, according to whom "20 years ago (ie 1933!)...positivism ruled uncontested" ["vor 20 Jahren...völlig unbestritten der Positivismus" "herrschte"], the Third Reich "took legal positivism at its word" ["den Rechtspositivismus beim Wort genommen"], "really followed positivist theory through" ["mit der positivistischen Lehre...wirklich Ernst gemacht"], which is why "even an order to kill all blue-eyed children was valid if issued by the person holding supreme state authority" ["selbst ein Befehl zur Tötung aller blauäugigen Kinder gültig sei, wenn er nur vom Inhaber der höchsten Staatsgewalt ausgeht"]; also Dahm (1956), p 15, according to whom there is "also" (!) ["auch"] "a development...from natural law to positivism and from positivism back to natural law" ["die Entwicklung...vom Naturrecht zum Positivismus und vom Positivismus zum Naturrecht zurück"] in international law; in detail including further references Foljanty (2013), p 23 ff (distinguishing between three lines of development).

489 Radbruch, *SJZ* 1 [1946], 105, 107.

490 *Cf* ch II 2. including fn 209 ff and this chapter's section 2. including fn 337, all with main text above.

491 *Cf* ch II 1. including fn 141 and this chapter's section 2. including fn 345, 374, all with main text above.

492 Ch III including fn 263 and main text above.

493 Dreier/Paulson [1999], p 248 ("einem pervertierten Gesetzespositivismus...und einem pervertierten 'Naturrechtsdenken'"); concurring Braun, *JZ* 2017, 454; also *cf* Marxen (1975), p 251–2 (rejection of strict legality because of a material, normative concept of crime and a strict binding only to NS legislation/*Führerbefehl*); Maus (1989), p 81 ff (two false premises of the positivism thesis, namely a failure to recognise NS norms' character as laws and as sufficiently defined orders [p 82 ff] and a failure to recognise the anti-positivist tendencies that already existed prior to 1933 [p 84 ff], in actual fact a "binding to values" ["Wertbindung"] instead of a binding to the law [p 92]); Walther,

"straw man" of positivism as a battle against NS legal thinking and after 1945 dedicated themselves to a renewal of the law that focused upon natural law to externalise their responsibility and displace their own guilt.[494] As a consequence, the "defencelessness thesis" turned victims of NS persecution such as Kelsen, Radbruch etc into perpetrators themselves[495] and served as an argument against punishing the perversion of the course of justice and for rehabilitating the NS judiciary as a whole.[496]

At any rate, "flawed law" still needs to be limited normatively through human rights. Precisely this is the lesson of Radbruch's relativisation of his authoritarian theory of the validity of law, which accorded primacy to le-

---

in: Dreier/Sellert (1989), p 325 ff, 335 ff (neither legal positivism nor *Geltungspositivismus*, "validity positivism", existed in the Weimar Republic, nor did National Socialism employ the argument of validity positivism); Wapler (2008), p 255 ff (no positivist turned to NS, NS doctrine was "radically anti-positivist" ["radikal antipositivistisch", p 257]; it was not positivism that rendered the German jurists defenceless, but their inability or unwillingness to defend the written law [p 257–8]); Foljanty (2013), p 19 ff (antipositivist "direction" ["Richtung"] since the First World War continued in NS); Ott (2016), p 25 ff (defencelessness thesis is "demonstrably wrong" ["nachweislich falsch", p 27], for anti-positivism already existed during the Weimar Republic and NS law is itself anti-positivist; most jurists were anti-liberal and believed in the authoritarian state); Lindner (2017), p 181 (NS ideology abhorred positivism and NS law was "metaphysical law, imbued with extra-legal ideologies of substance that used concepts such as blood, people, race, unworthiness to live etc to carve out a trajectory that was contemptuous and indeed destructive of human life" ["metaphysisches Recht, aufgeladen durch außerrechtliche Substanzideologien, die sich mit Hilfe von Begriffen wie Blut, Volk, Rasse, Lebensunwert etc. ihren menschenverachtenden und -vernichtenden Weg gebahnt haben"]); Frommel, *JZ* 2016, 913, 916, 919–20 (who rightly points out that positivism was the enemy of National Socialism); Whitman (2017), p 148 ("not... legal positivism at all...close to common law pragmatism"); against the myth also Rückert, *ZRG-GA* 103 (1986), 207–8; id, *JZ* 2015, 804; Rüping/Jerouschek (2011), p 111 (emphasising the general support of the regime); Stolleis (2016), p 11, 23 ("refuted" ["widerlegt"]).

494 *Cf* Walther, in: Dreier/Sellert (1989), p 350 including fn 42 *in fine*; in detail on this natural law "turnaround literature" ["Wendeliteratur"], "straw man" positivism and externalisation/guilt displacement Foljanty (2013), p 4 ff, 35–40, 37 ff; critically on the widespread silence, "networks" ["Netzwerken"] and "turnaround literatures" ["Wendeliteraturen"] Frommel, *JZ* 2016, 917 ff, 2017, 462 (on Welzel in particular) and Rüthers, *JZ* 2017, 457 ff; on the exonerating function of the positivism myth also Gross (2010), position 214.

495 Foljanty (2013), p 38–9.

496 Ibid, p 76 ff including further references.

gal certainty,[497] through the Radbruch Formula.[498] The formula is concerned with limiting "flawed law" through a turn towards individualism[499] —which increases the value-relativist, democratic element of Radbruch's

497 Radbruch (1932), p 81 [Dreier/Paulson, 1999, p 82] ("If nobody is able to ascertain what is just, then somebody needs to define what is to be lawful, and...put an end to the conflict between differing views of the law through an *authoritative fiat*...he who is able to implement the law thus proves that he is called to make laws" ["Vermag niemand festzustellen, was gerecht ist, so muß jemand festsetzen, was Rechtens sein soll, und...den Widerstreit entgegengesetzter Rechtanschauungen durch einen *autoritativen Machtspruch*...beenden...Wer Recht durchzusetzen vermag, beweist damit, daß er Recht zu setzen berufen ist", italics K.A.]) and p 83 [84] ("It is the judge's professional duty to bring the law's will to validity to bear, sacrificing his own sense of justice to the authoritative legal order, only asking what is lawful and never whether it is also just" ["Für den Richter ist es Berufspflicht, den Geltungswillen des Gesetzes zur Geltung zu bringen, das eigene Rechtsgefühl dem autoritativen Rechtsbefehl zu opfern, nur zu fragen, was Rechtens ist, und niemals, ob es auch gerecht sei"]). Thereto Dreier/Paulson (1999), p 245–6; critically (of all people!) Welzel, *FS Niedermeyer* (1953), p 279 ("schooled in such theories", "the German jurists" sallied forth "into the 'Third Reich'" ["in solchen Lehren ausgebildet", "die deutschen Juristen ins 'dritte Reich'"]) and Bockenförde, in Dreier (1990), 43 (according to whom Radbruch "released the German jurists" "into the NS regime" with this "orientation" ["die deutschen Juristen", "Orientierung", "in das NS-Regime entlassen"]); critically also Walther, in: Dreier/Sellert (1989), p 339–40 (which is why Radbruch's positivism thesis becomes a "self-accusation" ["Selbstanklage"]). However, it should be noted that Radbruch held fast to rationalism and relativism (fn 447 above) and even before 1933 did not advocate a purely positivist concept of the law, given his orientation towards the idea of the law and towards justice (fn 447 above) (thereto Wapler [2008], p 202 ff; similarly Frommel, *JZ* 2017, 460, who emphasises Radbruch's "relativist foundations" ["relativistischen Grundlagen"]).

498 Radbruch, *SJZ* 1 (1946), 105 (107) (limits to the basic priority of positive law if "the conflict between positive law and justice reaches a level so unbearable that the law, as 'flawed law', needs to make way for justice" ["der Widerspruch des positiven Gesetzes zur Gerechtigkeit ein so unerträgliches Maß erreicht, daß das Gesetz als 'unrichtiges Recht' der Gerechtigkeit zu weichen hat"; translation adapted from Litschewski Paulson and Paulson, *OJLS* 26 (2006), 1. Thereto including further references Dreier/Paulson (1999), p 247 ff; Wapler (2008), p 261 ff (who all assume, bz the way, that Radbruch's approach remained continuous); likewise against a natural law turn on Radbruch's part Frommel, *JZ* 2016, 916–7; however, in favour of such a turn (replying to Frommel) Braun, *JZ* 2017, 452 ff (contrasting Radbruch quotes from before and after 1945) and Rüthers, *JZ* 2017, 459; rejoinder by Frommel *JZ* 2017, 460, 462, who is willing to recognise only a "*personal* turn" ("*persönliche* Wende", italics in the original text), while Radbruch's earlier relativist (anti-positivist and anti-natural law) position is retained. Interestingly, Erik Wolf—whom Frommel sees as responsible for the natural law interpretation—himself identified a "seamlessness" ("Ungebrochenheit") and "continuity" ("Kontinuität") in Radbruch's works (thus Hollerbach, *JZ* 2017, 455, 456–7).

499 Wapler (2008), p 264; similarly Frommel, *JZ* 2017, 460 (emphasising the "importance of an individualist position" ["Wichtigkeit einer individualistischen Position"] after 1945).

theory—and through the recognition of inalienable human rights.[500] Thus it comes as no surprise that, in the (Bonn and Berlin) Republic of the *Grundgesetz*, *Wertungsjurisprudenz* ("value-based-jurisprudence") has persisted in different variations in the legal theory discourse[501] as well as in criminal law, Neo-Kantian, value-related thinking.[502]

500 *Cf* Wiegand (2014), p 194 ff (equality is rendered concrete by drawing upon human rights). – This recourse to human rights grounded upon natural law was of course to a certain extent the flipside of the positivism myth mentioned in fn 494 above, which is why it is hardly a surprise to encounter it more frequently among authors contaminated by National Socialism; *cf* in particular Dahm (1956), p 15, where he advocates a "heightened significance" ("erhöhte Bedeutung") of human rights within the context of a "historically and culturally relative natural and cultural law with a changing content" ("geschichtlich und kulturell relativierten Natur- und Kulturrechts mit wechselndem Inhalt"); also Welzel, *FS Niedermeyer* (1953), p 290 ff (293–4), where he recognises, besides "factual-logical structures" ("sachlogischen Strukturen") (which only bind the legislator in a "relative" manner, however ["nur relativ", p 293]), standards derived from natural law and human rights (Kant's "object formula", human dignity) as "intrinsic limits of positive law" ("immanente Grenzen des positiven Rechts"), "as intrinsic material principles that no state order may violate" ("als immanente materiale Prinzipien, die kein staatlicher Befehl verletzen darf") (in his criticism of Radbruch's relativism, fn 457 above, Welzel does not mention Radbruch's turn, however); as an author above suspicion (because born later) Amelung (1972), p 258 (recognising the theory of cultural value as restricting NS terrorism). On the glorification of NS statements through an "apparently safe and whole natural philosophy" ("scheinbar heile Naturrechtsphilosophie"), Eser, in: Hilgendorf (2010), p 77, 80 (referring to the public law scholar Günter Küchenhoff).

501 Rückert, in id (2018a), p 278 ff (distinguishing three variations); on the continuity of the methodological post-1945 discourse still clinging to the traditions of German idealism, Stolleis (2016), p 36 ff.

502 *Cf* Roxin (2006), § 7 mn 27 (refinement and development of the "Neo-Kantian...approaches of the interwar period, which...had become buried in the Nazi period" ["neukantianischen...Ansätze der Zwischenkriegszeit, die...in der Nazizeit verschüttet worden waren"]); thereto also Ziemann (2009), p 19; on the remaining "discoveries" ("Entdeckungen") Vormbaum (2015) p 151 ff.

Chapter V. The Independent National Socialist Criminal Law of the Kiel School

1. *Basic orientation and main representatives*

The Kiel School's aim—overcoming any last remnants of Enlightenment liberalism and distinguishing itself from the NS-imbued Neo-Kantianism of the Marburg School—was to develop an independent NS criminal law.[503] Accordingly, it became the NS regime's most important helpmate in the field of criminal law.[504] Zaffaroni rightly dedicates three chapters to the Kiel School, in which he outlines its central theory of breaches of duty (*Pflichtverletzung*)[505] and the path towards a unified concept of crime (*Delikttypus* or "offence type") through the abolition of the traditional (three-tier) theory of crime, in particular the categories of wrongdoing (*Unrecht*)[506] and guilt (*Schuld*).[507]

As far as the Kiel School itself is concerned, Zaffaroni—in line with German research[508]—describes it as a "shock troop" faculty.[509] Its protagonists in the field of criminal law were Georg Dahm (1904–1963) and Friedrich Schaffstein (1905–2001). Dahm,[510] who completed his *Habilitation* in Heidelberg in 1927 under Radbruch, already joined the NSDAP in 1933 and enjoyed a notable academic career—probably not least thanks to his National Socialist leanings[511]—first as a professor in

---

503 Also *cf* Zaffaroni (2017), p 231.

504 Zaffaroni (2017), p 171.

505 Zaffaroni (2017), p 197 ff (ch 6).

506 Zaffaroni (2017), p 231 ff (ch 7).

507 Zaffaroni (2017), p 255 ff (ch 8).

508 *Cf* Eckert, in: Säcker (1992), p 37 ff (37: "experiment of dedicating an entire faculty as a unit to ideologising and politicising science" ["Experiment, eine ganze Fakultät... geschlossen in den Dienst der Ideologisierung und Politisierung der Wissenschaft zu stellen"]). However, the Kiel School only existed from 1933 to 1937/38 because its members took up positions elsewhere, ibid, p 68.

509 Zaffaroni (2017), p 198.

510 *Cf* Lepsius, *FS Dilcher* (2003), p 389, 413 ff; Telp (1992), p 49 (according to whom Dahm only completed his *Habilitation* in 1930); Eckert, in: Säcker (1992), p 48–9, 55, 69; also Zaffaroni (2017), p 199 ff (imprecise in parts).

511 Lepsius, *FS Dilcher* (2003), p 413, 417–8 (according to whom "he owed" his positions "above all to his sustained efforts on behalf of National Socialism" ["vor allem seinem nachhaltigen Einsatz für den Nationalsozialismus zu verdanken hatte"] and his career would not have been "imaginable...without his close links" to National Socialism's

Kiel (1933–39, holding the position of rector 1935–37) and Leipzig

---

"political ideals" ["ohne seine enge Anbindung", "politischen Vorstellungen…nicht denkbar"]); similarly Zaffaroni (2017), p 232 ("Dahm asumía su condición de nazi…"). Dahm was also the only jurist in the *Führungsstab* or senior management of the National Socialist Association of Lecturers (Lepsius, *FS Dilcher* [2003], p 418) and was only 31 when he became rector in Kiel. According to Telp (1992), p 49, Dahm was "scarcely known" ("kaum bekannt") as a scholar before 1933. However, Hattenhauer (*JJZG* 7 [2005], 173) considers him one of the "last great jurists of the Kiel Faculty", and Zaffaroni (2017), p 238 also sees him as an "intelligent dogmatist" (on Zaffaroni's view, see ch IV 3. including fn 379 above). – Schaffstein ascribes Dahm's rapid rise within the university hierarchy to his "impressive personality" ("eindrucksvolle Persönlichkeit") and "charisma" ("Ausstrahlung"), although Dahm did not "hold or strive for a major political office" ("ein bedeutendes politisches Amt bekleidet oder…angestrebt hat"; Schaffstein, *JJZG* 7 [2005], 182). Despite joining the Party, he "continued to [regard] the NSDAP and its leadership with great aloofness and a certain scepticism" ("der NSDAP und ihren führenden Personen mit weiterhin großer Distanz und einer gewissen Skepsis"), albeit without "voicing this to others, of course" ("freilich nach außen hin… laut werden ließ"; ibid, 183). According to Schaffstein, Dahm and the other young *Privatdozenten* who now became professors could at most be accused of "opportunism" ("Opportunismus") in that "the Nazi takeover opened up unimagined fields of work in legislation and at the universities" ("als sich durch die Machtergreifung…ungeahnte Betätigungsfelder in der Gesetzgebung und an den Hochschulen eröffneten"; ibid). This essay's apologetic character becomes abundantly clear in several places, for example when Schaffstein explains Dahm's lack of a high position in the NS state by claiming that the "high functionaries suspected or as it were sensed his internal aloofness from them" ("hohen Funktionäre seine innere Distanz zu ihnen ahnten oder gleichsam fühlten"; ibid, 184), points out his mitigating role ("no death sentences" ["keine Todesurteile"]) as assessor at the Strasbourg Special Court (193–4), and mentions his popularity among the students, the "vast majority" of whom were, however, "enthusiastic Party members" ("ganz überwiegend begeisterte Parteigänger", 184). The account of Heinz Weil, a Jew studying in Kiel in 1933, sounds very different, however. Weil recalled "the tumultuous stamps of applause of my fellow students in their SA boots" ("das tosende Beifallsgetrampel der Kommilitonen in ihren SA-Stiefeln") in response to Dahm's exclamation in his lecture: "For us, instead of the mendacious *understand everything, forgive everything*, what counts is *understand everything, forgive nothing at all*" ("Statt des verlogenen *Alles verstehen, alles verzeihen* gilt für uns *Alles verstehen, gar nichts verzeihen*"; Weil [1986], p 31, italics in the original text). However, Schaffstein also rejects accusations that both he and Dahm were anti-Semitic (and racist) (Schaffstein, *JJZG* 7 [2005], 188: "accusation...is justified at most in that we remained silent then and later [!]" ("Vorwurf…allenfalls insofern berechtigt, als wir damals und später geschwiegen…hätten"), although Dahm at least certainly made anti-Semitic comments (see this chapter's section 2. including fn 550 and main text below). Dahm himself only commented upon his position during the NS period in a letter to Eb. Schmidt of 4 February 1948, which was published posthumously in *JJZG* 7 (2005), 199. Here, he responds to the assertions of Schmidt (1947), p 396–8, 413–4, although Schmidt only accuses Dahm (and Schaffstein) explicitly on p 397–8, namely in regard to their appearance at the meeting of the German national group of the *Internationale Kriminalistische Vereinigung* (IKV) in Frankfurt am Main in September 1932 (thereto Marxen [1975], p 92 ff) and their polemic against liberal criminal law (thereto section 2. including fn 521 below), with which they recommended themselves "to the future power" ("der kommenden Macht") and "drew the necessary dividing lines as a precaution" ("vorsorglich die erforderlichen Trennungslinien"; Schmidt [1947], p 398). Dahm defends himself against these accusations, but is certainly also self-critical: "I do not deny the errors and mistakes to which we all more or less fell victim. I, too, failed to foresee the external

(1939–41), and from 1941 onwards as a professor and deputy rector of the "Reich University" (!) of Strasbourg (which the National Socialists regarded as a "front university" in occupied France).[512] After the end of the War and denazification, Dahm was not permitted to hold a university position in Germany, but in 1951 managed to gain a post at the University of Dhaka (then in Pakistan, now in Bangladesh), where he taught international law in the English language as well as other subjects.[513] In 1955, he was able to return to Kiel and take up a chair in international law,[514] where he focused upon (Nuremberg) internation-

---

and internal development of the National Socialist state and cherished hopes that were bitterly dashed" ("Ich leugne nicht die Irrtümer und Fehler, denen wir mehr oder weniger alle zum Opfer gefallen sind. Auch ich habe die äussere und innere Entwicklung des nationalsozialistischen Staates nicht vorhergesehen und Hoffnungen gehegt, die bitter enttäuscht worden sind"; *JJZG* 7 [2005], 201). Schmidt continued to criticise Dahm and Schaffstein's text in subsequent editions, but removed the statement quoted above (Schmidt, 1951, p 420–1 and 1965, p 426–6), probably also because Dahm rightly reminded him of his speech as Hamburg rector of 7 November 1933, in which Schmidt—through the "triad of serving labour, serving the SA and serving science" ("Trias des Arbeitsdienstes, des SA.-Dienstes und des Wissenschaftsdienstes")—placed universities in the service of the NS regime and professed his allegiance to the NS state and Hitler (Schmidt, in: *Hamburgerische Universität* [1933], p 27–49 [46]; in greater detail thereto and on *Schmidt's involvement with National Socialism*, M. Vormbaum, in: Jeßberger/Kotzur/Repgen [2019], 399 ff; also Görtemaker/Safferling [2016], p 437). Dahm (1963), p 268–9, shies away from judging the National Socialists since "it is not yet the time" ("ist…noch nicht an der Zeit"); in any case, National Socialism is "not only the work of individuals" ("nicht nur das Werk von Einzelpersonen"), but also "a work of history ("ein Werk der Geschichte"), which is why "the political leader and perpetrator somehow" proves to have been "led" ("erweist sich der politische Führer und Täter irgendwie als der Geführte"), and "the personal share sinks, and the share of that imposed by fate rises" ("Anteil des Persönlichen sinkt, und es steigt der des vom Schicksal Verhängten"). A fine way to absolve oneself of any *personal* responsibility!

512 Schaffstein commented as follows on Dahm's move to Strasbourg: "For Dahm and myself, the offer of the positions in Strasbourg came at a time when it was possible to hope that the War had been won or would at least end in a stalemate, and that Alsace had been regained for Germany. The overwhelming majority of the Alsatian population were also of this opinion and were German-friendly at first, and the same applied to the Alsatian students in particular. Therefore I had no concerns about accepting the position" ("Der Ruf nach Straßburg traf Dahm und mich zu einem Zeitpunkt, in dem man hoffen durfte, daß der Krieg gewonnen sei oder doch zumindest mit einem Patt enden würde und das Elsaß für Deutschland wiedergewonnen sei. Auch die elsässische Bevölkerung war ganz überwiegend dieser Auffassung und zunächst durchaus deutschfreundlich gesonnen, was übrigens namentlich auch für unsere elsässischen Studenten galt. Ich hatte deshalb keine Bedenken, den Ruf anzunehmen"; Schaffstein, *JJZG* 7 [2005], 191).

513 According to the University of Leipzig's catalogue of professors, Dahm was Professor of Indian Criminal and Criminal Procedural Law at the University of Dhaka from 1951–55, < http://research.uni-leipzig.de/catalogus-professorum-lipsiensium/leipzig/Dahm_598/markiere:Georg%20Dahm/> (last accessed 9 May 2019); on this period, also see Schaffstein, *JJZG* 7 (2005), 195 ff.

al criminal law among other things.[515] Schaffstein,[516] a student of Robert von Hippel and a *Privatdozent* in Göttingen, became a profes-

514 According to Zaffaroni (2017), p 211 Dahm at first had to teach a kind of "Introduction to Law" ("explicar *enciclopedia del derecho*", italics in the original text). This information is probably derived from Schaffstein, *JJZG* 7 (2005), 196 ("Professorship for Legal Encyclopaedia" ["Professur für Rechtsenzyklopädie"]), who ascribed this restriction to the criminal law scholar Mayer and the international law scholar Menzel, who "were unwilling to accept any competition from such a brilliant speaker and teacher" ("die Konkurrenz einer so glänzenden Vortragenden und Lehrers...nicht akzeptieren wollten")—a further example of this Schaffstein article's apologetic tendencies, already mentioned in fn 512 above.

515 Dahm (1956). On international criminal law in other respects also Siegert (1953) (in the series of the Göttingen Institute for International Law), critically Halfmann, in: Becker (1998, p 130) and Henkel, *FG Kraft* (1955), p 122–3 (expectations concerning individual responsibility for international crimes).

516 On his career in general, Stefanopolou, *JoJZG* 2010, 111, 112, 117. A highly positive appraisal by Schaffstein's student Beulke, *MSchrKrim* 85 (2002), 81 (as far as his work during the NS regime is concerned, to Beulke "it appears mystifying" ["erscheint es", "rätselhaft"], that he "taught and wrote such problematic things" ["so problematische Dinge gelehrt und niedergeschrieben hat"] during this time; on the other hand, "perhaps he is a typical representative of our fathers' generation precisely in this epochal division of his life" ["vielleicht gerade in dieser epochalen Gespaltenheit seines Lebenswegs ein typischer Vertreter unserer Vätergeneration"], who "openly names the mistakes of the past" ["Fehler der Vergangenheit...offen beim Namen genannt"], however); similarly positive, Maiwald, *NJW* 2002, 1250 (according to whom Schaffstein's "experience" ["Erfahrung"] in the NS period was "extraordinarily painful" ["außerordentlich schmerzlich"] and he "ended up in proximity to the ideology of those in power at the time" ["in die Nähe des Gedankenguts der Machthaber jener Zeit geriet"], which sounds overly passive, of course—just like Beulke's statement (Beulke, *MSchrKrim* 85 [2002], 82) that Schaffstein repeatedly emphasised "that he had not been strong-willed enough as a young man" ["als junger Mann nicht willensstark genug gewesen zu sein"]—when Maiwald simultaneously highlights the exceptional significance of his *Habilitation*, which was "unusual for a 24-year-old scholar" ["für einen jungen 24-jährigen Wissenschaftler ungewöhnlich"]). *Schaffstein himself* first admitted to "errors" ("Irrtümer") in 1965. He explained these by the fact that National Socialism seemed "to offer the young people of the time...goals that transcended them" ("der Nationalsozialismus der Jugend von damals...über sie selbst hinausweisende Ziele zu bieten"; *MSchrKrim* 48 [1965], 67; also see his statement in this chapter's section 3. including fn 570 below in the context of the legality principle). Later he conceded that he (and Dahm) refused to let the NS interventions in justice ("bad cases" ["schlimme Fälle"]), about which they were informed by Hans von Dohnanyi (in the course of their work in the official criminal law commission), make any impression upon them, as they considered these to be "teething troubles in the revolutionary phase of a new beginning" ("Kinderkrankheiten in der revolutionären Phase eines Neubeginns"; Schaffstein, *JJZG* 7 [2005], 185–6); otherwise they were "blinded by the undeniable successes of the National Socialist regime" ("durch die unzweifelhaften Erfolge des nationalsozialistischen Regimes geblendet"; ibid, 187) and the "views of the criminal law doctrine of that time seem outdated to me today" ("strafrechtsdogmatischen Auffassungen aus dieser Zeit erscheinen mir heute als überholt"; ibid, 189). In an appraisal (with autobiographical traits) of his teachers Robert von Hippel and Curty Bondy, Schaffstein spoke of a "wrong track" ("Irrweg"; *RJ* 19 [2000], 647, 654), which is worth mentioning also because—as Schaffstein himself recognises—von Hippel and Bondy actually op-

sor in Leipzig[517] in 1933 and in Kiel in 1935; in 1941, like Dahm, he moved to Strasbourg, where he remained until 1944. After the end of the War, Schaffstein—who was initially suspended following denazification—was already able to return to Göttingen University in 1954 (as Welzel's successor),[518] where he taught until his retirement in 1969.

2. *Criminal policy: an authoritarian NS criminal law*

Perhaps the most important contribution of the Kiel School to NS criminal law—one which Zaffaroni only mentions in passing[519]—was the pro-

posed National Socialism (*RJ* 19 [2000], 649, 654), something that obviously failed to make an impression upon him *at the time* (according to Schaffstein, *RJ* 19 [2000], 651, von Hippel provided "a certain motivation" ["eine gewisse Anregung"] for his text "Liberales oder autoritäres Strafrecht" ("Liberal or authoritarian criminal law"), as "he, too...criticised Weimar criminal law as overly 'soft'" ["auch er das Weimarer Strafrecht...als zu 'weichlich' kritisierte"]). – What will the **victims of Nazi criminal policy** think when reading appraisals such as these? Were their experiences under National Socialism not far more painful than those of its intellectual protagonists, and did they not need to show far greater willpower? A more critical account, especially on Schaffstein's time in Göttingen, can be found in Schumann (2008), p 84, 89, 108, 114–5 (who states among other things that Schaffstein took over the chair of Richard Honig, who had been forced out, as acting professor in 1933, but refused to take this position on a permanent basis, even though Siegert wished him to; Siegert preferred Schaffstein to Welzel, as there was no comparable person who combined "political activity with sufficient academic achievements" ["politische Aktivität mit hinreichend wissenschaftlichen Leistungen"; ibid, p 89 including fn 94, 115]); on Schaffstein's role in the "renewal" of juvenile law, *cf* Schumann, *ZJJ* 28 (2017), 313, 315 ff; on his activity as a member of the Academy for German Law's Committee for Juvenile Law, Schumann, Der Ausschuss für Jugendrecht der Akademie für deutsches Recht 1934–1941, in Schumann/Wapler (2017), p 73, 87 ff. (93–4). Critically also Halfmann, in: Becker (1998), p 119; Görtemaker/Safferling (2016), p 393, who see Schaffstein's "distancing" ("Distanzierung") as unconvincing, "for in it Schaffstein attested a blindness to the values of National Socialism's political and ideological goals that is astonishing even for the situation at the time" ("denn Schaffstein bezeugte damit eine Wertblindheit gegenüber den politisch-ideologischen Zielen des Nationalsozialismus, die selbst für damalige Verhältnisse erstaunlich anmutet"). Also *cf* Zaffaroni (2017), p 199 ff (imprecise in parts, however) and previously Zaffaroni, in Zaffaroni, 2011, p 17 ff (critically on Schaffstein's abovementioned admission of error ["pero nada más", p 19–20], but considering him to be more dogmatic than Dahm [p 32]); critically also Guzmán Dalbora, *RDPC* VII (2017), 231 ("crocodile tears").

517 Counter to Zaffaroni's claims (Zaffaroni [2017], p 208), Schaffstein did not succeed Honig, he only covered his position, see Schumann (2008) in the previous fn.

518 Stefanopolou, *JoJZG* 2010, 117 calls his comparatively speedy return to Göttingen "striking" ("bemerkenswert")—quite an understatement! In actual fact, this return is a paradigmatic example of the existing (Nazi) networks and confirms the theory of **continuity** for the field of academia; thereto already Halfmann, in: Becker (1998), p 129 ff.

519 Zaffaroni (2017), p 203; however, *cf* Zaffaroni, ed (2011) with a lengthy introduction, where he acknowledges the text's "facetas múltiples", emphasising four aspects: (1)

grammatic text "Liberales oder autoritäres Strafrecht" ("Liberal or authoritarian criminal law"), co-authored by Dahm and Schaffstein.[520] The time of its publication—before the National Socialists came to power[521]—and its trend-setting description of the new criminal law of the future "authoritarian state"[522] quickly made it perhaps the most important text of the "anti-liberal movement for the renewal of criminal law",[523] though of course it also attracted criticism.[524]

> In this text, which is not quite 50 pages long, Dahm and Schaffstein seek to overcome "rationalist-individualist thinking" within the field of criminal law by means of National Socialism (p 4). They write that National Socialism is the "expression of a much broader and more profound intellectual movement" ("Ausdruck einer weit breiteren und tieferen geistigen Bewegung"), expressing the same "basic mood" ("Grundstimmung") in criminal policy, too; instead of radically breaking with the past, the aim is to link to grand conservative traditions

---

"conservative-authoritarian pamphlet", (2) destruction of Liszt/Beling's objective-subjective concept of crime, (3) destruction of the traditional understanding of the purpose of punishment, and (4) theoretical orientation towards the "immoral irrationalism" of C. Schmitt (Zaffaroni, in Zaffaroni, 2011, p 14).

520 Dahm/Schaffstein (1933). Zaffaroni quotes the Spanish translation.

521 This book was already completed over the course of 1932 and was published in the autumn of that year (Schaffstein, *JJZG* 7 [2005], 176–7, 178).

522 Dahm/Schaffstein (1933), p 40 ff., see presently main text above.

523 Marxen (1975), p 103 ("antiliberalen strafrechtlichen Erneuerungsbewegung") ("publication that attracted the most attention" ["meistbeachtete Veröffentlichung"]), 105 ("fundamental contribution to all later authoritarian criminal law programmes" ["grundlegenden Beitrag für alle späteren autoritären Strafrechtsprogramme"]); Feldmüller-Bäuerle (2010), p 47. Mittermaier, *SchwZStR* 52 (1938), 225–6, also saw it as representing a certain gain in knowledge, even though he basically agreed with Schwinge/Zimmerl (1937) (ch IV 2. including fn 322 above).

524 *Cf* eg Riemer, *MSchrKrimPsych* 24 (1933), 222 ff ("the valuations that are posited wholesale here lack any kind of justification grounded upon 'knowledge' or empirical insights" ["fehlt es den Wertungen, die hier in Bausch und Bogen gesetzt werden, an einer Begründung, die irgendwie auf ‚'Erkenntnissen' oder empirischen Einsichten… gründen", 222]; "science is the only authority that they [Dahm and Schaffstein, K.A.] do not recognise" ["Wissenschaft die einzige Autorität, die sie nicht anerkennen", 222 including fn 1]; "basic tenor...that, for all its detachment from material goals, for all the unworldliness with which it confronts concrete social problems, can have crucial repercussions" ["Grundstimmung…die bei aller Losgelöstheit von sachlichen Zielsetzungen, bei aller Weltfremdheit, mit der sie den konkreten sozialen Problemen gegenübersteht, zu ganz entscheidenden Auswirkungen…führen kann", 223]; "desire for an ultimate authority and an activism that lacks any defined content" ["Verlangen nach einer Autorität schlechthin und nach einem Aktivismus, dem es an jeder inhaltlichen Bestimmung gebricht", 223]; "purely formal affirmation of the hypostasised concept of authority" ["rein formale Bejahung des hypostasierten Autoritätsbegriffs", 224]). Also see Blasco y Fernández de Moreda, *Criminalia*, IX (4/1943), 238 (Dahm/Schaffstein as "teorizantes del más agudo extremismo").

such as those represented by Savigny and Hegel (p 4–5). After expounding the significance of individualism[525] in both liberalism and socialism, that is, in the social-liberal state (ch I, p 7 ff), the authors criticise the "alarming humanisation and weakening of the pain of punishment" ("bedenkliche Humanisierung und Abschwächung des Strafübels", p 18) and the "softening" ("Erweichung", p 22)[526] of criminal law and the penal system through the idea of education and the "over-emphasis on environmental influence as opposed to hereditary predisposition" ("Überbetonung der Umwelteinflüsse gegenüber der vererbten Anlage", p 17).[527] This, they claim, has led to "maximum advantages for the individual to the detriment of the interests of the state" ("ein Höchstmaß von Vorteilen für das Individuum zum Nachteil der Staatsinteressen", p 23); however, the idea of retribution that is "deeply rooted in the people's sense of justice" ("tief im Rechtsgefühl des Volkes", p 22)[528] could not be eradicated, which shows the need to "take into account the organic development of the law through the silent workings of the spirit of the people" ("Rücksichtnahme auf die organische Rechtsentwicklung durch den still waltenden Volksgeist", p 23) (ch II, p 13 ff). Then they lament the devaluation of protected (state, collective) interests by "individualism, rationalism and the tendency to detach law from ethics" ("Individualismus, Rationalismus und die Tendenz der Loslösung des Rechts von der Ethik", p 25), for example through the impunity for religious offences

525 Marxen (1975), p 118 sees the text's "main matter" ("Hauptsache") as an attack against "individualism in liberalism" ("Individualismus im Liberalismus").

526 However, much the same laments were already voiced in the earlier debate on the theory of guilt, *cf* Grossmann (1926), p 8 ("soft" ["weichlich"], "feminine" ["feminin"]) and Schumacher (1927), p 64 including fn 85 (leaving open the question of whether "the views of the new theory of guilt are based upon 'feminism'" ["die Anschauungen der neuen Schuldlehre auf 'Feminismus' beruhen"]); later also eg Gemmingen (1933), p 11 ff (referring to Frank's statement: "the criminal shall tremble once more" ["der Verbrecher soll wieder zittern", 11]). Also *cf* Eb. Schmidt (1965), p. 426–7 (defending the authority of the state "against the softening of the administration of criminal law allegedly brought about by the spirit of the reform of criminal law" ["gegen die vom Geiste der Strafrechtsreform angeblich bedingte Verweichlichung der Strafrechtspflege"]).

527 In this vein also Dahm, *MSchrKrimPsych* 24 (1933), 171–2, 176 (advance of special prevention "at the cost of retribution and general prevention" ["auf Kosten von Vergeltungs- und Generalprävention"] and of the idea of education to the detriment of security, significance of hereditary factors); Schaffstein, *ZStW* 55 (1936), 276, 277 ff (overemphasis on the idea of education and of special as opposed to general prevention; neglect of genetically proven hereditary factors). Critically on "educative punishment" ("Erziehungsstrafe") also Gemmingen (1933), p 21–2.

528 On retribution, see ch II 3. including fn 226 and main text above.

and the privileging of politically or religiously motivated offenders[529] (ch III, p 24 ff). Finally, they denounce the increase in the power of judges brought about by indeterminate elements of the *actus reus* and broad discretion—with a factual dissolution of the separation of powers (!) and an increasing "politicisation of the judiciary" ("Politisierung der Justiz", p 33), supported by the "liberal and democratic press" ("liberale und demokratische Presse", p 34), which in turn restrict the judges' power (p 36).[530] This, too, plays out in the individual's favour, so that "the combination of liberalist and socialist lines of thinking, which results in a special and exaggerated emphasis on their shared individualist starting point" ("die Verbindung liberalistischer und sozialistischer Gedankengänge mit dem Ergebnis einer besonderen und übertriebenen Hervorhebung des gemeinsamen individualistischen Ausgangspunktes", p 31) is evident in this regard, too; the StGB becomes the "magna carta of the criminal" ("magna charta des Verbrechers") instead of defending "state interests" ("Staatsinteressen", p 32) (ch IV, p 28 ff).

This (one-sided and simplistic)[531] analysis of the *status quo*—in sum, the authors lament a "softening of crime-fighting, a weakening of criminal law administration and a decrease in state authority" ("Erweichung der Verbrechensbekämpfung, Schwächung der Strafrechtspflege und Minderung der Staatsautorität", p 37)—is followed by the three programmatic chapters (p 37 ff), with a *draft of the future criminal law* developed in particular in ch VI (p 40 ff), although the authors do not want this draft to be understood as a "programme" ("Programm", p 40). Before this, in ch V on the "transition" ("Übergang", p 37 ff), they identify "signs of a shift" ("Anzeichen eines Wandels"), an "intellectual turn" ("geistige Wende", p 37), as part of which a "belief in the validity of generally binding values" ("Glauben an die Gültigkeit allgemeinverbindlicher Werte", ibid) is returning and a "new national

529 Against any "special treatment" ("Sonderbehandlung") in this regard see also Dahm, *DR* 4 (1934), 419 (because high treason should be seen as a crime not just against the state, but against the *Volk* itself, since the *Volk* forms the foundation of the NS state).

530 Also *cf* Dahm, *MSchrKrimPsych* 24 (1933), 169 ff.

531 Already *cf* Riemer, *MSchrKrimPsych* 24 (1933), 224 ("it is unnecessary to go into detail concerning the image drawn of the nature of liberal and socialist criminal law" ["Es erübrigt sich, im einzelnen auf das Bild einzugehen, das vom Wesen des liberalen und des sozialistischen Strafrechts gezeichnet wird"]); Marxen (1975), p 111 ff (pointing out the lack of an empirical foundation, especially concerning the development of criminality, and the "concealment" ["Unterschlagung"] of the expansion of criminal law in both case law and legislation); critically also Vogel (2004), p 61.

sense, a living state-focused mentality" ("ein neues Nationalgefühl, eine lebendige Staatsgesinnung", p 38) emerging, giving rise to a new "course in the development of criminal law" ("Kurs der Strafrechtsentwicklung"), which, "without being reactionary or antisocial [!], is based upon the unconditional primacy of the nation...over the interests of the individual" ("der ohne reaktionär und antisozial zu sein, auf dem unbedingten Primat der Nation...gegenüber den Interessen des Individuums beruht", p 38). At the same time, they draw attention to "some innovations" ("manche Neuerungen") that have already been brought about by emergency decrees and that "cannot be reconciled with the needs of an ordered state under the rule of law in the long term" ("mit den Bedürfnissen eines geordneten Rechtsstaats auf die Dauer nicht vereinbar sind", p 39). In the final ch VII (p 53 ff), the authors warn against placing overly great hopes in a comprehensive criminal law reform, because, first, the existing law is still quite close to popular sentiment (which is hard to define in any case), and second, no new "unified sense of justice" has as yet emerged that could underpin such a reform (p 54).[532] Thus it is more important first of all to create the intellectual foundations—"the imbuing of the administration of justice with a new spirit and a new mentality concerning the state and criminal law" ("die Durchdringung der Rechtspflege mit einem neuen Geist und mit einer neuen Staats- und Strafrechtsgesinnung", p 56).

532 The NS rulers failed to implement such a comprehensive reform (in the sense of a new Criminal Code; on their last attempt, the 1944 draft of a Reich Criminal Code, see Werle, 1989, p 53, 661 ff; also see Hartl [2000], p 276 ff, 379), which is why they shifted their focus to making individual laws (primarily executive ones); thereto Schreiber, in: Dreier/Sellert (1989), p 151 ff (153 ff, 167 ff); Hartl (2000), p 278 ff; on the executive nature of NS "legislation", Maus (1989), p 84; Werle (1989), p 59 ff, 203 ff; Vormbaum (2011), p 7; Arnedo, in Zaffaroni (2017), p 55.

Georg Dahm und Friedrich Schaffstein

Liberales oder autoritäres Strafrecht?

Hanseatische
Verlagsanstalt
Hamburg

Figure 15: Dahm and Schaffstein's anti-liberal and authoritarian booklet of just 50 p, 1933

But what do these **general guidelines of the new criminal law** of "the authoritarian state" consist of? After their preliminary reflections, it hardly comes as a surprise that Dahm/Schaffstein start from a "nationalist and *total understanding of the state*" ("nationalistischen und *totalen Staatsauffassung*"),[533] which, as the example of Italian fascism shows,[534] makes it possible "to develop a unified criminal law system that covers all areas of criminal policy" ("ein geschlossenes, alle kriminalpolitischen Bereiche umspannendes Strafrechtssystem zu entwick-

533 Cf ch II 1. including fn 208 and main text above (italics K.A.).

534 However, on the distinction between NS and fascist criminal law, see ch II 1. including fn 121 above.

eln", p 40). Such a criminal law is primarily a "means to preserve and establish state authority as such" ("Mittel zur Erhaltung und Bewährung der Staatsgewalt schlechthin", ibid);[535] the state uses punishment "to visibly demonstrate its power to all the world" ("um seine Macht aller Welt sichtbar vor Augen zu führen", p 41), as in it "the state's dignity is symbolically" revealed ("symbolisch die Würde des Staates", p 41), with the death penalty, which is an indispensable deterrent (p 49), making it "emphatically clear" ("eindringlich sichtbar") "that the individual may be surrendered to the state" ("daß der einzelne dem Staate preisgegeben werden darf", p 41). Here, the authors recognise that criminal law can "always only be one of many ways of upholding authority" ("immer nur eines unter vielen Mitteln der Autoritätswahrung sein", p 42), but then again make clear that *general preventive requirements* take precedence over the special-preventive application of criminal law:[536] "consideration of the criminal" can "go only as far as state authority is upheld and the wrong impression is not made upon the whole community" ("nur so weit gehen, daß die Staatsautorität gewahrt bleibt, der Eindruck auf die Gesamtheit nicht verfehlt wird", ibid), and at the same time punishment and its effects need to be "so long-lasting that not only the perpetrator, but also others are deterred in future" ("so nachhaltig sein, daß außer dem Täter auch andere für die Zukunft abgeschreckt werden", ibid). The authors want to retain the *idea of education*, but focus it upon the "education of the whole community" ("Erziehung der Gesamtheit", p 41) and restrict it considerably, with educatability "to be proven on a case-by-case basis" ("von Fall zu Fall zu prüfen"), taking "hereditary influences" ("Anlageeinflüsse") into account (p 45); in any case, the idea of education must be secondary (p 44) to "the necessities of the authoritarian administration of justice" ("den Notwendigkeiten der autoritären Rechtspflege"), such as punishing serious crimes "without any consideration of whether the perpetrator can be reformed" ("ohne jede Rück-

535 On the need for a stronger protection of the state, see ch II 2. including fn 104 above and Dahm, *MSchrKrimPsych* 24 (1933), 167–8 (although he considers the NS Draft Law "for the protection of the nation" ["zum Schutze der Nation"] of 12 March 1930 to be "unacceptable" ["untragbar"]). According to Dahm (1935b), p 21, "the fascist criminal law" ("das faschistische Strafrecht") (ie Italy) was "ahead of German criminal law" ("dem deutschen Strafrecht voraus") in this regard.

536 See also eg the emphasis on general vs special prevention in Schaffstein, *ZStW* 55 (1936), 280, 286, 288; as a secondary source Marxen (1975), p 147; however, also see Dahm, *MSchrKrimPsych* 24 (1933), 179, where he rejects a "fixed hierarchy" ("feste Rangfolge") of purposes of punishment.

sicht auf die Besserungsfähigkeit des Täters", p 44) and the "pre-satisfaction of minimum state requirements" ("Vor-Befriedigung staatlicher Mindestbedürfnisse", p 49).[537] Furthermore, the "educative enforcement of punishment in the authoritarian state needs to take a significantly different form than in the social-liberal state" ("Erziehungsstrafvollzug im autoritären Staate wesentlich anders aussehen als im sozial-liberalen Staat", p 46), since its aim is the ideological restriction of pedagogical autonomy, political education to convey the "traditional values of German culture" ("traditionellen Werte der deutschen Kultur", p 48) and the "significance of military tautness and discipline" ("Bedeutung militärischer Straffheit und Disziplin", p 49).[538] In the field of *sentencing*, Dahm and Schaffstein—contradicting their earlier criticism of the abolition of the separation of powers—advocate a "restriction of judicial discretion" ("Einschränkung des richterlichen Ermessens"), a stronger review by means of appeal ("Revision")[539] and "increasing minimum punishments" ("die Heraufsetzung der Strafminima"), "in short forcing the judge to take more drastic measures" ("kurz ein Zwang für den Richter zum Durchgreifen", p 50). The *separation of powers* is undermined under the catchphrase of fending off "harmful external influences" ("schädliche Einflüsse von außen") (meaning in particular the liberal, "indecent" press) and "the erosion of the idea of the state from within" ("der Aushöhlung des Staatsgedankens von innen", p 51); in particular, it must be ensured that "the judge actually applies criminal law in the interests of the authoritarian state leadership" ("der Richter das Strafrecht im Sinne der autoritären Staatsführung auch wirklich anwendet", ibid) and his discretion must be restricted in such a way that he cannot "use it one-sidedly in favour of the perpetrator" ("einseitig zugunsten des Täters verwendet") and thus "endanger the administration of criminal law by excessively watering down the law" ("die Strafrechtspflege durch eine zu weitgehende Aufweichung des Gesetzes gefährdet wird", p 52). Finally, as far as the theory of *protected legal interests* is concerned, the au-

537 Also *cf* Dahm, *MSchrKrimPsych* 24 (1933), 176 (education only of individuals who are capable of being educated).

538 *Cf* in more concrete detail Schaffstein, *ZStW* 55 (1936), 288 (pointing out the limits of educative punishment).

539 Critically Vogel (2004), p 65.

thors write that this theory should be retained at first,[540] but oriented more strongly towards the collective interests of the state—the "dignity of the state and honour of the nation" ("Würde des Staates und Ehre der Nation", p 50).[541] Concerning the *nulla poena* principle, Dahm/ Schaffstein follow Carl Schmitt[542] in stating that greater emphasis should be placed upon its constitutional aspects—the binding of the judge to the law as an expression "of the authoritarian understanding of the state" ("der autoritären Staatsauffassung", p 52). Later, Dahm explicitly advocated abolishing its liberal component[543]—a view that he calmly ignored after the War when dealing with the Nuremberg Trials.[544]

Now that the criminal policy **foundations of this new criminal law thinking**—in short: the NS ideology[545] of the total, racist *Volk* and *Führer state*, with the *Führerbefehl* that is equal to the law[546]—had been expound-

540 Arguing in favour of overcoming the theory of protected legal interests, however, Dahm, in: id et al (1935), p 62, 80 (cited imprecisely as a monograph by Zaffaroni); also Schaffstein, *ZStW* 56 (1937), 106 (wrongfulness cannot be defined by the concept of protected legal interests). On the anti-liberal battle against the "doctrine of the violation of protected legal interests", Marxen (1975), p 177 ff; Amelung (1972), p 228 ff; critically on Schaffstein's line of argument id, p 231 ff, 236 ff; critically also Amelung, in: Alexy (2002), p 368–9.

541 For a basic account of the intellectualisation or ethicisation of the concept of protected legal interests, see *Mittasch* (1939), p 86 ff; Amelung (1972), p 216 ff (217–8: loyalty to the people).

542 Ch II 1. including fn 162 above.

543 Dahm, *DStR* 80 (1934), 87, 92 (the principle no longer has any foundation, as the judge is bound to the will of the NS leadership); Dahm, in: Dahm et al (1935), p 78.

544 *Cf* Dahm (1956), p 55 ff, where he relativises this principle—based upon what is in fact a thorough study of comparative and international law—to the extent that he considers the unlawfulness of a certain conduct at the time of the act to be sufficient to establish criminal liability under international law (p 64–5), but simultaneously criticises this flexible approach of Nuremberg Law and case law (p 56 ff), only pointing out in passing that "the relaxation of this principle...in the National Socialist state...was sharply criticised" ("die Lockerung des Grundsatzes...im nationalsozialistischen Staat...scharf kritisiert"), blithely ignoring his own contribution to this "relaxation". See also Dahm (1963), p 515, where he justifies the relaxation of the principle, arguing that the sentiment of the people was itself limited by the reference to the "basic idea of a determinate statute" ("Grundgedanken eines bestimmten Gesetzes") and that the new provision was applied cautiously (it is a "legend" that the provision has "unleashed the arbitrariness of the courts" ["die Willkür der Gerichte entfesselt"]).

545 In regard to Nuremberg international criminal law, Dahm later ([1956], p 65) stated: "Professing a certain ideology does not provide a grounding for the law" ("Bekenntnisse zu einer bestimmten Ideologie begründen kein Recht").

546 Cf ch III including fn 263 above.

ed,[547] Dahm and Schaffstein were able to specify and develop their NS criminal law system further in numerous individual works. In doing so, they always rejected any attempts to position their methodological foundations in terms of *(legal) philosophy*. Thus Dahm strongly repudiated Schwinge and Zimmerl's classification of the "Kiel line" as Husserlian phenomenology,[548] if only because that this "traced a line of recent German legal science back to the theories of a Jewish [!] philosopher".[549] In reality, he claimed, the Kiel scholars' "basic methodological ideas" had no philosophical position at all, but sprang from "a certain basic view of the law and its relation to *völkisch* life".[550] Thus "the concept of the law is part of the völkisch order of life, which continues to develop and is founded upon popular sentiment, and like this sentiment is in a state of constant flux and in constant need of shaping".[551] However, the reference to völkisch life, concrete völkisch orders and so on expresses an (albeit vulgarising and simplifying) affinity to vitalist views,[552] with the recognition of the claim to leadership of the NS movement, the Führer state and the Führer principle

547 It is disputed whether the text already propagates an explicitly NS conception of criminal law, or "only" lays the ground for the totalitarian NS theory as an anti-liberal plea for authoritarianism (against the universally lamented "softening", fn 527 above) (thus Radbruch, 1933/1957, p 76, who calls it a German-national, authoritarian understanding of criminal law as opposed to the NS, racist-*völkisch* understanding; similarly Eb. Schmidt (1965), p 426–7; followed by Cattaneo (2001), p 201–2). This dispute is moot, however, for at the time the text was published the NSDAP had no explicit position on criminal policy (similarly Schmidt, 1965, p 426–7; likewise Marxen [1975], p 120); in any case, Dahm/Schaffstein contributed significantly to the development and elaboration of this position.

548 Ch IV 2. including fn 327 and main text above.

549 Dahm, *ZStW* 57 (1938) 225, 285 ("eine Richtung der jüngeren deutschen Rechtswissenschaft auf die Lehren eines jüdischen Philosophen zurückgeführt"); concurring with Dahm in this regard, Wolf, *DRWis* 4 (1939), 173–4, according to whom the term "Wesensschau" is "so hackneyed and general" ("so abgegriffen und allgemein") and "has been used by the Kiel authors, too, in such a popular, indeterminate sense" ("auch von den Kielern Autoren in einem so populär-unbestimmten Sinne verwendet worden"), "that one might be more likely to guess a lack of familiarity with Husserl's phenomenology" ("daß hieraus eher auf Unbekanntschaft mit der Phänomenologie Husserls….geschlossen werden könnte", 173).

550 Dahm, *ZStW* 57 (1938), 285 ("methodischen Grundanschauungen", "einer bestimmten Grundanschauung von Recht und seinem Verhältnis zum völkischen Leben").

551 Dahm, *ZStW* 57 (1938), 289 ("der Rechtsbegriff Teil der sich fortentwickelnden völkischen Lebensordnung und im Volksempfinden begründet, wie dieses ständig im Fluß und der Gestaltung bedürftig").

552 *Cf* Mittermaier, *SchwZStR* 52 (1938), 213–4, according to whom Dahm/Schaffstein never quoted Husserl, but "in substance" ("der Sache nach") are "supporters of a rather abundantly simplified phenomenologically oriented view" ("Anhänger einer etwas reichlich vereinfachten phänomenologisch gerichteten Anschauung"). Marxen (1975), p 236 ff likewise sees an affinity to phenomenology only in the sense of a vitalist vulgarisation and simplification.

as a Neo-Hegelian addition.[553] Furthermore, the *rejection of (Neo-Kantian)*[554] *methodological dualism* or *Trennungsdenken*[555] with the subsequent *ethicisation* of criminal law[556] is certainly a legal-philosophical or methodological stance, even if it is not specific to National Socialist criminal law thinking.[557]

3. *The role of the judge in the NS Führer state*

Before we take a closer look at individual aspects of "Kiel" criminal law theory, the role of the judge in the NS Führer state merits special consideration, for, as we have seen above,[558] the NS criminal law project could not

---

553 *Cf* Wolf, *DRWis* 4 (1939), 174–5, who sees the Kiel scholars, referring to Larenz among others, in the tradition of a Neo-Hegelian, "*völkisch* state metaphysics" ("völkischen Staatsmetaphysik"); on the Neo-Hegelian influence, also Marxen (1975), p 239–40; in general on the significance of Hegel's theory of punishment for National Socialism, Kiesewetter (1974), p 322 ("direct derivation" ["direkte Ableitung"]) and *passim*.

554 *Cf* ch IV 3. including fn 408 and main text above.

555 Concurring in this regard Zaffaroni (2017), p 235 ("no le faltaba razón"), which is hard to understand, considering that, according to the understanding espoused in ch IV 4. in fn 454 ff (main text), the anti-ethicisation of (criminal) law is one possible guarantee of a liberal, democratic (criminal) law.

556 Cf ch II 2. including fn 193–9 above (NS principles and literature) and here before fn 530, each with main text, and: Dahm, in: Dahm et al (1935), p 83, 89 and *passim*; Dahm (1940), p 37 ("concordance of law and morality" ["Übereinstimmung von Recht und Sittlichkeit"]); Schaffstein, *ZStW* 53 (1934), 606 ("linking law and morality more closely than hitherto...legal valuation should if possible be derived from ethical valuation" ["Recht und Sittlichkeit enger als bisher zu verknüpfen...gesetzliche Wertung möglichst auf die ethische zurückzuführen"]); Schaffstein, in: Dahm et al (1935), p 110 ("unity of criminal law and *völkisch* moral order" ["Einheit von Strafrecht und völkischer Sittenordnung"]); Schaffstein, *DStR* 81 (1935), 101 ("Trennungsdenken", namely the "separation of law and morality, of criminal legal and ethical valuation" ["Trennung vom[!] Recht und Sittlichkeit, von strafrechtlicher und ethischer Wertung"] as "characteristic of scientific individualism" ["charakteristisch für den wissenschaftlichen Individualismus"] and responsible for the destruction of the "unity of political being with its real communities and the concrete orders that correspond to them" ["Einheit des politischen Seins mit ihren echten Gemeinschaften und den ihnen gemäßen konkreten Ordnungen"]); Schaffstein, *FS Schmidt*, 1936, p 12 ("eradicate the division between ethical and legal valuation" ["Spaltung zwischen ethischer und rechtlicher Wertung zu beseitigen"]); Schaffstein, *DRWis* 1 (1936), 46 (against a "separation of criminal law and the völkisch moral order" ["Trennung von Strafrecht und völkischer Sittenordnung"]); Schaffstein, *ZStW* 57 (1938), 301, 314 ("ethical foundation of the theory of unlawfulness" ["ethische Grundlegung der Rechtswidrigkeitslehre"]), 325 ("ethical content of criminal law" ["ethische Gehalt des Strafrechts"]).

557 Already against this Liszt, *ZStW* 27 (1907), 91; quoted in ch IV 4. including fn 449 above.

558 Ch II 1. including fn 153 ff and ch IV 2. including fn 345, 374, all with main text above.

have been implemented without the active participation of the judiciary. Accordingly, it is hardly surprising to find that this topic is an important one in Dahm and Schaffstein's writings, even though their anti-liberal polemic only mentions it in passing.

In his inaugural lecture at Leipzig University in 1933—the same year the polemic was published—Schaffstein declared judicial interpretation of the law to be National Socialist "law-making" ("Rechtsschöpfung") and called for this interpretation to be submitted to the "will of the Führer embodied in the law".[559] One year later, he welcomed Schmitt's formula of "nullum crimen sine poena"[560] as an excellent way of combatting the formalism of legal certainty,[561] but at the same time feared that overly extensive judicial discretion would weaken the binding to the Führer principle that he advocated so emphatically.[562] Therefore, he states, in the "new criminal law" the "judges' application of the law" needs to "be form-bound, but not formalistic",[563] which simply means distinguishing between the "political formal principles of liberalism", which must be rejected, and "the real and necessary forms of National Socialist law".[564] The judge is bound to the latter, or in concrete terms to the "law that represents the Führer's will",[565] to the NS legislator as "leader",[566] and "all the more strongly" "the more probable" it is "that the law...truly represents the Führer's will", which is

559 *Cf* Schaffstein (1934), p 20, 24.

560 Ch II 1. including fn 162 above.

561 Schaffstein, *DR* 4 (1934), 349, 352.

562 Schaffstein, *DR* 4 (1934), 351–2.

563 Schaffstein, *DR* 4 (1934), 352 ("neuen Strafrecht", "richterliche Rechtsanwendung formgebunden, aber nicht formalistisch sein").

564 Schaffstein, *DR* 4 (1934), 349 ("politischen Formprinzipien des Liberalismus", "den echten und notwendigen Formen des nationalsozialistischen Rechts").

565 Schaffstein, *DR* 4 (1934), 352 ("den Führerwillen repräsentierende Gesetz").

566 Schaffstein, *ZStW* 53 (1934), 619 and 607 (judicial discretion determined by recourse "to the people's healthy sense of justice" ["auf das gesunde Rechtsempfinden des Volkes"]), 618–9 (raising judicial sentencing decisions "from the level of arbitrariness to conscious planning in line with the National Socialist understanding of criminal law" ["aus dem Bereich der Willkür in den der bewußten Planung im Sinne der nationalsozialistischen Strafrechtsauffassung"]), 628 (the judge's position is "more important and more responsible" ["wichtiger und verantwortungsvoller"]); id, *FS Schmidt*, 1936, p 50 ("proceed in the same manner as the National Socialist legislator" ["wie der nationalsozialistische Gesetzgeber zu verfahren"]), 52 ("binding to the supreme leadership's legal policy goals and valuations" ["Bindung an die rechtspolitischen Ziele und Wertungen der obersten Führung"]), 63 ("binding...to the Führer's will" ["Bindung... an den Führerwillen"]). Against Cattaneo (2001), p 213–4, there is no "problem of interpretation" ("Interpretationsproblem") concerning the Schaffstein essays quoted in the previous and present footnote. In both cases, Schaffstein essentially emphasises that the judges are bound to the Führer's will; "ultimately" ("letztlich"), as Cattaneo (2001), p 214, says himself, there is thus "no difference", although there is no need to focus

the case particularly for laws inspired by National Socialism, such as *Rasseverrat* or "racial treason".[567] This shows that NS legislation and especially the *Führerbefehl* set boundaries to the looser binding to the law associated with the material concept of wrongdoing and *Wesensschau* (thereto 5. below); the *Führerbefehl* in particular must be strictly observed (provided it has been expressed clearly),[568] and judges are not completely free to determine the law. Schaffstein distanced himself from this view in 1974, however.[569]

In his inaugural lecture at Heidelberg University in 1931, two years before the Nazis came to power, Dahm gave a comparatively innocuous explanation for the "increase in judicial power", seeing it as stemming from judicial work on a law that was becoming increasingly normativised through "the modern tendency towards the softening of legal forms" and the loosening of the "components of the concept of crime" (normative characteristics of the elements of the *actus reus*, substantive unlawfulness, normative concept of guilt), thus creating scope for "valuations and will-based decisions" in more areas than just sentencing.[570] Dahm's National Socialist turn only came in 1934, when he tasked judges with implementing the demands of the NS legislator—standing on the same level as the legislator, as it were—and the political leadership in the light of the "*völkisch* idea of justice" and the "healthy sentiment of the people" and in

upon the abolition of the separation of powers. However, this also renders Schaffstein's "contact with legal certainty" ("Kontakt mit der Rechtssicherheit"; Cattaneo, 2001, p 213) worthless, as legal certainty is represented by the "will of the Führer".

567 Schaffstein, *DR* 4 (1934), 352 ("umso stärker", "je wahrscheinlicher", "das Gesetz wirklich…den Führerwillen repräsentiert").

568 *Cf* ch III including fn 263 and main text above.

569 Schaffstein, in Ellscheid/ Hassemer (1974), p 417 ("this proved to be an erroneous understanding not only...in a political sense. Beyond this, it leads to an inadmissible abbreviation of the methodological questions at stake. The belief in a totalitarian ideology curtails one of the most important questions …, namely how to determine the standards and criteria according to which the judge has to balance conflicting interests and values when interpreting and filling in gaps in the law" ["Als Irrweg erwies sich jene Auffassung nicht nur…im eigentlich politischen Sinne. Darüber hinaus bewirkt sie auch eine unzulässige Verkürzung der behandelten methologischen Fragestellungen. Der Glaube an eine totalitäre Ideologie schneidet eine der wichtigsten Fragen … ab, nämlich wie die Maßstäbe und Kriterien zu gewinnen sind, nach denen der Richter bei der Auslegung und Lückenausfüllung den Ausgleich der widerstreitenden Interessen und Werte vorzunehmen hat"]). Zaffaroni (2017) overlooks this distancing.

570 Dahm (1931), p 4 and *passim* (brief reference to the southwest German school of Neo-Kantianism on p 5) ("Zunahme der Richtermacht", "die neuzeitliche Neigung zur Erweichung der Rechtsformen", "Bestandteile des Verbrechensbegriffs", "Wertungen und Willensentscheidungen"). Zaffaroni (2017), p 245 including fn 446 quotes this source imprecisely, namely as a journal (*Recht und Staat*). On the sentencing system in this context, Hartl (2000), p 243 ff.

reference to the "concrete *Lebenstatbestand*" (the concrete, life-based definition of the *actus reus*).[571] The increase in judicial power, Dahm concludes, is ultimately more illusion than reality in the NS Führer state (a "pseudo-increase"), as judges are "now more strongly bound to the will of the political leadership and the *Volksgemeinschaft's* view of the law than ever before".[572] This qualitative leap in Dahm's work—from legal problem analysis (1931) to an NS-inspired description of the judge's personality (1934), that is, from an analytical to a decidedly ideological approach—is often overlooked,[573] but is certainly typical of the (criminal) law literature of the time.

4. *Loyalty, breaches of duty, honour punishments*

Schaffstein's **theory of breaches of duty** is particularly significant.[574] He developed this theory in response to the "individualist subversion of criminal law of the past decades"—represented by the liberal theory of violations of rights or protected legal interests (*Rechtsgüter*) (thereto below)[575]—

571 Dahm, *DStR* 80 (1934), 87 ff ("völkischen Rechtsgedankens", "gesunden Volksanschauung", "konkreten Lebenstatbestand") (89: "law and judge's verdict...on the same level" ["Gesetz und Richterspruch...auf gleicher Ebene"], expressing "the völkisch idea of justice" ["den völkischen Rechtsgedanken"] and the "völkisch order" ["völkische Ordnung"], at the same time, the judge is subject to "the decision of the political leadership expressed in the law" ["im Gesetz zum Ausdruck kommende Entscheidung der politischen Führung"]; 90: the judge must "make value judgements that correspond to the National Socialist view of the law and the will of the political leadership" ["Werturteile zu fällen, die der nationalsozialistischen Rechtsanschauung und dem Willen der politischen Führung entsprechen"]; 91: "the judge will reach the appropriate decision through obedience to the will of the political leadership" ["durch Gehorsam gegenüber dem Willen der politischen Führung findet der Richter die zutreffende Entscheidung"]). Here, too, Dahm is cited imprecisely by Zaffaroni (2017), p 245 including fn 448, namely with *Deutsches Recht* as the source (which is a different journal).

572 Dahm, *DStR* 80 (1934), 96 ("Scheinzunahme", "an den Willen der politischen Führung und die Rechtsanschauung der Volksgemeinschaft heute stärker gebunden als je").

573 Thus also Zaffaroni (2017), p 245, who only mentions the earlier work (1931) in passing and suggests a continuity to the later work (1934)—a continuity that is not supported by textual analysis.

574 Schaffstein, in: Dahm et al (1935), p 108 ff (once again cited imprecisely by Zaffaroni, namely as a monograph). Also see Schaffstein, *DRWis* 1 (1936), 39 (42 ff: replacing the liberal-individualist theory of the violation of the law/protected legal interests by the völkisch-collectivist theory of breaches of duty); thereto also Marxen (1975), p 185–6; Hartl (2000), p 106 ff; critically Hoyer (1997), p 54 ff (pointing to "possibilities of abuse" ["Mißbrauchsmöglichkeiten"] and a lack of legitimacy); Cattaneo (2001), p 222–3; summarising the contemporary criticism Stefanopolou, *JoJZG* 2010, 113–4.

575 Critically on the liberal theory of protected legal interests Schaffstein, in: Dahm et al (1935), p 112–3, 117; similarly Schaffstein, *DStR* 81 (1935), 97 ff (protected legal inter-

and the "criminal attacks on the völkisch community".[576] Thus Schaffstein advocated abandoning the opposition between individual and community, as the former can only exist as part of the latter, namely as a *Volksgenosse* with intrinsic duties (including moral duties) to the *Volksgemeinschaft*, which always takes precedence.[577] Not fulfilling these duties—that is, a (morally objectionable)[578] omission[579]—can be sanctioned under criminal law (in the worst case as treason, as we will see below).

---

ests as a concept whose "Enlightenment, individualist content needs to be exposed" ["aufklärerisch-individualistischen Gehalt es zu entlarven gilt", 97], whose "intellectualisation" appears "particularly dangerous" ["Vergeistigung...als besonders gefährlich"], because it allows "the poison of Enlightenment ideology" ["dem Gift der Aufklärungsideologie"] to find its way "into many cracks and crevices of criminal law" ["in viele Ritzen und Spalten des Strafrechts", 101]).

576 Schaffstein, in: Dahm et al (1935), p 108–9 ("individualistische Strafrechtszersetzung der vergangenen Jahrzehnte", "verbrecherischen Angriffe gegen die völkische Gemeinschaft").

577 Schaffstein, *ZStW* 53 (1934), 605 ("protection of the *Volksgemeinschaft*...precedes the protection of the individual *Volksgenosse*" ["Schutz der Volksgemeinschaft...geht dem Schutz des einzelnen Volksgenossen voraus"]); id, in: Dahm et al (1935), p 109; id, *DStR* 81 (1935), 104 (the opposition between collective and individual crimes is abolished "as soon as the isolated single person becomes a member of the community, as soon as the individual becomes the *Volksgenosse*" ["sobald aus dem isolierten Einzelnen das Gemeinschaftsmitglied, aus dem Individuum der Volksgenosse wird"]); id, *DRWis* 1 (1936), 46–7 ("the individual's status as a member of the whole organism is expressed...in his duties towards the community...the *Volksgenosse* is bound into the community as a member...which is why crime appears precisely as a breach of duty" ["Gliedhaftigkeit des einzelnen im völkischen Gesamtorganismus bekundet sich...in den Pflichten gegenüber der Gemeinschaft...gliedmäßige Verbundenheit des Volksgenossen in der Gemeinschaft...Grund dafür, warum uns das Verbrechen gerade als Pflichtverletzung erscheint"]).

578 *Cf* eg Preußischer Justizminister (1933), p 132 (moral duty to act based upon healthy popular views) and § 13 of the Draft StGB of 1936 (those whose omissions constitute a breach of duty are punished "like agents...according to the healthy sentiment of the people" ["wie ein Handelnder...nach gesundem Volksempfinden"], quoted from Hartl [2000], p 141); also Mezger, *DJZ* 39 (1934), col 104 ("justified" ["berechtigt"] in principle); Schaffstein, *DJ* 98 (1936), 767 ("every duty springing from the *völkisch* moral order as a legal duty" ["jede der völkischen Sittenordnung entspringende Pflicht als Rechtspflicht"]). This corresponds to the ethicising abolition of the distinction between law and morals, see thereto ch II 2. including fn 194 above.

579 On the corresponding upgrading of (improper) omission offences, Schaffstein, in: Dahm et al (1935), p 140 ff (what is decisive is not the violation of a protected legal interest, but the "unique characteristics of the respective duty breached" ["Eigenart der jeweils verletzten Pflicht"]; wrongfulness is based upon the breach of duty, not upon a causal violation of a protected legal interest); id, *FS Gleispach* (1936), p 73 ff; id, *DJ* 98 (1936), 767 ff (problem of types of perpetrator, expansion of omission offences as a consequence of the emphasis on the "Volksgemeinschaft" [767]); also Mezger, *DJZ* 39 (1934), col 102 ("comparison of the image of the act" ["Vergleich des Tatbildes"]; also see the following section (5.) at fn 670 and Hartl (2000), p 139 ff; Hoyer, *GS Eckert* (2008), p 358; Stefanopolou, *JoJZG* 2010, 114–5.

GRUNDFRAGEN DER NEUEN RECHTS-WISSENSCHAFT

Von

Georg Dahm / Ernst Rudolf Huber
Karl Larenz / Karl Michaelis / Friedrich Schaffstein / Wolfgang Siebert
sämtlich Professoren der Rechte in Kiel

1935
JUNKER UND DÜNNHAUPT VERLAG / BERLIN

Figure 16: Schaffstein's main text on the central theory of breaches of duty (*Pflichtverletzung*), published in Dahm et al (1935), p 108 ff

The concepts of *duty*,[580] *honour* (of the *Volks*- or *Rechtsgenossen*)[581] and *loyalty*[582] (towards the Führer, people and state)[583] lay the ground for the (oft-

580 On duty, especially as the duty of loyalty towards the Volksgemeinschaft, see Frank (1935), p 11 ff (with specific reference to duty [of loyalty] in principles 3, 4, 5, 20 and 38).

581 On the significance of the concept of honour, see ch II 2. including fn 192 above, referring to the NS guidelines (Frank, 1935), which refer to it specifically in nos 5 and 27 as a (criminal) legal consequence of the loss of honour in breaches of the duty of loyalty. Specifically on honour in NS criminal law, Dahm, *DR* 4 (1934), 416 ("crucial precondition for the existence and preservation of a true community and as such an immediate völkisch legal interest" ["wesentliche Voraussetzung für den Bestand und die Erhaltung einer wirklichen Gemeinschaft überhaupt und insofern unmittelbar ein völkisches Rechtsgut"], "more valuable than life" ["wertvoller als das Leben", referring

mentioned) radical **ethicisation** or moralisation of criminal law;[584] concrete "spheres of duties"—modelled on Carl Schmitt's[585] "*concrete orders*"[586]—are to overcome "the old opposition between the criminal law of the act and an agent-focused criminal law".[587] A breach of the duty of loyalty towards the Volksgemeinschaft is "treason",[588] although this applies only to Germans as *Volksgenossen* with particular duties of loyalty, while foreigners only violate their right of abode (as evident in "Landesverrat", treason to one's country);[589] the link between loyalty and honour explains the particular significance of honour punishments,[590] symbolising a

---

to the Prussian Memorandum (1933)]); on honour punishment, see fn 591 and main text below.

582 On the significance of the concept of loyalty, see ch II 2. including fn 192 above, referring to the NS guidelines (Frank, 1935), which refer to the (völkisch) duty of loyalty specifically in nos 3, 4, 5 and 38; also Siegert, *DR* 4 (1934), 528 ff (blood-based loyalty to the völkisch community); Schaffstein, *DStR* 81 (1935), 104; from a historico-political perspective Gross (2010), position 813 ff (936), 1077 ff and *passim*; from a legal history perspective Kroeschell (1995), p 158 ff (162: danger of exaggeration into "a Germanic mystery of the law" ["einem germanischen Rechtsmysterium"]); Kroeschell, in: Rückert/Willoweit (1995), 60–1, 66 ff.

583 Thierack, in Frank (1934), p 27.

584 References in section 3. including fn 557 above.

585 Ch IV 2. including fn 340 above.

586 Explicitly Schaffstein, *DRWis* 1 (1936), 45 (the "nature of the crime" ["Wesen des Verbrechens"] derives from the "nature of the concrete community" ["Wesen der konkreten Gemeinschaft"]), 47 (duty arises "from the concrete order of the völkisch community" ["aus der konkreten Ordnung der völkischen Gemeinschaft"]; the individual is integrated not only into the "totality of the Volksgemeinschaft, but also into the 'lower orders' of a variety of estate-based and other communities" ["Volksgemeinschaft in ihrer Gesamtheit, sondern darüber hinaus in eine Vielzahl ständischer und sonstiger Gemeinschaften 'niederer Ordnung'"]). Schaffstein himself later acknowledged Schmitt's influence, Schaffstein, *JJZG* 7 (2005), 187–8. On this link, also see Schwinge/Zimmerl (1937), p 53.

587 Schaffstein, in: Dahm et al (1935), p 114 ("Pflichtenkreise", "den alten Gegensatz von Tatstrafrecht und Täterstrafrecht"); id, *DRWis* 1 (1936), 49 (abolition of the "antithesis between agent and act" ["Antithese von Täter und Tat"]).

588 Schaffstein, in: Dahm et al (1935), p 114. Critically Schwinge/Zimmerl (1937), p 50–1. On treason and violations of honour, Dahm, in: Dahm et al (1935) p 103 ff. On "crime as treason" ("Verbrechen als Verrat"), also Marxen (1975), p 186 ff; Hartl (2000), p 111 ff.

589 Thereto Dahm (1935a), p 13; Dahm (1935b), p 29–30; Schaffstein, *DRWis* 1936, 48; similarly Siegert, *DR* 4 (1934), 530; also Freisler, *DJ* 97 (1935), 1251 (high treason as a "severe breach of loyalty towards the people themselves" ["schwerer Treubruch gegenüber dem Volke selbst"]).

590 Schaffstein, in: Dahm et al (1935), p 115; thereto also Schaffstein, *DStR* 80 (1934), 273; Schaffstein, *DJZ* 39 (1934), col 1179 (civil law concept of the "right to punish" ["Strafanspruch"] cannot be reconciled with honour punishment); Schaffstein, *ZStW* 53 (1934), 625–6; Schaffstein, *ZStW* 55 (1936), 286, 288 (emphasis of punishment's "effect upon honour" ["Ehrenwirkung"], "loss of honour" ["Ehrenminderung"] should

(morally reprehensible)[591] *loss of honour* due to a breach of the duty of loyalty.[592] Even though the duty of loyalty should in principle be restricted to "those cases in which the act characterised as such attacks and questions the essence of the perpetrator's belonging to the community",[593] Schaffstein also transfers the idea of loyalty to breaches of duty in private (economic) dealings, such as breaches of professional, official and trade duties, family and marriage duties, and embezzlement ("Untreue").[594]

In the case of embezzlement, this continues to have an effect in § 266 StGB, [595] since its emphasis on the abstract duty to safeguard property derives from the replacement of the casuistic version of 1871, which referred to particular perpetrators,[596] by the Criminal Law Provisions Amendment Act of 26 May 1933.[597] Even if, like the BVerfG, we regard the "values underpinning" today's version of § 266 "not as National Socialist thought"[598] and emphasise the reference to a protected legal interest (property) rather than a pure breach of duty,[599] this does not alter the fact that the NS legislator's orientation towards the idea of loyalty enabled an "extensive use of the elements of the *actus reus* according to National Socialist ideas",[600] which is why embezzlement

---

also be involved in prison sentences); also Dahm (1935a), p 6 ff (punishment as a shame sanction, including exclusion from the community); Dahm, *DJZ* 39 (1934), col 821 (critically on the neglect of honour punishments [and the death penalty] and in favour of their renewal).

591 Radbruch's attempt at de-moralisation by abolishing honour punishments in his 1922 Draft is thus consistent, thereto Goltsche (2010), p 304–5, 360, 376–8.

592 Fn 582 above.

593 Schaffstein, in: Dahm et al (1935), p 115–6, 118 ("diejenigen Fälle", "in denen die so gekennzeichnete Tat die Gemeinschaftszugehörigkeit des Täters wirklich in ihrem innersten Kern angreift und in Frage stellt").

594 Schaffstein, in: Dahm et al (1935), p 127 ff (four groups of breach of duty offences, although these are not exhaustive). On the anti-liberal movement's demands concerning the Special Part, see Marxen (1975), p 124 ff.

595 *Cf* explicitly on the connection with the NS concept of loyalty, Siegert, *DR* 4 (1934), 531; also Dahm (1935a), p 14.

596 RGBl I 1871 127 (§ 266 RStGB).

597 RGBl I 1933 295.

598 BVerfG, Decree of 23 June 2010 [constitutionality of § 266 StGB] – 2 BvR 2559/08 et al, subparagraph 88 ("zugrunde liegenden Wertungen nicht als nationalsozialistisches Gedankengut").

599 Thus in general on the current special offences Hoyer, *GS Eckert* (2008), p 362; Stefanopolou, *JoJZG* 2010, 117.

600 BVerfG, 2 BvR 2559/08, subparagraph 16 ("extensive Handhabung des Tatbestands im Sinne nationalsozialistischer Vorstellungen") (albeit with an uncritical reference to the text by Bruns, 1938, the quality of which as a *Habilitation* thesis was disputed, *cf* Jeßberger, in: Jeßberger/Kotzur/Repgen (2019), p 244 including fn 44; critically on Bruns Wolf, *JuS* 1996, 189).

continues to constitute a "legacy" of National Socialist legislative technique to this day.[601] The amendment's early date—only a few months after the Nazis had (formally) taken power—confirms the theory of (retrospective) **continuity**.

In a criminal law that is dominated by loyalty and duties towards the Volksgemeinschaft, the (external) *violation of the law or of protected legal interests* no longer holds any significance in its own right. It is replaced by the internal attitude ("Gesinnung") towards these duties of loyalty, so that crime becomes a breach of duty that expresses a culpable inner attitude in regard to the abovementioned duties of loyalty.[602] Thus Schaffstein moves from a "criminal law of the violation of protected legal interests" ("Rechtsgutsverletzungsstrafrecht") to an **"attitude-based criminal law or criminal law of duty"** ("Gesinnungs- oder Pflichtenstrafrecht"),[603] although abandoning the concept of protected legal interests altogether would not have been necessary (we will come to the punishment merely of the "evil will" below), as it was (and is!) "elastic" enough[604] to be imbued with National Socialist ideology through the teleological understanding[605] propagated by Schwinge/Zimmerl.[606] This is why the Kiel School ultimately had no problems with the "content- and substance-filled" concept of

601 Wolf, *JuS* 1996, 193 ("Vermächtnis"); Safferling, *NStZ* 2011, 376, 377 left col. Commentaries usually uncritically reproduce the 1933 amendment, *cf* eg Dierlamm, in: *MüKoStGB* (2014), § 266 mn 20; Kindhäuser, in: *NK-StGB* (2017), § 266 mn 17.

602 Schaffstein, *DRWis* 1 (1936), 45 (crime as the "expression of a reprehensible attitude that is hostile to the people" ["Ausdruck einer verwerflichen und volksfeindlichen Gesinnung"]); thereto Marxen (1975), p 188–9.

603 Schaffstein, in: Dahm et al (1935), p 110; in greater detail on breaches of duty and attitude id, p 119 ff, 125; to some extent also Schaffstein, *DStR* 81 (1935), 105 (understanding of crime as a breach of duty as the "cornerstone" ["Grundstein"] of the "newly constructed National Socialist criminal law system" ["Neubau des nationalsozialistischen Strafrechtssystems"]); id, *DRWis* 1 (1936), 45 ff; on attitude-based criminal law, Hartl (2000), p 126 ff.

604 Amelung (1972), p 238 ("geschmeidig").

605 Ch IV 2. including fn 350–358 and main text above. – Hartl (2000), p 102 overlooks the (albeit superficial) disagreement between the Kiel and Marburg scholars concerning the question of protected legal interests in assuming that the anti-liberal reform movement's struggle was unanimous (at least he quotes Schwinge/Zimmerl on p 109 including fn 401).

606 In this context also Murmann (2005), p 138 (protected legal interest is "open enough to be filled with any content" ["für jede inhaltliche Auffüllung offen"]; Hoyer, *GS Eckert* (2008), p 361 (criminal liability for impossible attempt justified by considerations related to protected legal interests). On the (traditional) concept of protected legal interests' low restrictive potential, also Ambos, *FS Wolter* (2013), 1285, 1288 ff including further references (English version in *Criminal Law and Philosophy* 9 [2015], 301, 304 ff); critically, instead emphasising the principle of offensiveness (*principio de ofensividad*) advocated in Italy in particular, Zaffaroni (2017), p 228–9.

protected legal interests[607]—just like other NS jurists[608]—and their main target was Feuerbach's (subjective) theory of the violation of rights ("Rechtsverletzungslehre").[609] Essentially, then, the dispute between the Kiel and the Marburg scholars boiled down to the question of which approach—the breach of duty theory or the teleological theory of protected legal interests—was better suited to overcoming the hateful liberal thought;[610] especially given that the Marburg scholars also saw guilt as manifest in an attitude conflicting with National Socialism.[611] Seen from this angle, the dispute was (as already stated above[612]) a mock battle.

The subjectivised breach of duty theory has direct consequences for the concept of crime. On the one hand, it *subjectivises unlawfulness*[613]—as a subjective conflict with duty (although the duty should be understood objectively, measured against the "völkisch moral order")[614]—which on the other hand leads, in turn, to a *conflation with guilt*,[615] since guilt after all consists only in the flawed inner attitude, as expressed in the act, towards duty. In other words, the breach of duty theory renders the distinction between unlawfulness and guilt superfluous, as both consist equally of the (subjective) breach (non-fulfilment) of duty towards the Volksgemein-

607 *Cf* Dahm, *ZStW* 57 (1938), 231 ("inhaltlichen und substanzerfüllten"); id, *Tätertyp* (1940), p 31 including fn 56 (agreement reached in principle); Schaffstein, *DRWis* 1 (1936), 43–4 (according to whom the true "essence of the theory of protected legal interests" ["Kern der Rechtsgüterlehre"] lies in its protection of certain values of the Volksgemeinschaft). Also *cf* Amelung (1972), p 249 (adaptation to NS thinking as "Volksgutlehren" or "theories of popular interest"), 251 ff.

608 *Cf* eg the plea for an expansion of the protection of legal interests in a National Socialist sense by Strauß, in Frank (1934), p 31 ff.

609 Accurately Günther, in: Institut für Kriminalwissenschaften (1995), p 445, 452 ff.

610 *Cf* in this sense against Schaffstein also Schwinge/Zimmerl (1937), p 48–9, 67 (where they attempt to prove the breach of duty theory's closeness to the individualist thinking of liberalism among other things).

611 Ch IV 2. including fn 355 and main text above.

612 Ch IV 3. including fn 429 and main text above.

613 Schaffstein, in: Dahm et al (1935), p 123; also Schaffstein, *DRWis* (1936), 49 (subjectivisation of unlawfulness).

614 Schaffstein, in: Dahm et al (1935), p 139 ("objectivisation of contravention of duty" ["Objektivierung der Pflichtwidrigkeit"]); also Schaffstein, *DRWis* 1 (1936), 49 ("objectivisation of a normatively understood guilt" ["Objektivierung einer normativ verstandenen Schuld"]).

615 See eg Schaffstein, in: Dahm et al (1935), p 123; Schaffstein, *DRWis* 1 (1936), 49 (conflation of wrongdoing and guilt); on the abolition of this distinction, also Marxen (1975), p 222 ff; in greater detail on the debate, particularly in the official Criminal Law Reform Commission (Gürtner, 1934 and 1935), Hartl (2000), p 159 ff (according to whom the "advocates of the unification of unlawfulness and guilt...ultimately...were unable to assert" themselves ["Befürworter einer Vereinheitlichung von Rechtswidrigkeit und Schuld...letztlich...nicht durchsetzen", 162]).

schaft[616]—fully in line with the "attitude-based criminal law or criminal law of duty" mentioned above. For example: a witness who believes she is lying but is actually telling the truth is committing the completed offence of giving false testimony, as her intention was to lie. Thus, she has expressed a flawed attitude towards the duty of truth, and in any case is guilty of a breach of duty in this subjectivised sense.[617]

Thus the breach of duty theory clearly contains an element of ***Willensstrafrecht***, the criminal law of the will: on the one hand, the subjectivisation of unlawfulness through the theory of breaches of duty leads to an (attitude-focused) "criminal law of the will";[618] on the other hand, it is the theory of breach of duty that "gives the concept of Willensstrafrecht its proper content in the first place",[619] since it is the will (attitude) hostile to the people's community expressed in the breach of duty that is decisive.[620] Schaffstein had previously already made the emphasis on the "evil will" the foundation of the National Socialists' "ethicising understanding of criminal law".[621] We will return to this and to further consequences for the concept of crime in the following two sections.

---

616 Schaffstein, in: Dahm et al (1935), p 132 ff (134, 137); in particular against a three-part division into the elements of the offence, unlawfulness and guilt, ibid p 123, 132; also Schaffstein, *DRWis* 1 (1936), 46 ff (breach of duty as a violation towards the völkisch community with concrete consequences for the concept of crime).

617 Schaffstein, in: Dahm et al (1935), p 128–9; also see Gallas, *FS Gleispach* (1936), p 52 (who criticises not only the theory of protected legal interests but also the theory of breach of duty because of its "one-sidedness" ["Einseitigkeit"]—raising the ethical standpoint "to the essential principle" ["zum wesensbestimmenden Prinzip", p 67–8]) [also quoted by Zaffaroni (2017), p 221 including fn 420, albeit without giving page numbers and imprecise also because he cites both Schaffstein and Gallas as monographs]. Critically Schwinge/Zimmerl (1937), p 68, according to whom the teleological concept of protected legal interests (ch IV 2. including fn 358 above) enables the subjective "interpretation of the meaning of an offence" ["Sinndeutung eines Delikts"]; however, against the teleological method in principle Schaffstein, *FS Schmidt* (1936), p 59 ff. At any rate, an emphasis on the (dis)value of the act/action leads to the same results, *cf* Welzel, *FS Kohlrausch* (1944), p 101, 107–8.

618 Schaffstein, in: Dahm et al (1935), p 123 (subjectivisation and conflation lead to "Willensstrafrecht"), 137 (crime as a breach of duty categorised as part of *Willensstrafrecht*); Schaffstein, *DRWis* 1 (1936), 45 (link between attitude and breach of duty in the future "Willensstrafrecht"). Thereto also Hartl (2000), p 160–1.

619 Schaffstein, in: Dahm et al (1935), p 114 ("Begriff des Willensstrafrechts erst seinen eigentlichen Gehalt").

620 *Cf* eg Schaffstein, *DRWis* 1 (1936), 49 ("occurrence of the breach of duty" ["Eintritt der Pflichtverletzung"] is "independent of the occurence of the harmful result" ["Eintritt des schädigenden Erfolgs unabhängig"]).

621 Schaffstein, *ZStW* 53 (1934), 609 ff (good or evil "will decisive" ["Wille entscheidend"], result "irrelevant" ["gleichgültig"] for moral evaluation; "focusing on the evil will alone" ["Abstellen allein auf den bösen Willen"] corresponds to an "ethicising understanding of criminal law" ["ethisierenden Strafrechtsauffassung"]; "standpoint of an

5. Concrete Wesensschau (focus on the substance of the offence), Täterstrafrecht (agent-focused criminal law) and Willensstrafrecht (criminal law of the will)

The rejection of dualist thinking leads to a comprehensive view that focuses on the essence or substance of an offence (**"wesensmäßige Gesamtbetrachtung"**). This view is oriented towards the reality of the Volksgemeinschaft, towards the "völkisch being" of Schmitt's concrete order:[622] "'Killing' ("Tötung") cannot be seen separately, it cannot be ascertained 'as such' and then labelled as 'murder' ("Mord"). It is murder from the very start where it destroys the community. Those whose thinking starts from the community will not [merely] see a killing, but murder".[623] For "abstract thinking carries in itself the seed of destruction"[624] and abstract elements of crime alone are meaningless;[625] they gain their meaning only in reference to the Volksgemeinschaft, "from their being and effect within

---

ethicising criminal law of the will" ["Standpunkt eines ethisierenden Willensstrafrechts"]).

622 Dahm, in: Dahm et al (1935), p 86 ("völkisch being" ["völkisches Sein"] as an "order" ["Ordnung"], law as a "concrete order" ["konkrete Ordnung"], crime as "concrete disorder" ["konkrete Unordnung"]), 101 (law as the "expression of an essential reality of life, the living order of the German people and the *Führerbefehl*" ["Ausdruck einer wesenshaften Lebenswirklichkeit, der lebendigen Ordnung des deutschen Volkes und des Führerbefehls"]); also Dahm (1940), p 35 (the law strives for an "order of things in accordance with life" ["lebensmäßiger Ordnung der Dinge"]); Schaffstein, *DRWis* 1 (1936), 47 (morality "arises from the concrete order of the völkisch community" ["ergibt sich aus der konkreten Ordnung der völkischen Gemeinschaft"], reference to "low" ["niedere"] estate-based orders). On Schmitt in this regard, ch IV 2. including fn 339 above. On *Wesensschau* and order-based thinking also Marxen (1975), p 221–2; briefly Vogel (2004), p 65–6.

623 Dahm, in: Dahm et al (1935), p 86 ("Die 'Tötung' kann nicht für sich gesehen, sie kann nicht 'als solche' festgestellt und alsdann mit dem Stempel 'Mord' versehen werden. Sie ist von vorneherein Mord, wo sie die Gemeinschaft zerstört. Wer von der Gemeinschaft her denkt, sieht gar nicht die Tötung, sondern den Mord").

624 Dahm, in: Dahm et al (1935), p 63–4 ("abstrakte Denken trägt den Keim der Zerstörung in sich") ("subversive thinking at work here" ["zersetzendes Denken, das hier am Werke ist"]). On the fight against abstract concepts and *Trennungsdenken*, also Marxen (1975), p 214 ff including further references.

625 Against Beling's theory of *Tatbestand*, especially the thesis of normative neutrality ("Wertfreiheit"), and its liberal implications (principle of legality etc), also Dahm, in: Dahm et al (1935), p 63 ff, 78 ff, 89 and 107 (abolition of the concept of "Tatbestand", which is "artificial" ["künstlich"] and an example of "spectral, depleted and dead words" ["gespensterhafte, ausgelaugte und tote Worte"]); differently however Dahm (1940), p 37 (*Tatbestand* as the sole "starting point for any study of the...type" ["Ausgangspunkt jeder Untersuchung über den...Typus"], the "type" ["Typus"] as the "shadow of the *Tatbestand*" ["Schatten des Tatbestands"]). At other points in this later text, Dahm likewise uses the term *Tatbestand* as if he had never called for its abolition. On the fight against abstract concepts and valuating unlawfulness, also Marxen (1975), p 219 ff.

the community, that is, from people and race".[626] Human actions cannot be seen in any other way "than in the community, not as an individual, independent or natural process...instead, they bear their meaning or conflict with meaning within themselves, that is, in their völkisch being";[627] what is at stake here is thus the action springing from the "völkisch moral order".[628] Criminal wrongdoing cannot be captured by the purely rational and logical analysis of the elements of the *actus reus*, but only in its essence or "true being",[629] that is—"substantively"[630]—by taking into account its

626 Dahm, in: Dahm et al (1935), p 86 ("aus ihrem Sein und Wirken in der Gemeinschaft, verstanden aus Volk und Rasse").

627 Dahm, in: Dahm et al (1935). p 86–7 ("sehen als in der Gemeinschaft, nicht als einzelnen, selbständigen und natürlichen Vorgang..., sondern es trägt seinen Sinn oder Widersinn in sich, das heißt in seinem völkischen Sein"). On the battle against the naturalist concept of action, also Marxen (1975), p 217 ff.

628 Dahm, *ZStW* 57 (1938), 250 ff ("essence of legal institutions" ["Wesen der Rechtsinstitute"] or the "concept of legal science" ["Begriff der Rechtswissenschaft"] as the "replica of a reality full of meaning" ["Nachbildung einer sinnerfüllten Wirklichkeit", 251–2], "ideas that have developed historically, live in the consciousness of the people, and are significant for communal life in specific ways" ["geschichtlich gewordene, im Volksbewußtsein lebendige, für das Gemeinschaftsleben in bestimmer Weise bedeutsame Vorstellungen", 252], "going back to more profound ideas that live in the people" ["Zurückgehen auf tieferliegende, im Volke lebende Vorstellungen", ibid], "popular view working behind the law...a popular feeling for justice and injustice" ["hinter dem Gesetz wirkende volkstümliche Anschauung...ein Volksempfinden für Recht und Unrecht", 255], "standard in the moral order that has developed historically, in the internal law of life and the communal orders of the people" ["Maßstab in der geschichtlich gewordenen Sittenordnung, in dem inneren Lebensgesetz und den Gemeinschaftsordnungen des Volkes", ibid]); also Dahm (1940), p 34–5 ("popular sentiment" ["Volksempfinden"] stands "behind every legal concept" ["hinter jedem Rechtsbegriff"], it is the foundation and "raw material" ["Rohstoff"] of legislative and judicial work).

629 Dahm, in: Dahm et al (1935), p 89 ("wirklichen Sein") ("For the core, the nature of crime cannot be comprehended 'logically'" ["Denn der Kern, das Wesen des Verbrechens ist eben 'logisch' gar nicht zu fassen"]); Dahm (1935b), p 14 (core NS concepts such as honour, loyalty etc elude "final rational comprehension" ["sich einer letzten rationalen Erfassung"]). Prior to Dahm, however, Mittermaier (*ZStW* 44 (1924), 8–9) had already focused upon the "inner nature" of a conduct when defining it as a crime ("Something can be legally defined as an offence that is nevertheless not a crime according to its inner nature" ["Es kann aber etwas vom Recht in einem Tatbestand ausgeprägt werden und ist seinem inneren Wesen nach doch kein Verbrechen", 8]). Dahm himself later recognised the fundamental value of a logical-rational structure of crime ("task of science to identify the constituent parts of the concept of crime that are most accessible and most in need of rational assessment and shaping, and structure the entirety of crime in a meaningful way" ["Aufgabe der Wissenschaft, die einer rationalen Erfassung und Gestaltung im weitesten Umfange zugänglichen und bedürftigen Bestandteile des Verbrechensbegriffs zu ermitteln und das Ganze des Verbrechens sinnvoll zu gliedern"], but still maintained that the holistic view ("crime as part of a whole, as part of an internal context of meaning" ["Verbrechen als eines Ganzen, als eines inneren Sinnzusammenhangs"]) was "of greater importance" ("von größerer Bedeutung"; Dahm (1940), p 60–1).

"significance for the völkisch order".[631] Thus the war crimes of German soldiers in the First World War are—according to their essence—no more manslaughter or even murder[632] than the confiscation of a Catholic organisation's flag by the Hitler Youth is a theft.[633]

This focus on essence/substance or *Wesensbetrachtung* can thus lead both to a "restriction of the elements of crime" as well as to their expansion.[634] Ultimately, elements of crime and unlawfulness (as well as guilt) are subsumed in a type of offence that is only vaguely defined by its substance—which means that it is actually undefined (thereto section 6. below)—thus doing away with the specificatory and limiting function of the elements of

630 Eg Schaffstein, *ZStW* 53 (1934), 612 ("principle of the material exclusion of wrongdoing in accordance with the National Socialist idea of the law" ["Prinzip des materiellen Unrechtsausschlusses im Sinn der nationalsozialistischen Rechtsidee"]).

631 Dahm, in: Dahm et al (1935), p 102 ("Bedeutung für die völkische Ordnung"); auch Dahm (1940), p 21 (definition of the völkisch type of perpetrator through "popular opinion" ["Volksanschauung"], from which the "image of the perpetrator" ["Täterbilde"] arises), 34 ("popular sentiment" ["Volksempfinden"] and the "völkisch moral order" ["völkische Sittenordnung"] as the foundation of the law), 37 (perpetrator type as a "guideline" ["Richtlinie"] for the "sensible" ["vernünftige"] application of the law). Drawing more strongly on Schmitt's order-based thinking, Dahm (1935a), p 16 ("thinking from the concrete community and the living order" ["Denken aus der konkreten Gemeinschaft und aus der lebendigen Ordnung heraus"]).

632 Dahm, in: Dahm et al (1935), p 71 ff (critically on the Leipzig War Crimes Trials), 91 ("Nowadays jurists actually have to relearn the fact that a soldier at war is not a murderer, nor does he commit killing 'as such'" ["Der Jurist muß heute tatsächlich wieder lernen, daß der Soldat im Kriege kein Mörder ist, daß er auch 'an sich' keine Tötung begeht"]).

633 Dahm, in: Dahm et al (1935), p 102 ("The nature of theft is not exhausted in the sum of the elements of its definition" ["Das Wesen des Diebstahls erschöpft sich nicht in der Summe seiner Tatbestandsmerkmale"]), 103 ("Basically it is not the law that says what theft is; rather, this arises from the nature of the matter" ["Was Diebstahl ist, sagt ja im Grunde nicht das Gesetz, sondern das ergibt sich aus dem Wesen der Sache"]). Nor do the taking away of something belonging to a woman by her husband (ibid p 92–3) or the taking away of French flags, which according to the Treaty of Versailles are to be surrendered, constitute theft, as these acts correspond neither to the nature of theft nor to the underlying type of act or agent (Dahm, *ZStW* 57 (1938), 253–4; thereto also Marxen (1975), p 207).

634 Dahm, in: Dahm et al (1935), p 102. Dahm, *ZStW* 57 (1938), 254 speaks more generally of a "limitation of the offence type" ["Einschränkung des Deliktstypus"], which is contradictory if one, as he does (in: Dahm et al, 1935, p 68), already sees the elements of the offence (*Tatbestandsmäßigkeit*) as an "incrimination" ("Belastung"). Also *cf* Dahm (1940), p 42–3 ("limitation" ["Einschränkung"] by "typification" ["Typisierung"], "perpetrator type" ["Tätertypus"] and reference to "the typical living condition" ["das typische Lebensverhältnis"]), 49 ("expansion" ["Ausdehnung"] through "appropriate application" ["entsprechende Anwendung"] by referring to the perpetrator type). Likewise Schaffstein, *FS Gleispach* (1936), p 104 (limitation when the perpetrator type diverges from the elements of the *actus reus*).

the *Tatbestand (actus reus)*.[635] In this regard, we can point to the contemporary criticism of the vague concept of *Wesensschau*, which has already been mentioned at several places in this study.[636]

> I note in passing that Hans Welzel arrives at the same conclusion through his theory of social adequacy (*Sozialadäquanzlehre*), for "in combat situations during war", "actions that are appropriate and normal during war" do not constitute "offences in the first place"; ultimately, "the idea that the army when fighting is committing criminal offences—albeit lawfully—is too absurd, is constructed too woodenly to be correct".[637]

Dahm recognises **perpetrator/attitude types** and the **criminal law of the will** in that a crime is more than the mere violation of interests or goods, but he steers clear of a *pure* criminal law of the will or attitude (thereto below)[638] in that he emphasises the *act-relatedness* of agent-focused criminal law (*Täterstrafrecht*)[639] and for this reason seeks to uphold the distinction

---

635 Critically also Marxen (1975), p 203 ff ("undefined hints and vague paraphrases" ["unbestimmte Andeutungen und vage Umschreibungen", 221]); Hoyer, *GS Eckert* (2008), p 355 (certain types of offence or perpetrator only hinted at).

636 *Cf* in particular Schwinge/Zimmerl (1937) and Schwinge (1938), thereto ch IV 2.; also Mittermaier, *SchwZStR* 52 (1938), 213, 217 ("abundantly emotional '*Wesensschau*'" ["reichlich gefühlsmäßige 'Wesensschau'"]); Wolf, *DRWis* 4 (1939), 173 (the concept of *Wesensschau* is "hackneyed and general" ["abgegriffen und allgemein"] and "used in a popular, undefined sense" ["populär-unbestimmten Sinn verwendet"]).

637 Welzel, *ZStW* 58 (1939) 491, 516 ff. ("in den kriegerischen Kampfsituationen", "kriegsadäquate, kriegsnormale Handlungen [unterfallen] von vorneherein nicht deliktischen Tatbeständen"; "der Gedanke, daß das Heer im Kampf um Leben und Tod lauter strafrechtliche Tatbestände—wenn auch rechtmäßig—verwirkliche, zu absurd, zu papieren konstruiert, als daß er richtig sein könnte" [527]). Critically on the social adequacy theory because of its affinity to National Socialism, Llobet (2018), p 301 ff including further references; in German scholarship, criticism of this concept is limited mainly to its vagueness (*cf* eg Loos, in: Loos (1987), p 502 ff [503: "vagueness of the concept" ("Vagheit des Begriffs")]; Eser, *FS Roxin* [2001], p 199, 205 ff), which is precisely what enables it to be "filled" with NS ideology (critically in this regard more recently Kindhäuser, in: Kindhäuser et al [2019], p 160 ["concept of the *Völkisch* not rendered very concrete" ("wenig konkretisierten Begriff des Völkischen")], 178–9 [wrongdoing defined by a "'will of the people' that cannot be captured even halfway precisely in empirical terms" ("empirisch auch nicht halbwegs exakt einzufangenden 'Volkswillen')].

638 On *Täterstrafrecht* as a theory competing with *Willensstrafrecht*, *cf* Hartl (2000), p 116 ff (according to whom, among other things, "Willensstrafrecht" affected primarily the General Part, while "Täterstrafrecht" rather served the creation of new offences and originated not only in the criminal law of the will, but also in community-related criminal law thinking [121]).

639 Dahm (1940), p 55 (*Täterstrafrecht* "shaped by the act's external course of events" ["äußeren...Tatvorgang geprägt"] and "control of the act" ["Tatherrschaft", Lange] as a

between perpetration and secondary participation.[640] For Dahm, it comes down to the perpetrator or agent's role and position within the community—"the external conditions under which he lives, the belonging to a certain profession or estate etc"[641]—and the way these are evaluated. The focus lies—against "an overly one-sided" emphasis on the "nature of the perpetrator"[642]—on an objectivisation that uses as its measure the essence of the concrete act, which arises from the völkisch moral order[643] (*connection between Wesensschau and Willensstrafrecht*),[644] on "the deepening and correct assessment of the criminal law of the 'act'" through the perpetrator type,[645] on a perpetrator type—oriented towards the "idea living within the people of the murderer, the thief" and so on[646]—, an "idea of personality", an "image of a human person",[647] a type of crime,[648] on "act and agent as a unit",[649] thus ultimately on "a certain way of being in the com-

---

characteristic of "perpetration" ["Täterschaft"]); also later Dahm (1963) p. 511 ("will externalised/activated" ["Wille betätigt"]; concurring in essence Mezger, *DJZ* 39 (1934), col 100 (relation to the elements of the *actus reus* cannot be dispensed with in *Willensstrafrecht*, either, whose "backbone" ["Rückgrat"] is the "will to carry out a certain legally defined offence" ["Verwirklichenwollen eines bestimmten gesetzlichen Tatbestands"]), col 103 ("objective correction" ["objektive Korrektur"]).

640 Dahm (1940), p 54 ff (the "starting point" of *Willensstrafrecht's* "equal treatment of all forms of participation...is already misguided" ["Gleichbehandlung aller Beteiligungsformen…schon im Ansatz verfehlt", 54]). Schaffstein, *ZStW* 57 (1938), 319 ff likewise adheres to this distinction, but differentiates where the accessoriness of secondary participation is concerned, depending on whether the conditions of criminal liability for the main act establish its nature ("wesensbegründend") (if so, then accessoriness, otherwise—regarding personal grounds for excluding criminal liability and responsibility—independence of the participation). On *Willensstrafrecht* in this regard, *cf* ch II 3. including fn 251 and main text above.

641 Dahm, in: Dahm et al (1935), p 88–9 ("die äußeren Bedingungen, unter denen er lebt, die Zugehörigkeit zu einem bestimmten Beruf oder Stand usw.").

642 Dahm, *ZStW* 57 (1938), 256 ("zu einseitig", "Wesen des Täters").

643 Dahm, *ZStW* 57 (1938), 253 ("essence of the perpetrator type meant in this rule" ["Wesen des in dieser Vorschrift gemeinten Tätertypus"], "essence of the ideas of the act and the agent underlying the legal definitions" ["Wesen der den gesetzlichen Umschreibungen zugrundeliegenden Tat- und Tätervorstellungen"]).

644 *Cf* Dahm, in: Dahm et al (1935), p 89 ("where the perpetrator can be named in one key word—traitor, murderer, thief, fraudster, blackmailer—that is where the essence usually lies in the 'will'" ["Wo der Täter mit einem Hauptwort genannt werden kann—Verräter, Mörder, Dieb, Betrüger, Erpresser—dort liegt das Wesen in der Regel im 'Willen'"); Dahm (1935a), p 11 ("nature of crime" ["Wesen des Verbrechens"] as the "degeneration of the will" ["Entartung des Willens"]).

645 Dahm (1940), p 25 ("die Vertiefung und richtige Erfassung des 'Tat'-Strafrechts").

646 Dahm (1940), p 24 ("im Volk lebende Vorstellung vom Mörder, vom Diebe") ("as murder corresponds linguistically to murderer and dealing [in stolen goods] to dealer" ["wie in der Sprache ja auch dem Mord der Mörder und der Hehlerei der Hehler entspricht"]).

647 Dahm, *ZStW* 57 (1938), 257 ("Persönlichkeitsvorstellung", "Menschenbild").

648 Accurately Zaffaroni (2017), p 253.

munity",[650] which finally also must find expression in the statutory recognition of certain types of perpetrator.[651] Against this background it is striking that the NS murder type, introduced on 4 September 1941 in § 211 RStGB[652] and abolishing the premeditated murder rule of the 1872 Code,[653] is still valid today (apart from the death penalty)—another example of the said future-oriented **continuity**.[654]

In this context—in contrast to the theory of breaches of duty, which was more subjectivised[655]—Schaffstein likewise emphasises the external aspects of *Willensstrafrecht*, as it is "not the criminal will as such" that makes the act unlawful, "but its realisation in a particular external event".[656] He also

---

649 Dahm, in: Dahm et al (1935), p 92 ("Tat und Täter als Einheit"); Dahm (1940), p 24.

650 Dahm, in: Dahm et al (1935), p 88 ("ein bestimmtes Sein in der Gemeinschaft").

651 In this regard, in his later work on the *Tätertyp* ("perpetrator type") (1940), already quoted at several points—and which Zaffaroni only mentions in passing—, Dahm, despite recognising a "legal subjectivism" ("Gesetzessubjektivismus") and the role of case law "as pioneering the new 'criminal law of the will'" ("als Vorkämpferin des neuen 'Willensstrafrechts'", p 5), laments that "even today criminal law is stil first and foremost a criminal law of the act" ("auch heute noch das Strafrecht zunächst einmal Tatstrafrecht ist", p 7), as it has not been possible to go beyond criminological perpetrator types and develop a theory of the "criminal's personality as a whole" ("Gesamtpersönlichkeit des Verbrechers", p 8, 9) that can be applied beyond sentencing, that is, already on the level of wrongdoing (p 7–8). He attempts to remedy this—sympathising with Mezger's "lifestyle-based guilt" ("Lebensführungsschuld"; ch IV 1. including fn 305 and main text above) (p 11 ff) and reactiving the "atonement" used above all by Freisler (ch II 3. including fn 245 and main text above) (p 11, 38, 40)—by developing the perpetrator type—in the sense of a "culpable being-a-perpetrator" ("schuldhaftes Tätersein", p 9)—as a "third track" ("dritte Spur") by means of a detailed analysis of relevant (NS) norms (including the Habitual Offenders Act, special war legislation ["Volksschädling", p 34]) (p 9 ff; on different perpetrator types p 27 ff), although his (abstract) attempt at definition remains vague: "After all, the idea of the perpetrator type aims to say that where the *actus reus* is in itself sufficiently detailed and coherent, the act constitutes the idea of a perpetrator or agent too" ("Will doch der Gedanke des Tätertypus besagen, daß, wo das Tatbild in sich hinreichend anschaulich und geschlossen ist, mit der Tat auch die Vorstellung eines Täters gegeben sei", p 24). What is actually surprising is that Dahm distances himself from the text "Liberales oder autoritäres Strafrecht" (Dahm/Schaffstein, 1933), as "today's [1940] criminal policy situation is different to what is was then [1933]" ("kriminalpolitische Lage heute eine andere als damals"), for the "goal" ("Ziel") of the "forceful prosecution and destruction of true crime...has now essentially been achieved" ("kraftvolle Verfolgung und Vernichtung des wirklichen Verbrechens...heute im Wesentlichen erreicht", p 44).

652 RGBl I 549.

653 This rule was criticised as "overly intellectual" ("überintellektualistisch[en]") by Freisler, *DJ* 103 (1941), 935.

654 On the various reform attempts see Eser and Sternberg-Lieben, in Schönke/Schröder, *StGB* (2019), p 2056 ff including multiple references.

655 In this regard, see section 4. including fn 620–4 and main text above.

656 Schaffstein, *ZStW* 57 (1938), 313 ("nicht der verbrecherische Wille als solcher", "sondern erst seine Verwirklichung in einem bestimmten äußeren Geschehen"). Also *cf*

recognises the "unity" of act and agent[657] and its significance for the "formation and interpretation of the elements of the *Tatbestand*",[658] referring to Erik Wolf's theory[659]—which will be discussed below (ch VI)—concerning the manner in which perpetrator types should be taken into account when defining wrongdoing (Dahm, however, considers Wolf's theory to be overly subjective).[660] Thus the theories of breaches of duty and of perpetrator types both have attitude (*Gesinnung*) as a point of reference and the punishment of attitudinal disvalue (*Gesinnungsunwert*) as their shared theoretical foundation:[661] the former sees the lack of loyalty to the NS moral order (and thus a deficient, wrong or even malevolent attitude), the latter the deficient personality of the perpetrator (the perpetrator's attitude) as the reason for punishment, with the abovementioned stronger emphasis upon the external aspects (of the act) restricting criminal law. In any case, *pure* attitude- or duty-focused criminal law in the abovementioned Schaffsteinian sense[662] leads to an expansion of criminal law on a subjec-

---

ibid, p 315, according to which "the nature of crime as the implementation of the will necessarily leads to a distinction between the will and its implementation, between the intent and the external event in which the intent realises itself in the act" ("aus der Natur des Verbrechens als Willensverwirklichung zwangsläufig eine Unterscheidung zwischen dem Willen und seiner Verwirklichung, zwischen dem Vorsatz und dem äußeren Geschehen, in dem er sich in die Tat umsetzt, folgt"). Also Schaffstein, *DRWis* 1 (1936), 43 (external manifestation of "will and attitude" ["Wille und Gesinnung"]). Likewise Mittermaier, *SchwZStR* 52 (1938), 221–2 (definition of the object of the will); Mittasch (1939), p 133–4 (*Willensstrafrecht* inconceivable without an external result, mere "social inferiority" ["soziale Minderwertigkeit"] could at most lead to measures of "racial hygiene" ["rassehygienisch"], but not to punishment).

657 Schaffstein, *ZStW* 57 (1938), 332 ("Einheit") ("the perpetrator is he who commits the act, and the act is shaped in turn by the perpetrator. The act cannot be imagined without a perpetrator, or the perpetrator without an act" ["Täter ist wer die Tat begeht, und die Tat wiederum erhält durch den Täter ihr Gepräge. Die Tat kann nicht ohne einen Täter und der Täter nicht ohne eine Tat gedacht werden"]); also Schaffstein, *DRWis* 1 (1936), 49 (abolition of the "antithesis of agent and act" ["Antithese von Täter und Tat"]).

658 Schaffstein, *ZStW* 57 (1938), 336 ("Tatbestandsbildung und Tatbestandsauslegung").

659 Schaffstein, *ZStW* 57 (1938), 334–5; Schaffstein, *FS Gleispach* (1936), p 70, 103; on types of "perpetrator" ["Täter"] and "attitude" ["Gesinnungstypen"] also Schaffstein, *DRWis* 1 (1936), 46.

660 Dahm (1940), p 25–6. However, he refers to Wolf's work cited below in ch VI 1. including fn 692, while Schaffstein refers to the later essay of 1936, see ch VI 2. including fn 750 below.

661 *Cf* explicitly on the connection between the breach of duty theory and the criminal law of the will, Schaffstein, in Dahm et al (1935), p 137 ("breach of duty...allocated to *Willensstrafrecht*" ["Pflichtverletzung...Willensstrafrecht...zugeordnet"]); also *cf* Stefanopolou, *JoJZG* 2010, 113.

662 Section 4. including fn 604 and main text above; on Freisler's approach, see ch II 3. including fn 230 ff and main text above.

tive-cerebral basis, to the punishment of mere evil will,[663] which is why the emphasis on the external side (relatedness to the elements of the *Tatbestand*, manifestation of the will) seems like mere lip service,[664] and drawing a distinction between *Willens-* and *Gesinnungsstrafrecht* (criminal law of the will versus criminal law of the internal attitude), while theoretically attempted,[665] appears an unfeasible endeavour.[666] This is also as far as the justification of punishment through a teleological, National Socialist concept of legal interest ("Rechtsgut") can go, if this concept is not to be robbed of any tangible content (evil will as an—abstractly dangerous—attack on the National Socialist moral order?).[667]

In the field of **omission**, too—enhanced by the breach of duty theory[668] —Schaffstein sees the "perpetrator type", the characteristics that "typify the perpetrator" and express the nature of the act, as the decisive criteria defining wrongful omission.[669] Beyond their subjective nuances, the criminal law of the will and the theory of perpetrator types can be regarded as an

---

663 *Cf* Schaffstein, *DStR* 81 (1935), 102 (punishment of non-dangerous impossible attempt can only be explained as an expression of evil will).

664 Or as a mere procedural concession as in Freisler, ch II 3. including fn 240 above.

665 *Cf* Mezger (1936), p 29, who distinguishes between an act-based ("Betätigung") criminal law of the will, *Willensstrafrecht* (which is no criminal law of the attitude, *Gesinnungsstrafrecht*) and a pure criminal law of the will focusing on the internal attitude (which, however, also needs to be inferred from some form of conduct ["die Tat entsprungen"]), ultimately for evidentiary reasons, see fn 240 above). Perhaps the most important and, as far as I can see, only legislative attempt at a pure *Gesinnungsstrafrecht* can be found in the NS draft of a "Gesetz über die Behandlung Gemeinschaftsfremder" ("Law on the Treatment of Those Foreign to the Community") whereby, *inter alia*, a "group of criminals" ("Verbrechergruppe") was defined by focusing on their "personality and lifestyle" ("Persönlichkeit und Lebensführung"), which shows that their "type of mentality is focused upon committing serious crimes (criminals hostile to the community and criminals by inclination)" ("Sinnesart auf die Begehung von ernsten Straftaten gerichtet ist (gemeinschaftsfeindlicher Verbrecher und Neigungsverbrecher)"); Art. I § 1 no. 3, reprinted in Ayaß (1998), Nr. 153; thereto also Werle (1989), p 636 ff.

666 Critically also Hartl (2000), p 93 ff ("ambivalent distinction" ["ambivalente Abgrenzung"]).

667 According to Hoyer, *GS Eckert* (2008), p 361 the punishability of impossible attempt can be justified only through considerations related to legal interests ("abstract danger that reality could indeed be constituted as the perpetrator imagines it to be, and that the violation of a legal interest could thus ensue" ["abstrakte Gefahr, dass die Realität tatsächlich so beschaffen sein könnte, wie sie sich der Täter vorstellt, und es deshalb zu einer Rechtsgutsverletzung kommen könnte"]), but this does not apply to *non-dangerous* impossible attempts, which Schaffstein refers to explicitly.

668 *Cf* this chapter's section 4. including fn 580 and main text above.

669 Schaffstein, *FS Gleispach* (1936), p 102 ff (perpetrator type as a "new criterion...that meaningfully restricts criminal responsibility for the result" ["neues Kriterium..., das in sinvoller Weise die strafrechtliche Haftung für den Erfolg beschränkt", 102], "nature of the perpetrator" ["Wesen des Täters"] "determined primarily by the manner of per-

"ideological unit" in that both, on the one hand, are a logical consequence of the orientation towards an attitude inspired by the healthy sentiment of the people;[670] on the other hand, they focus upon subjectivisation and anticipation to the detriment of anti-National Socialist perpetrators while at the same time limiting punishability in favour of perpetrators who are faithful to National Socialist principles.[671] This not only has concrete consequences for the theory of crime, such as the abovementioned[672] abolition of the difference between attempt and completion,[673] but also establishes a "**double legal morality**" ("doppelte Rechtsmoral"), a "double law, a law for the members of one's own Party, and another for political opponents" on the level of criminal policy—a danger already identified by Radbruch in 1933.[674]

---

petration, through the perpetrator's concrete position in regard to his duties, by the attitude...and the motives of the act" ["vor allem durch die Art der Ausführung, durch die konkrete Pflichtenstellung des Täters, durch die Gesinnung...und durch die Motive der Tat bestimmt", 105]; "concrete kind and strength of the duty breached by the omitter, the attitude...the intensity of the criminal will" ["konkrete Art und Stärke der vom Unterlassenden verletzten Pflicht, die Gesinnung...die Intensität des verbrecherischen Willens"] as the criteria significant for "the measure of wrongfulness" ["das Maß des Unrechts"] that typify the perpetrator [107]); followed by Dahm (1940), p 46–7; previously Preußischer Justizminister (1933), p 132 (also consideration of the "perpetrator's personal circumstances" ["persönlichen Verhältnisse des Täters"]). Thereto also Marxen (1975), p 229 ff (general duty towards the *Volksgemeinschaft* to act, drawing upon the breach of duty theory and abolishing the distinction between action/omission through the theory of perpetrator types), 260 (critically on today's § 13 StGB as a "holistic, essential and thus fuzzy definition of the duties to act and the offenders" ["ganzheitliche, wesenhafte und damit verschwommene Bestimmung der Handlungspflichten und des Täterkreises"] that stands in the tradition of NS essence-focused thinking; Zaffaroni (2017), p 256 ff.

670 In this vein on perpetrator types Cattaneo (2001), p 238 ff.

671 Similarly Frommel, in: Reifner/Sonnen (1984), p 86, 88; Marxen, in ibid, p 81 (limitation of offence definitions at most in favour of NS perpetrators); in greater detail on the theory of perpetrator types as an (attempted) restriction of criminal liability in ideologically neutral areas (not in wartime criminal law, for example), Marxen (1975), p 208 ff.

672 Ch II 3. including fn 249 and main text above.

673 See eg Schaffstein, in Dahm et al (1935), p 137; Schaffstein, *DRWis* 1 (1936), 48–9; thereto also Stefanopolou, *JoJZG* 2010, 115–6.

674 Radbruch (1933/1957), p 75, "zweifache Recht, eines Rechts für die eigenen Parteigänger, eines anderen für die politischen Gegner"; italics K.A.).

6. *A comprehensive actus reus defined by overall disvalue ("offence type") instead of a structured theory of crime*

The breach of duty theory thus leads to a merging of wrongdoing and guilt in the form of the diffuse "attitude-/duty-focused criminal law" (*Gesinnungs-/Pflichtenstrafrecht*, section 4. above), and the mysterious *Wesensschau* (section 5. above) brings everything together in a unified definition of a comprehensive *Tatbestand (actus reus)* focused upon overall disvalue (**Gesamtunwerttatbestand**).[675] Schaffstein already stated the reasons for the abolition of the distinction between unlawfulness and guilt that follows from such a holistic view[676] in 1936.[677] He accuses the "old system" of "inadequacy" regarding its unclear distinguishing criteria and its antithetical, "unnatural tearing apart of systemic connections and relations and the...concepts of criminal law, which should be understood holistically".[678]

Schaffstein only recognises the traditional structured concept of crime in conceptual terms through categories of offences ("*Strafandrohungstatbestände*")[679] (elements of wrongdoing and guilt) and exclusionary grounds ("*Strafausschließungsgründe*")[680] as negative elements of the offence,[681] but essentially merges these with the abovementioned comprehensive Tatbestand defined by overall disvalue as an *"offence type"* ("*Deliktstypus*").[682] This comprehensive Tatbestand defined by overall disvalue incorporates everything, with the exception of personal exclusionary grounds, including

675 *Cf* earlier Zaffaroni, in Zaffaroni, 2011, p 36 (elements of the *actus reus* as "a kind of window" that is completed by the judge by adding the act and the agent ["ventana que le permitía al juez completarlo con un tipo de delito y de autor"]).

676 See section 4. including fn 616 and main text above, referring to Schaffstein, *DRWis* 1 (1936), 49; rudimentarily already Schaffstein, *FS Schmidt* (1936), p 77 (distinction very doubtful in light of *Gesinnungs-* and *Willensstrafrecht*); thereafter Schaffstein, *ZStW* 57 (1938), 295. Thereto also Marxen (1975), p 222 ff; Stefanopolou, *JoJZG* 2010, 114.

677 Zaffaroni (2017), p 266 ff assumes 1938.

678 Schaffstein, *ZStW* 57 (1938), 327 ("alten System", "Unzulänglichkeit", "unnatürlichen Zerreißung der Systemzusammenhänge und der...ganzheitlich zu verstehenden Strafrechtsbegriffe"). At the same time, while he recognises the logic and rationality of a structured concept of crime, he considers it to be systematically "impractical" ("unbrauchbar"; ibid, 330).

679 Zaffaroni (2017), p 267 incorrectly terms these "Strafdrohungstatbestände".

680 Schaffstein, *ZStW* 57 (1938), 311 ("all exclusionary grounds...limitations of the *Strafandrohungstatbestände* in the form of negative elements of the *actus reus*" ["alle Strafausschließungsgründe...Einschränkungen der Strafandrohungstatbestände in Form negativer Tatbestandsmerkmale"]).

681 Schaffstein, *ZStW* 57 (1938), 302, 305, 305–6, 311. Ambiguously Zaffaroni (2017), p 267, who assumes a structured concept of crime in material terms also.

682 Schaffstein, *ZStW* 57 (1938), 315–6 ("offence type"). Zaffaroni (2017), p 269 believes this term is borrowed from Beling.

those concerning sound mind/legal sanity.[683] This offence type takes its content from the breach of duty theory and the (new) NS criminal law ethics, fed by the völkisch moral order, the völkisch sense of justice and the holistic *Wesensschau*.[684] The aim is to perfect the material concept of crime through extreme ethicisation, renouncing even the—likewise considerably ethicised—normative concept of guilt.[685]

The rejection of **Unzumutbarkeit**—a situation in which the perpetrator cannot reasonably be expected to comply with the law—as a supra-legal ground excluding guilt (which was already justified in 1933[686])[687] is merely a further consequence of the new authoritarian, general-preventive criminal law, for (additional) grounds excluding punishment are the "expression of an individualist shaping of the law"[688] and only weaken the threat of punishment of the total NS state, which after all must spare no effort in taking action (through criminal law) against dissidents ("Volksschädlinge"). Not just criminal policy, but criminal law doctrine likewise needs to combat the subversive tendencies of traditional liberal criminal law: "the greater the hold of individualism upon the people's sense of justice, the more disastrous it would be to accommodate this individualism by relativising the concept of guilt."[689]

683 Schaffstein, *ZStW* 57 (1938), 305 ("overall disvalue" ["Gesamtunwert"] with *Strafandrohungstatbestände* and exclusionary grounds). Critically Marxen (1975), p 226–7; also *cf* Zaffaroni (2017), p 271 ff (type of act and perpetrator includes everything).

684 Schaffstein, *ZStW* 57 (1938), 301, 322, 327.

685 Also *cf* Zaffaroni (2017), p 273.

686 Schaffstein (1933).

687 Thereto also Stefanopolou, *JoJZG* 2010, 115; Zaffaroni (2017), p 258 ff.

688 Schaffstein (1933), p 60 ff ("theory of reasonableness as expressing an individualist shaping of criminal law" ["Zumutbarkeitslehre als Ausdruck individualistischer Strafrechtsgestaltung"]).

689 Schaffstein (1933), p 82 ("je stärker der Individualismus von dem Rechtsbewusstsein des Volkes Besitz ergriffen hat, desto verhängnisvoller wäre es, ihm auch noch durch die Relativierung des Schuldbegriffs entgegenzukommen"); thereto also Zaffaroni (2017), p 265.

Chapter VI. Erik Wolf: From Perpetrator Types to an Attitudinal Theory of Agency

1. *Authoritarian-social criminal law and theory of agency*

While Erik Wolf (1902–1977) was not formally a member of the Kiel School, his normative theory of agency (*Täterlehre*) aligned him very closely with its thinking, as we will see below. Zaffaroni's appraisal of Wolf—appended to the chapter on the Kiel School's approach to wrongdoing[690] —does not do justice to this fact, especially as he fails to take all of Wolf's relevant writings into account. Thus he only mentions Wolf's seminal 1932 inaugural lecture at Freiburg University, "Vom Wesen des Täters" ("On the Nature of the Perpetrator"),[691] in passing,[692] and completely ignores his Heidelberg and Freiburg lectures of 1933 ("Krisis und Neubau der Strafrechtsreform" ["The Crisis and Rebuilding of the Criminal Law Reform"][693] and "Richtiges Recht im nationalsozialistischen Staat" ["Right Law in the National Socialist State"][694]), and concentrates more or less exclusively on an essay that was only published in the *ZStW* in 1935.[695] This is problematic because on the one hand, the (published) texts of 1932/1933 ("Wesen" and "Krisis") were not yet *unambiguously* National Socialist, while on the other hand Wolf's National Socialist turn occurred at the latest towards the end of 1933 when he was writing "Richtiges Recht", the text of which was published in 1934 (meaning that his turn took place before the 1935 *ZStW* essay).[696]

---

690 Zaffaroni (2017), p 246 ff.

691 Wolf (1932). On the influence of phenomenology ("new theory with a personalistic-existentialist orientation" ["personalistisch-existentialistisch ausgerichtete neue Lehre"]), see Wolf himself, ibid, p 12 (individualism is supplanted by a "phenomenological personalism" ["phänomenologischen Personalismus"]) and in a letter to K. Barth (Wolf, 2009, p 305); also see Hollerbach, in: *Heidegger-Jahrbuch* 4 (2009), p 284, 326 ff.

692 Zaffaroni (2017), p 247.

693 Wolf (1933).

694 Wolf (1934).

695 Wolf, *ZStW* 54 (1935), 544. Thereto Zaffaroni (2017), p 247 ff.

696 Likewise, overly apodictically, Guzmán Dalbora, *RDPC* VII (2017), 231 ("otro jurista nazi").

FREIBURGER UNIVERSITÄTSREDEN

Heft 13

Richtiges Recht im nationalsozialistischen Staate

von

Erik Wolf

Freiburg im Breisgau
Fr. Wagnersche Universitätsbuchhandlung
1934

Figure 17: Wolf's first truly National Socialist text on "Right Law in the NS State", 1934

In "*Vom Wesen des Täters*" (1932), Wolf—engaging critically with Liszt's account of the concept and the different types of perpetrator[697] —proclaims a normative (anthropological-cultural) perpetrator type with "legal personality" ("Rechtspersonalität") and "attitude" ("Gesin-

697 *Cf* ch III including fn 270 above and Wolf (1932), p 7 ff (without clear references, although he rejects Liszt's perpetrator concept as overly cause-oriented and naturalist and thus as a "fatal error" ["verhängnisvolle Irrtum"], p 9 ff, 32).

nung").[698] Whatever our view of this approach,[699] in taking it Wolf was not spreading National Socialist ideology.[700] Rather, he derived five types of perpetration from the current law (as set out in definitions of criminal offences)[701] and thus ultimately only revealed what this law already contained.[702] In "*Krisis und Neubau*" (1933), Wolf follows his critique of current law and the reform movement thus far[703] with a call for "a criminal policy of authoritarian criminal law" with

698 Wolf (1932), p 12, 14 ff (16: the perpetrator is "according to his nature a person and member of the legal community with a deteriorating attitude towards the law" ["seinem Wesen nach ein personales Glied der Rechtsgemeinschaft mit verfallender Rechtsgesinnung"]; 18: "within the sphere of culture" as a "current, unique perpetrator" ["im Raum der Kultur", "jetzige, einmalige Täter"]; 19: as a "legal concept...dependent upon certain preconditions of the German legal system" ["juristische Begriff...abhängig von bestimmten Voraussetzungen des deutschen Rechtssystems"]; 32: "human as standing in the world of law" ["Mensch, wie er in der Welt des Rechts steht"]; 36: "human way of being in the law" ["Seinsweise des Menschen im Recht"]); on the distinction between legal person and legal subject ibid, p 16; on stages of "attitudinal decay" ("Gesinnungsverfalls") ibid, p 17 ff.

699 From a modern perspective, this tendency towards an agent-focused criminal law naturally elicits criticism, as does Wolf's opposition to humanising punishment, which he believes would undermine effective deterrence: according to Wolf, there is a need for "courage to loosen the supposedly sacrosanct guarantees of the idea of the rule of law in the interest of the idea of a member-based social state whose basic unit is the person" ("Unerschrockenheit, scheinbar geheiligte Garantien des Rechtsstaatsgedankens im Interesse eines sozialen Gliedstaatsgedankens auf personaler Grundlage aufzulockern"; Wolf [1932] p 35–6). On the other hand, Wolf always opposed corporal punishment, Wolf, *ZStW* 54 (1935), 560–1.

700 However, Marxen (1975), p 84, 190 sees this text as "already" containing "groundbreaking themes of anti-liberal criticism" ("bereits wegweisende Motive der antiliberalen Kritik") and as the foundation of the new theory of agency.

701 "Types of perpetration" ("Typen der Täterschaftsmäßigkeit"), *cf* Wolf (1932), p 26 ff (perpetrators who are dangerous, in conflict with, hostile to, neglectful of and harmful to the community ["gemeingefährlich", "gemeinwidrig", "gemeinfeindlich", "gemeinlässig" and "gemeinschädlich"]). These typify "kinds of attitudinal deterioration in persons" ("Arten des personalen Gesinnungsverfalls"), ibid p 27.

702 Wolf (1932), p 31, states quite convincingly: "There needs to be an open catalogue of types of perpetration, instead of a secret one that, as is the case today, is hidden within a catalogue of types of defined offences" ("Es muß ein offener Katalog von Täterschaftstypen werden, an Stelle eines heimlichen, der sich, wie es heute der Fall ist, in einem Katalog von Tatbestandstypen verbirgt").

703 Wolf (1933), p 6 ff. Here, he sees the current law as a "compromise between conflicting worldviews and political and social ideals" ("Kompromiß widerstreitender Weltanschauungen und politisch-sozialer Ideale", p 9), which on a practical level merged to become a "two-track liberal-authoritarian criminal law" ("zweispuriges liberal-autoritäres Strafrecht", p 11) and ultimately led to the "failure of criminal law" ("Versagen des Strafrechts", p 13). Wolf identifies Italian-inspired criminal-biological naturalism (p 13 ff), sociologism (p 15–6) and "the idea of the social" ("die Idee des Sozialen", p 16–7) as the main traits of the reform movement; in criminal-political terms, the latter manifesting itself in social democracy's influence on criminal policy and the "very powerful socialist influence upon the shaping of German criminal law"

the aim of a "national-social reconstruction of criminal law".[704] He states that the time for this criminal policy has come with the "turn from a liberal authoritarian state to a liberal-social state of the people",[705] in the sense of a "turn towards a national criminal law in a national state under the rule of law",[706] to an "authoritarian-social" instead of a "social-liberal" or a "social-authoritarian" instead of an "authoritarian-liberal" attitude towards criminal law (thereby seeking to replace the pairing "National Socialist"-"German national").[707] Wolf thus emphasises the "social element" of the new criminal law—an element that was already present in the existing reform movement (but of course also formed part of National *Socialism*!)—but wants to grant it greater prominence at the expense of the liberal element by having it "merge with the ideas of the authoritarian-conservative state leadership and represent a new sense of the community of the people".[708] This "merging of the social and authoritarian element in criminal law"[709] is evident in three points of view that differ fundamentally from the reform efforts undertaken thus far (which is why these need to be dismantled and not just altered): in a phenomenological rather than an idealist-philosophical orientation; in an understanding of society based upon a hierarchy of classes or "estates" rather than a formal-liberal perception of society; and above all in the conception of the state as a national social state rather than a formal state based upon the rule of law or welfare state.[710] The new criminal law centres around "state" and "person" instead of around society and the individual.[711] The state re-

---

("mächtigsten sozialistischen Einflüssen auf die Gestaltung des deutschen Strafrechts", p 17–8). Wolf (p 18 ff) sees the reform movement's image of humanity as scientific-deterministic, economic-liberal and (politically) liberal-authoritarian, with the individual norm addressee manifesting in three different ways (p 20 ff): as a citizen with rights, as a subject ("object of welfare measures" ["Objekt wohlfahrtspflegerischer Maßnahmen"], p 20), and as a "normal criminal of opportunity or chance" ("normale Gelegenheits- oder Zufallsverbrecher", p 22).

704 Wolf (1933), p 6 ("eine Kriminalpolitik des autoritären Strafrechts", "national-soziale Neubau des Strafrechts").

705 Wolf (1933), p 13 ("Wendung vom liberal-autoritären Obrigkeitsstaat zum liberal-sozialen Volksstaat").

706 Wolf (1933), p 25 ("Wendung zum nationalen Strafrecht im nationalen Rechtsstaat").

707 Wolf (1933), p 30, 31 ("autoritärsozial", "sozialliberal", "sozial-autoritärer", "autoritärliberaler", "Strafrechtsgesinnung", "nationalsozialistisch"-"deutschnational").

708 Wolf (1933), p 30 ("mit den Gedanken der autoritär-konservativen Staatsführung verschmolzen, einen neuen Sinn von Gemeinschaft des Volkes repräsentieren").

709 Wolf (1933), p 31–2 ("Verschmelzung des sozialen und des autoritären Elements im Strafrecht").

710 Wolf (1933), p 32.

711 Wolf (1933), p 33.

alises itself ever anew "as a real union of the will of the nation" and becomes "the fundamental idea giving meaning to the entire system of protected legal interests", which is why "*every* attack upon the legal order" must "be regarded as an attack upon the whole".[712] The "person" is no longer "understood as an egoistic individual", but as part of the state, with duties towards it (including preventing crime);[713] the perpetrator is not only an "object of welfare, but a responsible member of the legal community",[714] which lays the foundation for the theory of perpetrator types that Wolf later developed in greater detail (more thereto below).[715] Ultimately, this new understanding of criminal law also leads to a collectivist, normative reshaping of the theory of crime in a narrower sense,[716] to a social-preventive view of punishment,[717] and to the increased creation of crimes against the state.[718]

Even though Wolf's authoritarian-social criminal law model comes close to National Socialism and he refers explicitly to both National Socialism[719]

---

712 Wolf (1933), p 33 ("als realer Willensverband der Nation", "zur sinngebenden Grundidee des gesamten Rechtsgütersystems", "*jeder* Angriff auf die Rechtsordnung...als Angriff auf das Ganze gelten"; italics in the original text).

713 Wolf (1933), p 34 ("als egoistisches Individuum verstanden").

714 Wolf (1933), p 35 ("Objekt der Wohlfahrtspflege, sondern ein verantwortliches Glied der Rechtsgemeinschaft").

715 Wolf (1933), p 35–6 ("rejection of a merely causal theory of perpetration" ["Ablehnung einer bloß kausalen Lehre von der Täterschaft"] and instead recognition of perpetrator types and a "type of attitude with a corresponding type of action" ["Gesinnungstypus mit entsprechendem Handlungstypus"]).

716 Wolf (1933), p 36 ff (normativisation of the concept of action ["expression of attitude" ("Gesinnungsausdruck")] within the context of the *elements of the offence*; *wrongdoing* as "contravening the state" ["Staatswidrigkeit"], subjectivisation of the grounds of wrongfulness and emphasis on the collective-social element in justificatory grounds ["social defence" ("Sozialwehr")]; normative, socio-ethical concept of *guilt*, "contravening duties towards the state" ["Staatspflichtwidrigkeit"]).

717 Wolf (1933), p 40 ff ("adapting the criminal to the *Volksgemeinschaft* or excluding him from it" ["Anpassung des Verbrechers an die Volksgemeinschaft oder Ausschluß von ihr"], putting an end to or discrediting the perpetrator "in his social existence" ["in seiner sozialen Existenz"], in "his specific estate-based existence" ["seinem spezifisch-ständischen Dasein"], "narrowing his options to act as a legal person" ["Einengung seiner rechtspersonalen Handlungsmöglichkeiten"], social-preventive means of education).

718 Wolf (1933), p 43 (eg protection of national honour, *Volkstum*, labour power, estate-based honour). *Cf* ch V 2. including fn 536 above.

719 Wolf (1933), p 30 ("active incorporation of social ideals into the idea of a National Socialist criminal code" ["aktive Hineinnahme sozialer Wertvorstellungen in die Idee eines nationalsozialistischen Strafgesetzbuchs"]), 31 ("young people" ["junge Menschen"] as an "element of the National Socialist renewal movement" ["Element der nationalsozialistischen Erneuerungsbewegung"]). Referring to Wolf as "National Socialist" ("nationalsozialistisch") "in a wider sense" ("in einem weiteren Sinne") in this regard, Gemmingen (1933), p 7–8.

and the "Kiel scholars",[720] "Krisis and Neubau" cannot be classed as an unambiguously National Socialist text, and for four reasons. Firstly, its references to National Socialism tend to be descriptive; terminologically, we could even see Wolf's choice of "social-authoritarian" and "authoritarian-social" as an attempt to distance himself from National Socialism. Secondly, Wolf wanted to retain liberalism and the rule of law with their corresponding "rights of personality",[721] and to uphold "freedom *in* the state";[722] in this regard, however, it should be pointed out that he did not want "so-called basic rights" to be understood as absolute and thus advocated relativising them if they conflicted with state interests.[723] Furthermore, "freedom *from* the state" was to "disappear"[724] (which raises the question of how "freedom *in* the state" can exist without "freedom *from* the state"—a question that Wolf fails to address). Thirdly, Wolf's reflections focus not upon the *Volksgemeinschaft*, but upon the state as the collective element, which betrays a fascist rather than a National Socialist tendency.[725] Finally, Wolf placed his criminal law model under a so-called religious or divine reservation and thus deprived it of any absoluteness.[726]

2. *Wolf's turn towards and away from National Socialism*

Wolf's real turn towards National Socialism[727] took place in late 1933/early 1934, when he declared his commitment to the NS state (in front of the

---

720 Wolf (1933), p 24–5 including fn 1 (concurring with and quoting from the "manifesto" ["Programmschrift"] by Dahm/Schaffstein, 1933).

721 Wolf (1933), p 29 ("Persönlichkeitsrechten") (in favour of a "social-national" ["sozial-nationalen"] instead of a "social-liberal" ["sozial-liberalen"] state under the rule of law, "but the rule of law remains" ["aber es bleibt beim Rechtsstaat"]).

722 Wolf (1933), p 32 ("Freiheit *im* Staat"; italics in the original text).

723 Wolf (1933), p 29 ("sogenannten Grundrechte") (basic rights are "not absolute rights" ["keine absoluten Werte"]; there is a need to "prevent their excessive or even harmfully exclusive protection" ["verhindert werden, daß sie in übertriebener Weise oder gar schädigener Ausschließlichkeit geschützt sind"]).

724 Wolf (1933), p 32 ("Freiheit *vom* Staat", "verschwinden"; italics in the original text).

725 On this difference between (Italian) fascism and NS, see ch II 1. including fn 121 above.

726 Wolf (1933), p 43–4 (criminal law reform requires "religious effort of attitude" ["religiösen Gesinnungseinsatz"] and a "constantly adhered-to will to justice" ["dauernd festgehaltenen Willen zum Recht"]; while the state is "the law's highest value" ["höchste Wert des Rechts"], it is "not an absolute" ["kein Absolutes"]).

727 Ignored by Ziemann (2009), p 113 ff.

local Freiburg group of the Association of National Socialist German Jurists')[728] and its "right law".[729] This law still needed to develop, of course,[730] starting from the National Socialist concept of *Volk* and race and becoming realised "in the total state".[731] For criminal law, this meant, from a principled perspective, a radical shift in its "intellectual foundations" towards a *Feindstrafrecht* or criminal law of the enemy in order to "uphold state authority";[732] in concrete terms, it meant offering better protection "against exploitation harmful to the people"[733] by "excluding harmful elements".[734]

---

728 Wolf, *ARSP* 28 (1934), 348 ("Volkstum" and "Führertum" as sources of the law and "hallmarks of the authenticity of the National Socialist revolution" ["Kennzeichen der Echtheit der nationalsoz. Revolution", 348], "idea of the hierarchical estate-based honour of the *völkisch Rechtsgenossen*" ["Gedanke ständisch gestufter Ehre der völkischen Rechtsgenossen"] and thus honour as a National Socialist legal ideal [348–9]).

729 Wolf (1934), p 10 ("Right law...our real law can thus only be the law of National Socialism in the Third Reich" ["Richtiges Recht...unser wirkliches Recht kann deshalb nur das Recht des Nationalsozialismus im Dritten Reich sein"]). Here, Wolf also proclaims his commitment to the Führer, albeit without mentioning Hitler's name (ibid, p 28–9).

730 Wolf (1934), p 10ff (no "fully visible complete form" ["vollkommen sichtbare abgeschlossene Gestalt"] exists thus far, only a "preliminary stage of the future law of the *Volk*" ["Vorstufe zum künftigen Volksrecht", as developed in Hitler's "Mein Kampf" among other sources).

731 Wolf (1934), p 13ff ("*Volk* and race" ["Volk und Rasse"] as "facts of natural-historical life" ["Tatsachen des natürlich-geschichtlichen Lebens"], from which "communal benefit and a sense of sacrifice" ["Gemeinnützigkeit und Opfersinn"] arise as "demands" ["Forderungen"] made of each individual, demands that in turn are realised through the "unity of the nation and the social community" ["Einheit der Nation und soziale Gemeinschaft"] in the "total state" ["totale Staat", 13]); in this regard also ibid, p 28 on the "characteristics" ["Kennzeichen"] of "National Socialist life in general" ["nationalsozialistische Leben überhaupt"] ("belonging to *Volk* and race, pursuing communal benefit and a sense of sacrifice, surrendering to the national and social community" ["Zugehörigkeit zu Volk und Rasse, Betätigung von Gemeinnützigkeit und Opfersinn, Hingabe an Nationalgemeinschaft und Sozialgemeinschaft"]). Concerning the total state, Wolf (ibid, p 23ff) emphasises its hierarchical, profession-based character, and refers in particular to *Forsthoff's* (1933, p 42) "beautiful phrase" ("schöne Wort") [!] of "each individual's total obligation to the nation" ("totale Inpflichtnahme jedes einzelnen für die Nation"; Wolf, [1934], p 25). Otherwise, "the totality of the state" needs to be "justified by the highest authority of God" ("die Totalität des Staates...der Rechtfertigung durch die höchste Autorität Gottes"; ibid, p 27).

732 Wolf (1934), p 23 ("staatlichen Autoritätsbewährung") ("crime...as disobedience and rebellion" ["Verbrechen...als Ungehorsam und Auflehnung", the "criminal" ["Verbrecher"] as an "enemy of the state" ["Feind des Staates"]). Similarly Thierack, in Frank (1934), p 29 ("upholding authority" ["Autoritätswahrung"] as the "goal of punishment" ["Ziel der Strafe"]).

733 Wolf (1934), p 22 ("gegen volksschädliche Ausbeutung").

734 Wolf (1934), p 23 ("Ausschliessung von Schädlingen"). Wolf (ibid) lists as measures in this regard: "forced sterilisation and castration of genetically defective sex offenders, revoking the rights held as a citizen, preventive detention of professional criminals and

Wolf links to this text and earlier writings in the abovementioned *ZStW* essay, commenting favourably upon the NS system of punishments and developing it further on the basis of a report of the official Criminal Law (Gürtner) Commission and the Memorandum of the Central Committee of the Academy for German Law's Criminal Law Department.[735] On the one hand, Wolf highlights the "reduction of the perpetrator's legal personality within the community"[736] as a consequence of punishment, that is, the destruction of not only his "private", but also his "social" existence. This in turn is explained by Wolf's understanding firstly of the nature of punishment "as a value judgement of the *Volksgemeinschaft*" on the perpetrator as part of the Volksgemeinschaft, and secondly of the protection of the Volksgemeinschaft as constituting the sole function of punishment.[737] On the other hand, he develops his normative perpetrator type further into a *völkisch "attitude type"* and the *"type of the enemy of the people"*.[738] Wolf also uses the National Socialist worldview to justify capital punishment through *decapitation* [!]—as an "expression of the absolute dominance of the whole over the individual"[739]—explicitly dismissing rational concerns (the irrevocability of a false judgment).[740] Furthermore, he rejects any privileging of politically motivated offenders,[741] understands honour punishments as a "punishment of attitude" that aims to "put an end to" the perpetrator's professional existence,[742] and advocates ostracism in cases dis-

---

those who pose a threat to the community" ("Zwangsunfruchtbarmachung und Entmannung erbkranker Triebtäter, Entziehung des Staatsbürgerrechts, Sicherungsverwahrung der Berufsverbrecher und Gemeingefährlichen").

735 Frank, ed (1934); thereto Wolf, *ZStW* 54 (1935), 544 including fn 1.

736 Wolf, *ZStW* 54 (1935), 545 ("Minderung der Rechtspersönlichkeit des Täters in der Gemeinschaft"); previously Wolf (1932), p 33 (retribution as a "reduction of legal personality" ["Verminderung der Rechtspersonalität"]) and section 1. in this chapter including fn 718 above.

737 Wolf, *ZStW* 54 (1935), 545–6 ("als Werturteil der Volksgemeinschaft").

738 Wolf, *ZStW* 54 (1935), 550–1 ("Gesinnungstypus", "Typus des Volksfeinds") (referring to the "healthy opinion of the people" ["gesunde Volksanschauung"]). On the significance of the right attitude, previously Wolf (1934), p 25 ff (referring to the "connection between National Socialism and Christianity that is crucial to their essence [!]" ["wesensnotwendige Verbindung von Nationalsozialismus und Christentum", p 26]).

739 Wolf, *ZStW* 54 (1935), 547 ("Ausdruck der absoluten Herrschaft des Ganzen über den Einzelnen") (referring to the Commission's report in fn 8).

740 Wolf, *ZStW* 54 (1935), 546 ff (547: "ideologically rooted in the nature of the National Socialist state" ["weltanschaulich im Wesen des nationalsozialistischen Staates verwurzelt"]).

741 Wolf, *ZStW* 54 (1935), 548–9 (548: "The total state knows no 'decent criminals'" ["Der totale Staat kennt keine 'anständigen Verbrecher'"], referring to the Commission's report in fn 18); see ch V 2. including fn 530 above.

742 Wolf, *ZStW* 54 (1935), 561–2 ("Gesinnungsstrafe", "Decapitierung").

playing an increased "deterioration in völkisch attitude".[743] In the field of sentencing—in order to emphasise the protection of the Volksgemeinschaft as the "fundamental principle of National Socialist criminal law" and the "fruitful idea of *Willensstrafrecht*"[744]—Wolf calls for a general sentencing rule that renders the "degree of punishment" dependent upon the "protection of the völkisch living conditions in regard to the act's harmfulness to and the hostility of the perpetrator's attitude towards the people".[745] He advocates stricter punishments for habitual offenders[746] as well as in cases where "the perpetrator's will" is "particularly reprehensible";[747] grounds for mitigation should be used "sparingly", so as not to unsettle the people's sense of justice.[748]

One year later, Wolf suggests replacing the three-part concept of crime by a two-part concept oriented towards the type of act and the type of perpetrator—a suggestion that Zaffaroni ignores.[749] In this regard, Wolf adheres to his *völkisch-communal concept of person and perpetrator*—an attack on a victim as an attack on "the substance of the Volksgemeinschaft" itself[750] that simultaneously weakens the Volksgemeinschaft through the perpetrator's "attitudinal deterioration" as "intellectual criminal harm"[751] —and wants to materially define act/perpetrator type by referring to popular opinion and ultimately the will of the Führer.[752] However, he retracts

743 Wolf, *ZStW* 54 (1935), 562–3 ("völkischen Gesinnungsverfall").

744 Wolf, *ZStW* 54 (1935), 569 ("Grundgedanken des nationalsozialistischen Strafrechts", "fruchtbaren Gedanken des Willenstrafrechts").

745 Wolf, *ZStW* 54 (1935), 569 ("Maß der Strafe", "Schutz der völkischen Lebensbedingungen im Hinblick auf den Grad der Volksschädlichkeit der Handlung und auf die Volksfeindlichkeit der Gesinnung des Täters"). He thus goes beyond the official recommendation—"degree of the infringement of the people's living conditions" ("Grad des Verstoßes gegen die Lebensbedingungen des Volkes"; ibid, 568).

746 At the beginning of this article he already comments positively upon the Habitual Offender's Act (Wolf, *ZStW* 54 [1935], 544) and wants to place dangerous habitual offenders in preventive detention (ibid, 571).

747 Wolf, *ZStW* 54 (1935), 570–1 ("besonders verwerfliche Wille des Täters").

748 Wolf, *ZStW* 54 (1935), 571–2 ("sparsam").

749 Wolf, *ZAkdR* 3 (1936), 358.

750 Wolf, *ZAkdR* 3 (1936), 361 ("die Substanz der Volksgemeinschaft selbst") (which "questions...its power...as a political whole" ["Kraft...als politisches Ganzes...in Frage gestellt"]).

751 Wolf, *ZAkdR* 3 (1936), 362 ("Gesinnungsverfall", "intellektueller Verbrechensschaden").

752 Wolf, *ZAkdR* 3 (1936), 360 ff (to be determined by legal characteristics, the continued creation of law by judges and "unwritten law" ["ungeschriebenes Recht"] that feeds upon "popular opinion" ["Volksanschauung"], but can also be defined by a "possible decision by the supreme leader" ["etwaige oberste Führerentscheidung", 361] or "a concrete instruction by the supreme leader" ["eine konkrete Weisung des obersten Führers", 362]).

his earlier subjectivisation somewhat by viewing act type and perpetrator type as equally significant.[753] This line of dialectic synthesis is also evident his 1939 opinion statement on the controversy between the "Kiel scholars" (Dahm/Schaffstein) and the "Marburg scholars" (Schwinge/Zimmerl),[754] which Wolf in the end considers to be a purely methodological dispute, with both schools building upon the same (National Socialist) criminal policy foundation.[755] He thus argues in favour of overcoming this controversy through a "synthetic combination of the two extreme starting points of criminal law conceptualisation"[756] by finding a "higher synthesis" inspired by Hegel and Heidegger[757]—fully in line with the abovementioned conceptualisation abolishing contrasts and antitheses[758]—relying on a material, National Socialist basis.[759]

Accordingly, in Wolf's works we can observe a *shift* first from perpetrator types that draw upon classical theory (1932) and the demand to "rebuild" criminal law (1933) to a commitment to the NS state and NS law (1933/34), an NS-inspired *Gesinnungstypus* or attitude type (1935), an equation of act type and perpetrator type (1936) and a higher (NS) inspired synthesis (1939) that brought him very close to the Kiel School indeed —also and in particular in his orientation towards Hegel.[760] This development

753 In this regard, Schaffstein's concurring reference, ch V 5. including fn 660, is understandable.

754 Wolf, *DRWis* 4 (1939), 168 (simultaneously a review of Schwinge's book on irrationalism, for more detail see ch IV 2. including fn 363 ff and main text).

755 Cf ch IV 2. including fn 335, 371 above.

756 Wolf, *DRWis* 4 (1939), 176 ("synthetischer Verbindung der beiden extremen Ausgangspunkte strafrechtswissenschaftlicher Begriffsbildung"). Concretely ibid, 178–9 ("crime constitutes not only a breach of duty, but also harm to a protected legal interest...not only the perpetrator's attitude, but also the result of his act determines the content of crime..., law evinces both concrete and abstract elements of order" ["Verbrechen nicht nur Pflichtverletzung, sondern auch Rechtsgüterschaden…nicht nur die Gesinnung des Täters, sondern auch der Erfolg seines Tuns den Verbrechensgehalt bestimmt…, das Recht sowohl konkrete als auch abstrakte Ordnungselemente aufweist"]) and 179 ("perpetrator to be understood as the 'perpetrator of an act' and the act as the 'act of a perpetrator'", as a "synthesis" ["Täter als 'Täter einer Tat' und die Tat als 'Tat eines Täters' zu begreifen", "Synthese"]).

757 Wolf, *DRWis* 4 (1939), 181 ("höheren Synthetis").

758 Ch IV 4. including fn 467 above.

759 Wolf, *DRWis* 4 (1939), 177 ("for the substantive content of justice in the area of present-day German law is constituted by National Socialism" ["denn die materiellen Inhalte der Gerechtigkeit im Raum des deutschen Rechts der Gegenwart sind durch den Nationalsozialismus gegeben"]). Similarly Mittasch (1939), p 99 ff, who argues for ethicisation and the theory of breaches of duty while retaining the concept of protected legal interests.

760 Wolf, *DRWis* 4 (1939), 181 and his identification of the Kiel line with a Neo-Hegelian, "völkisch state metaphysics" ("völkischen Staatsmetaphysik", ibid, 174–5).

clearly shows how the attitude type increasingly subjectivised the initially act-focused perpetrator type.[761] In doing so, act and perpetrator type take on the function of not just aggravating, but also justifying punishment.[762] However, Wolf does not go quite as far as the Kiel scholars, who assume that wrongfulness is restricted in acts that do not conflict with the völkisch-inspired essence of the offence[763]—for example in the abovementioned case of the Hitler Youth confiscating a flag.[764]

However, contrary to some suggestions,[765] Wolf's (literary) support for National Socialism did not end in 1936/1937 with his turn to the "Confessing Church" ("Bekennende Kirche") and his subsequent calls for the separation of religion and state. While Wolf himself expressed, in two letters (never sent) to Karl Barth, a feeling of guilt and admitted to "errors and wrong paths from 1933 onwards", at the same time he asked for understanding, referring to the historical context and the expectations associated with the NS movement.[766] At any rate, his ongoing support of National

761 Also *cf* Vogel (2004), p 81–2, 84 (criminal law of the will as guilt of the will and dangerousness with the addition of attitude; orientation towards the perpetrator as the second step in its radicalisation).

762 Overlooked by Zaffaroni (2017), p 248.

763 *Cf* ch V 5. including fn 634 and main text above.

764 Ch V 5. including fn 672 and main text above.

765 Thus Wapler (2008), p 252–3, 259–60 (who considers the text quoted in fn 750 above to be his last NS one and furthermore assumes an "early and clear" ["frühe und deutliche"] dissociation); Foljanty (2013), p 140 ff including further references (who herself mentions both years—1936 and 1937—however, p 140 including fn 24); also Vogel (2004), p 32.

766 The letters (of 15 October 1945 and another of 11 November 1968) were later published (Wolf, 2009, p 288 ff, relevant references at p 290 ["Irrtümer und Fehlwege ab 1933"] and 291 ff). Wolf further said there that, he, in the run-off between Hindenburg and Hitler in 1932, voted for the former (307), but gradually began "to take the 'social' ideas of these people more seriously in political terms" ("den 'sozialen' Gedanken dieser Leute politisch ernster zu nehmen", 309) and joined the NS Association of Jurists in the summer of 1933 "to demonstrate willingness towards self-criticism of the mistakes of the postwar bureaucratic state" ("um guten Willen zur Selbstkritik an den Fehlern des bürokratischen Beamtenstaats der Nachkriegszeit zu beweisen", 317). However, in 1933 he already witnessed and condemned NS attacks within and beyond the University of Freiburg (where he was Dean of the Faculty of Law, appointed by Rector Heidegger) (312–3, 315, 319–20), himself became a victim of "spying" ("Bespitzelung", 317) and grew increasingly isolated (317–8), which is why he resigned from the deanship in March 1934 (at the same time as Heidegger) (318). His "real turn" ("eigentliche Wende") came in 1937 (when he wrote a report on behalf of the priest Martin Niemöller that was used in the latter's trial) (321–2): "I saw that the fine revolutionary vigour of the NS movement had been permanently extinguished and had given way to a power politics without ethical legitimacy that needed to be resisted" ("Ich sah, daß der gute revolutionäre Elan der ns Bewegung endgültig erloschen war und einer Machtpolitik ohne ethische Legitimation gewichen war, der man widerste-

Socialisme clearly follows from the 1939 text quoted above[767] as well as from a lecture on NS juvenile criminal law—(probably) only published in Spanish—held at the University of Valladolid, Spain, in 1942.[768] Against this (literary) backdrop, Wolf's disciple Hollerbach's view that "nowhere" in Wolf's texts "was there a complete affirmation" of National Socialism and that they "remained an episode in contemporary discourse"[769] is not fully convincing. Likewise, with this background in mind the recent controversy on Wolf's role in Radbruch's (alleged) natural law turn[770] casts a different, less favourable light on Wolf.[771]

hen müsse", 322). This fits with Wolf's disciple Hollerbach's claim that Wolf protested against the co-opting of the entire young national and young conservative movement by National Socialism at the IKV conference in Frankfurt am Main in 1932 (in: *Heidegger-Jahrbuch* 4, 2009, p 306 including fn 78, referring to entries in Wolf's diary; likewise —referring to the minutes of the meetings—Marxen [1975], p 97–8).

767 Fn 755 above.

768 Wolf, *REP* II (1944/45), 7 ff. This is a translation by Juan de Rosal for which I was unable to find the German original. There (12 ff) Wolf describes the new NS juvenile criminal law in favourable terms (claiming that his aim is to reintegrate adolescents into "la vida comunitaria popular", 23), nor does he distance himself from NS criminal law in any other way. Critically Torino y Roldan, *RDP* 1 (1945), 507–514 (calling for the denunciation and destruction of this so-called New Criminal Law, "para que no vuelva más a erguirse enhiesto en ningún país de la tierra, ni hoy ni nunca, ni en la teoría ni en la práctica, ni en la doctrina ni en las leyes, ni en los maestros ni en los discípulos, ni en los legisladores ni en los jueces y ejecutores, ni en nada, ni en nadie.").

769 Hollerbach, in: *Heidegger-Jahrbuch* 4 (2009), p 330 ("nirgendwo Totalaffirmation", "im zeitgenössischen Diskurs Episode geblieben") (arguing in particular against Emanuel Faye's "completely distorted image" ["völliges Zerrbild"] of Wolf as a "prominent NS legal philosopher" ["prominenten NS-Rechtsphilosophen"]); also ibid, p 346–7 (there can be "no question" ["keine Rede"] that Wolf wanted to provide National Socialism with "a legal-philosophical foundation" ["ein rechtsphilosophisches Fundament"]).

770 *Cf* ch IV 4. including fn 499 and main text above.

771 Hollerbach, *JZ* 2017, 455 ff plausibly disproves Frommel's hypothesis (*JZ* 2016, 913 ff) that Wolf made Radbruch turn towards natural law after 1945, but remains silent on Wolf's own literary contributions to National Socialism (which are also ignored by Frommel, however).

Chapter VII. Some (preliminary) conclusions

1. *Selective reception of German (NS-inspired) criminal law in Latin America*

Zaffaroni's final chapter[772] is an important contribution on the history of the reception of German criminal law in Latin America and the current relationship between German and Latin American criminal law. Zaffaroni first addresses the relation between criminal law doctrine and the political system, arguing in favour of a humane criminal law—along the lines of his parallel publication, already mentioned in the opening chapter[773]—and warning against the inhumane tendencies of modern (Latin-American) criminal law that could have been taken from National Socialist criminal law doctrine.[774] Zaffaroni repeats his conviction that legal science is conditioned by its cultural and socio-political context and thus also cautions against any kind of blind adoption where the reception of criminal law science, in this case of German criminal law doctrine, is concerned.[775] He writes that attention always needs to be paid to two aspects when making such adoptions: on the one hand, to a methodological aspect that concerns the adoption of the actual doctrine to perfect and consolidate one's own law; on the other hand, to a—frequently neglected—political aspect that relates to this doctrine's content.

Zaffaroni had previously—knowledgably and self-critically—already denounced the reception of German criminal law in Latin America in the mid-20th century as one-sided, namely as a reception of NS-inspired criminal law, whether in the form of Neo-Kantian authors, especially Mezger, or of the authors of the Kiel School, although only the latter were regarded as Nazis according to Zaffaroni.[776] Ultimately, this (first) reception of German criminal law in Latin America thus focused upon the "vestiges of a doctrinal war among National Socialists",[777] namely between the NS criminal law theorists inspired by Neo-Kantianism and the Kiel School. Accord-

772 Zaffaroni (2017), p 277 ff.

773 See ch I 1. including fn 10 above.

774 Zaffaroni (2017), p 277–8.

775 Zaffaroni (2017), p 279–80. Concurring Guzmán Dalbora, *RDPC* VII (2017), 230, 232.

776 Zaffaroni (2017), p 172.

777 Zaffaroni (2017), p 172 ("arribaron los restos de una *guerra dogmática* entre nazistas" [italics in the original text, translated K.A.]).

ing to Zaffaroni, the purported scientificity and neutrality of these criminal law theories contributed to the disorientation of Latin American criminal law science, which seemed to have forgotten that there "can never be *ideological purity* where decisions of power are at stake, as the *nature of the matter* itself prevents this."[778]

Zaffaroni does consider criminal law doctrine to be a suitable instrument for developing a humane criminal law, but argues that the experience of National Socialism shows that such doctrine can also be perverted, leading to the loss of the humane purpose that should inform all criminal law.[779] In this regard, Zaffaroni accuses Neo-Kantianism of a purely scientific, apolitical understanding of criminal law doctrine,[780] which made its co-option by National Socialism possible in the first place. As already explained above (ch IV 3.), this does not do justice to the complexity and diversity of the various lines of Neo-Kantianism. However, we can certainly concur with Zaffaroni that in times of regime change or transition, from democracy to totalitarianism, there is a danger that the methodological tools developed by criminal law doctrine may as likely be used to carry out a genocide as to establish a democratic *Rechtsstaat*.[781] In this context, Zaffaroni repeats his (convincing) hypothesis that the Kiel School was more consistent in this regard, as its aim right from the start was to create—upon the ruins of the liberal-individualist criminal law of the Enlightenment—a new, independent NS criminal law.[782]

---

778 Zaffaroni (2017), p 172 ("nunca puede haber *asepsia ideológica* cuando se proyectan decisiones de poder, porque lo impide la propia *naturaleza de las cosas*." [italics in the original text, translated K.A.]); concurring Guzmán Dalbora, *RDPC* VII (2017), 230. Critically on the uncritical reception of German (including NS-inspired) criminal law also Matus, *ZIS* 9 (2014) 622–3, 627–8, who doubts (Latin American) criminal law doctrine's democratic fitness and ability to resist dictatorship in general, however.

779 Zaffaroni (2017), p 281.

780 Zaffaroni (2017), p 282 ("mito de la *ciencia pura*" [italics in the original text]). Also *cf* his accusation of technocracy, ch IV 3. including fn 379 above.

781 Zaffaroni (2017), p 282.

782 Zaffaroni (2017) emphasises the greater consistency of the Kiel School in this regard at several points, *cf* eg p 284 ("darle la razón a los autores de Kiel"), 290 ("consecuencias más coherentes"); previously Zaffaroni, in Zaffaroni (2011), p 13 ff, 51 (destruction and reconstruction). Similarly Mittermaier, *SchwZStR* 52 (1938), 210 ("progressive, almost revolutionary line" ["fortschrittliche, ja fast revolutionäre Richtung"]).

2. Did Hans Welzel truly overcome (Neo-Kantian) NS criminal law?

This heading sums up Zaffaroni's (untenable) hypothesis as a rhetorical question. His hypothesis consists of two premises: firstly, that the (supposedly homogenous) philosophy of Neo-Kantianism laid the ground for NS criminal law; and secondly, that finalist ontologism as defined by Welzel[783] overcame NS criminal law once and for all. We cannot concur with either premise, for on the one hand, as seen above (ch IV 3. and 4.), National Socialist criminal law was precisely *not* Neo-Kantian and categorically rejected methodological dualism in particular, calling for an "ethicisation" instead. On the other hand, Welzel, too, was always critical of Neo-Kantianism (and especially of methodological dualism)—already in his *Habilitation* thesis,[784] but also in the post-war period[785] (even though his late works recognised the theory of separation as a "basic difference"[786])—and the ontological approach of his *Habilitation* thesis in particular displays an

783 For a brief explanation, see ch I, fn 34, and the following fn; for further explanation, see Ambos, *Cardozo Law Review* 28 (2007), 2649–50.

784 Welzel (1935), p 41 ff ("when values are deeply rooted in the ontic" ["wenn die Werte tief im Ontischen wurzeln"], "the ontic...itself [is] 'valuable' or 'valued'" ["das Ontische...selbst 'wertig' oder 'wert'"], "ontic being forms part of the matter of any value" ["das ontische Sein gehört zur Materie jedes Wertes", 55], "overcoming naturalist positivism" ["Überwindung des naturalistischen Positivismus"], "all higher intellectual life with its concrete value relations" ["das ganze höhere geistige Leben mit seinen konkreten Wertbeziehungen"] forms part of reality [74], legal concepts "do not refer only to neutral characteristics of being, but to ontic being that stands in concrete value relations" ["beziehen sich...nicht lediglich auf wertfreie Seinsmerkmale, sondern auf in konkreten Wertbeziehungen stehendes ontisches Sein", 75]); thereto also Loos, in: Loos (1987), p 505; Loos, *JZ* 2004, 1118 including fn 47.

785 Welzel (1962), p 190 ("the deeper reason for the failure of Neo-Kantian legal philosophy lies in its retention and reinforcement of the positivist concept of law" ["im Beibehalten und Verfestigen des positivistischen Rechtsbegriffs liegt der tiefere Grund für das Versagen der neukantianischen Rechtsphilosophie"]).

786 *Cf* Welzel (1966), p 22 ff ("Grunddifferenz") (where he sees the distinction between "Sein" [being] and "Sollen" [ought] not "merely" ["lediglich"] as "a product of Neo-Kantian epistemological theory" ["einen Ausfluß der neukantianischen Erkenntnistheorie"], however, but considers it to be relevant "completely independently" ["völlig unabhängig"] of that theory; this distinction is correct in that the content of the "ought" cannot be defined out of itself, but only out of "being" [p 22]); differentiating, Loos, in: Loos (1987), p 505 ff ("separation of being and ought" ["Trennung von Sein und Sollen"], but the "main concern is to show the normative boundaries of possible legislation...antithesis of relativist positivism à la Kelsen or Radbruch" ["Hauptanliegen, normative Grenzen möglicher Rechtssetzung aufzuzeigen...Gegenbild zum relativistischen Positivismus à la Kelsen oder Radbruch"]); also see Loos, *JZ* 2004, 1118 including fn 50.

astonishing affinity to the ethicising unified thinking of National Socialism.[787]

NATURALISMUS
UND WERTPHILOSOPHIE
IM STRAFRECHT

Untersuchungen
über die ideologischen Grundlagen
der Strafrechtswissenschaft

Von

Dr. HANS WELZEL
Dozent der Rechte an der
Universität Köln

1935

DEUTSCHES DRUCK- UND VERLAGSHAUS GMBH.
VERLAG FÜR RECHTS- UND STAATSWISSENSCHAFTEN
MANNHEIM · BERLIN · LEIPZIG

Figure 18: Welzel's Habilitation thesis, 1935

Regardless of this, Zaffaroni praises Welzel in particular and—despite criticising Welzel's deeply conservative views, especially of criminal law as an ethical minimum (in the sense of a necessary criminal minimalism)—does not see him as an "official criminal law theorist" ("penalista oficial") of the NS regime, and thus regards him as only of "secondary importance" in this regard.[788] For Zaffaroni, the crucial factors are that Welzel—and here Zaffaroni's well-nigh fanatical antipathy to Neo-Kantianism is revealed once

787 Fn 785 above.
788 Zaffaroni (2017), p 287. The only critical source Zaffaroni mentions is the essay by Matus, *ZIS* 9 (2014) 622 (giving another source).

more—was the "architect who constructively overcame the destroyed Neo-Kantian system" in the post-war period,[789] and that his theory of rational-logical structures in particular facilitated the development of an independent Latin American criminal law science.[790] According to Zaffaroni, the Latin American perception of the dispute between causalism and finalism was distorted, because too little attention was paid to the political context, and (this seems to be the intended thrust of Zaffaroni's subsequent elaborations) scholars failed to recognise that Welzel's post-war writings, especially his "das neue Bild des Strafrechtssystems" ("the new picture of the criminal law system"),[791] should be understood first and foremost (also) as a response to the Kiel School.[792] In particular, Welzel repudiated the Kiel scholars' unified concept of crime, showing that the elements of the structure of crime were not simply an aggregate of unrelated parts, but constituted a logical and internally consistent system.[793] In Latin America, however, Welzel's finalism became erroneously associated with Marxism in the context of the National Security Doctrine.[794]

In this, Zaffaroni is remaining true to himself as an orthodox finalist, upholding the widespread narrative (prevalent particularly in the Spanish-language legal sphere) that Welzel was silently opposed to National Socialism, and that his rational-logical structures proved a bulwark against all authoritarian criminal law, including that of the NS ilk.[795] However, this completely uncritical picture of Welzel fails to stand up to an objective

789 Zaffaroni (2017), p 287 ("arquitecto de la superación constructiva del demolida sistema neokantíano").

790 Zaffaroni (2017), p 287–8.

791 Welzel (1961).

792 The Argentinian-Spanish criminal law scholar Enrique Bacigalupo, Jiménez de Asúa's other important disciple and a supporter of Welzel, emphasises the latter's opposition to the Kiel School in a similarly apologetic manner, *cf* Bacigalupo, *FS Eser* (2005), p 61, 69 ff (although he refers mainly to Welzel's essay in the *FS Kohlrausch* [1944] and his reception of Welzel is thus highly selective); against Bacigalupo, Llobet (2018), p 343 (according to whom Bacigalupo overemphasises the protection of legal interests in Welzel's thinking).

793 Zaffaroni (2017), p 289.

794 Zaffaroni (2017), p 289.

795 *Cf* Bacigalupo, *FS Eser* (2005), p 61, 69 ff and—exemplifying a position typical of uncritical (blind) finalism—Donna, in: Moreno et al (2005), p 45, 51–2, 56–7 (who sees Welzel's theory as a response to NS irrationalism among other things, but fails to quote even one of his NS-inspired writings); more recently in a similarly apologetic tone, Aller (2009), p 45 ff ("lucha de Welzel por sobrevivir al oprobioso sistema nazi" [45], "abordó topicos penales ajenos al interés del extremismo nacionalsocialista…Los adelantos y ensayos sobre la acción penal…no agradaron a los penalistas de esa época" [48]); further references in Llobet (2018), p 321 ff (with a comprehensive analysis of Welzel's reception, not only in Spanish-language sources).

analysis of his works between 1933 and 1945,[796] regardless of Welzel's personal motivations.[797] The opening chapter already alluded to Welzel's political understanding of criminal law science,[798] an understanding that ultimately was oriented towards the NS state as the final *telos*—in line with the finalist stance of all theories of criminal offences in the Third Reich (a stance likewise mentioned at the beginning of this study[799]).[800] Welzel's abovementioned *Habilitation* thesis (1935) can be characterised at least as a legal-philosophical legitimation and, in its histrionic, ethicising language, an idealisation of the NS renewal of the law.[801] For, contrary to Kubiciel's assertions,[802] not only is it concerned with an (over)emphasis on commu-

796 Welzel's earlier writings, especially "Kausalität und Handlung" (*ZStW* 51 [1931], 703), are highly significant in that they lay the ground for the concepts of finalist action and person-based wrongdoing as well as for the theory of rational-logical structures. However, they are not important in the context we are interested in here (Welzel's theory's affinity to National Socialism).

797 *Cf* in this regard Kubiciel, in: Frisch et al (2015) p 135, 150–1 (suspecting that Welzel was motivated more by career-related opportunism than by political conviction) and p 155 (attesting Welzel great tactical and strategic "skill" ["Geschick"]).

798 Ch I 2. including fn 35 and main text above.

799 Ch I 2. including fn 44 and main text above.

800 Also *cf* Marxen, in: Rottleuthner (1983), p 59, 63.

801 Frommel, in: Reifner/Sonnen (1984), p 90–1; critically also Sticht (2000), p 19 ("a tone that sometimes smacks of ideology" ["zuweilen ideologielastige Ton"]), at the same time convincingly refuting a statement produced by Welzel's Habilitation supervisor Bohne during his denazification procedure in which Bohne—referring among other things to a review by Adami, *JW* 64 (1935), 2348—claims that Welzel's Habilitation thesis engaged in ideology critique (Sticht [2000], p 25–6); likewise critically Politoff (2001), p 64–5 (*Wertphilosophie* as supporting the dominant NS system, including the Führer principle, following Frommel); also see Radbruch (1936) in Radbruch (1990), p 29, according to whom Welzel employed "curiously dark and immature phrases" ("merkwürdig dunkler und unausgereifter Wendungen") to describe the current "revolution" ("Umbruchs", p 30) and, like "his like-minded colleagues" ("seine Gesinnungsgenossen"), emphasises "everywhere the conceptual indissolubility of the units of life" ("überall die begriffliche Unauflösbarkeit von Lebenseinheiten"), even though "the strongest possible permeation of manifestations of the law with 'corroding' reason [should be seen as] a guarantee of legal certainty" ("in der möglichsten Durchdringung der Rechtserscheinungen mit dem 'zersetzenden' Verstand eine Garantie der Rechtssicherheit", p 31); recently, at least implicitly critically, Kindhäuser, in: Kindhäuser (2019), p 160, 180, 181, 187 (emphasising Welzel's reference to völkisch thinking and the Volksgemeinschaft) and p 164 and *passim* (pointing to Welzel's sometimes imprecise representation of Radbruch's position); on the affinity of Welzel's text to National Socialism and his influence, particularly on the Kiel School, Stopp (2018), p 17 ff and *passim*.

802 Kubiciel, in: Frisch et al (2015), p 146 ff ("commitment to the values of a völkisch-statist community...embedded in a broad narrative arc and justified through philosophical positions, in short: comparatively strongly coded" ["Bekenntnis zu den Werten einer völkisch-staatlichen Gemeinschaft…in einen weiten Erzählbogen eingebettet und mit philosophischen Positionen begründet, kurz: vergleichsweise stark codiert", p 147]), referring among others to Radbruch (p 148).

nity-based thinking[803]—which may simply have followed the trend of the times—but it also contains (further) traces of National Socialist thought.[804] The finalist theory of action follows the trend towards a subjective understanding of wrongdoing.[805] In any case, in his later writings—and even beforehand through his membership of certain Nazi organisations[806]—Welzel clearly commits himself to National Socialism;[807] his contributions

803 *Cf* the quotes in ch I 2. including fn 35, which in themselves constitute an anti-liberal idealisation of community-based thinking; also Welzel (1935), p 36 (idea of the Volksgemeinschaft as "the mighty programme of National Socialism...with which our future independent existence as a state and nation stands and falls" ["das gewaltige Programm des Nationalsozialismus...mit der unser künftiges staatliches und nationales Eigenleben steht und fällt"]), 76 ("Volksgemeinschaft" rendered concrete in the "will of the Führer" ["Führerwillen"]).

804 *Cf* eg Welzel (1935), p vii ("the tremendous political events of the National Socialist revolution" ["das ungeheure politische Geschehen der nationalsoz. Revolution"] forces "us all to enquire into where we stand in history" ["uns allen die Frage nach unserem geschichtlichen Standort"]), 49 ("significance of the mixing of races for the fall of ancient Rome" ["Bedeutung der Rassenmischung für den Verfall des alten Rom"]), 72 ("idea of the state" ["Staatsidee"] as "the metaphysically rooted political 'stance' of a concrete *Volkstum*" ["die im Metaphysischen wurzelnde politische 'Haltung' eines konkreten Volkstums"], "race and *Volkstum*" ["Rasse und Volkstum"] as that which is "real" ["Reale"]), 74–76 (concrete order-based thinking, referring to C. Schmitt and culminating in the "expressed will of the Führer" ["geäußertem Führerwillen", 76]), 77 (significance of "eugenics and racial research...for the reshaping of criminal law" ["Eugenik und Rassenforschung...für die Neugestaltung des Strafrechts"]), 88 ("irreplaceable significance" ["unersetzliche Bedeutung"] of the "intellectual revolution of 1933...for our science" ["geistige Umbruch des Jahres 1933...für unsere Wissenschaft"]); thereto Stopp (2018), p 23 ff.

805 Welzel, *ZStW* 58 (1939), 501–2 thus also sees "a commitment to or at least tendencies towards a finalist concept of action" ("ein Bekenntnis oder mindestens Tendenzen zu einem finalen Handlungsbegriff") in statements made by E. Wolf, Dahm and Schaffstein among others. Also see Hartl (2000), p 135 (Kiel School as the "model" ["Vorbild"] for Welzel's polemic against the theory of the violation of protected legal interests; finalist theory of action "as a product of that intellectual line of criminal law doctrine...in which there was a clear shift from the objective to the subjective when defining the essence of substantive wrongfulness" ["als Ausfluß jener geistigen Strömung der Strafrechtsdogmatik..., in der sich bei der Wesensbestimmung des materiellen Unrechts eine deutliche Wendung vom Objektiven zum Subjektiven vollzog").

806 Such as the NSDAP and the National Socialist German Association of University Teachers (*NSD-Dozentenbund*), thereto Sticht (2000), p 18–9, for whom Welzel's "membership in not just one, but several NS organisations makes an internal dissociation from the regime seem unlikely" ("gleich mehrfache Mitgliedschaft in NS-Organisationen eine innere Distanz zum Regime nicht plausibel erscheinen läßt"). *Cf* in this regard also the statements reproduced in Sticht (2000), p 22 ff on Welzel's National Socialist fitness and reliability in the context of his appointment at Göttingen University. Likewise Stopp (2018), p 10 ff and previously Halfmann, in: Becker (1998), p 123 (who overlooks Welzel's membership of the NSDAP, probably because he was denied access to the files, among others by the dean at the time, Welzel's (former) student Fritz Loos, ibid note 5).

on Hegel's political philosophy (1937) and community honour (1938) are of particular significance not only for their content,[808] but also for the National Socialist context of their publication.[809] National Socialist tendencies can also be found in further texts by Welzel[810] practically up until the end of the NS regime,[811] including in the 1944 edition of his influential

807 Likewise Kubiciel, in: Frisch et al (2015), p 148 ff (148, 150), emphasising the two texts mentioned in the following. For Sticht (2000), p 19, these writings "increase the impression that Welzel's distance to the dominant ideology cannot have been emphatic" ("verstärken den Eindruck, daß Welzels Distanz zur herrschenden Ideologie nicht dezidiert gewesen sein kann").

808 Welzel, in: Schürmann (1937), p 87, 102 ff (agreement with Hegel in regard to his "anti-individualism" ["Anti-Individualismus", 104], but dissociation in regard to the state's significance as a "reification of the world spirit" ["Konkretion des Weltgeistes", 102], belonging to which "is ultimately a matter of attitude" ["letztlich eine Sache der Gesinnung ist", 103] [which is why Hegel was also in favour of integrating the Jews [!]] and instead an emphasis on "blood-based connections" ["blutmäßige Zusammenhang", 103], of the "natural and motherly soil of *Volkstum*" ["naturhaft-mütterliche Boden des Volkstums"] as the "creative foundation" ["schöpferische Grund"] of the state [102], as its "'substance', on the basis of which we seek to comprehend the institutional forms of the state and the creative forms of the mind" ["'Substanz', von deren Grundlage aus wir die institutionellen Formen des Staates und die Bildungsformen des Geistes zu begreifen suchen", 104]; Welzel, *ZStW* 57 (1938) 28, 40 ff (material-historical definition of the community as the "bearer of history" ["Geschichtsträger", 40], rooted "in völkisch being" ["im völkischen Dasein", 42], demanding that criminal law protect the honour "of the historical achievements of the German people" ["der historischen Leistungen des deutschen Volkes", 41] and "the supreme leadership" ["der höchsten Führung", 42]; individual is "historical only within the community" ["geschichtlich nur innerhalb der Gemeinschaft", 40]).

809 Welzel's cooperation with the Nazis of Göttingen University's Faculty of Law was documented by his participation in the essay collection edited by the avowed Nazi Schürmann to celebrate the University's 200th anniversary, as well as by his membership of the newly founded National Socialist Academy of Sciences (Schumann, in: Schumann [2008], p 90–1 including fn 103). The *ZStW* essay originated in a lecture held at a conference of the criminal law working group of the "university professors" panel of the NS Association of Legal Professionals ("Rechtswahrerbund") on 30/31 March 1937 in Eisenach (*ZStW* 57 [1938] 28 including fn *).

810 *Cf* in the context of social adequacy ch IV 5. including fn 638 above; there, Welzel defines as "socially adequate" ("sozialadäquat") those actions that "take place functionally within the historically evolved order of the communal life of a people" ("funktionell innerhalb der geschichtlich gewordenen Ordnung des Gemeinschaftslebens eines Volkes bewegen"; *ZStW* 58 [1939], 516); previously Welzel, *DRWis* 3 (1938), 113, 119 ("biological foundations are of crucial importance" ["biologische Grundlagen von entscheidender Bedeutung"] for "historical life and fate" ["geschichtliche Leben und Schicksal"]); later Welzel, *ZStW* 60 (1941), 428 (461–2 including fn 61a, where, in the context of the debate on perpetrator types, the "Volkschädling" in the sense of the abovementioned NS decree [fn 275] is—almost innocuously—characterised as a particular attitude type that, as it bears within itself "the seed of the corrosion of the cumulative unity of the people" ["den Zersetzungskeim für die geballte Volkseinheit"], needs to be "struck with the full severity of the criminal law [ie the death penalty]" ["mit der ganzen Schärfe des Strafrechts getroffen werden"]); thereto also Stopp (2018), p 45 (51 ff on *DRWis* 3 [1938], 113).

treatise on German criminal law (which approves of the relaxation of the prohibition of analogy)[812] and in his article in the *Festschrift für Kohlrausch* (1944),[813] even though after the war Welzel himself interpreted this paper as a dissociation from National Socialism.

811 It is thus incorrect for Loos (*ZStW* 114 (2002), 657, 674 ff), in his debate with Sticht, to see only Welzel's 1935–1937 writings as betraying a Nazi involvement; after this point in time, Loos argues, scarcely any traces of involvement can be detected, "which we could interpret as a retreat into the ivory tower of criminal law doctrine" ("was man als Rückzug in den Elfenbeinturm der Strafrechtsdogmatik einschätzen könnte", ibid, 674–5); inaccurately also Kubiciel, in: Frisch et al (2015), p 150, who believes that "such textual passages" ("derartige Textstellen") can only be identified for 1937, which actually contradicts his own analysis of *ZStW* 57 (1938 [sic!]) 28.

812 Welzel (1944), p 23–4 ("basis of punishment is...the legal conscience of the people" ["Grundlage der Bestrafung ist...das völkische Rechtsbewusstsein"]). In the post-war edition Welzel (1947, p 14–5) re-interpreted his former view as having contained more radical Nazi views (*inter alia* of Freisler) that wanted to renounce any statutory reference as contained in § 2 RStGB as amended in 1935 (see discussion fn 181 ff above and main text).

813 Welzel, *FS Kohlrausch* (1944), p 105 (value of the facts and act "indispensable for shaping the community" ["für die Gestaltung der Gemeinschaft unentbehrlich"]), 109 ("loyalty towards the *Volk*, Reich, leadership" as "act values of a lawful attitude" ["Treue gegenüber Volk, Reich, Führung", "Aktwerte rechtlicher Gesinnung"]), 112 (turn from the disvalue of the facts to the disvalue of the act to "uphold a lawful attitude" ["Bewährung rechtlicher Gesinnung"] in order to safeguard "the strength and survival of the state" ("die Kraft und den Bestand des Staates"), 118–9 ("exceptional crisis" ["ausnahmebedingte Krisis"] of the "idea of the elements of the offence" ["Idee der Tatbestandlichkeit"] and emphasis on the "value of the facts" ["Sachverhaltswert"] by the norms of wartime criminal law, although Welzel still considers "the abiding values of the act and attitude of lawful action" ["die bleibenden Akt- und Gesinnungswerte rechtlichen Handelns"] to be "the pillars sustaining the state" ["die tragenden Pfeiler des Staates"] in this situation). Critically also in regard to Welzel's commitment to a "new state law" ("neues Staatsrecht") in this text, Sticht (2000), p 28 including further references.

DAS DEUTSCHE STRAFRECHT

in seinen Grundzügen

Eine systematische Darstellung

von

Dr. HANS WELZEL

Professor in Göttingen

Zweite Auflage

Berlin 1949

WALTER DE GRUYTER & CO.

Vormals G. J. Göschen'sche Verlagshandlung — J. Guttentag, Verlagsbuchhandlung
Georg Reimer — Karl J. Trübner — Veit & Comp.

Figure 19: Welzel's very influential textbook, first published in 1940 as a "General Part" and right after WWII in its 4th edition of 1949 with a slightly changed title (our picture), the final 11th edition appearing in 1969

In a case note of 1949 discussing an OGH judgment on the criminal responsibility of the NS euthanasia doctors,[814] Welzel on the one hand designates them as accessories (with Hitler as the sole perpetrator) using his theory of subjective control over the act ("subjektive Tatherrschaftslehre"), and on the other hand recognises, in principle, an exclusion of criminal liability based upon extra-statutory necessity ("übergesetzlicher Notstand") or an unavoidable mistake of law.[815] In our context, it is not so much Welzel's doctrinal remarks that are of

814 Judgment of 5 March 1949, StS 19/49, published in part in *MDR* 3 [1949] 370.

815 Welzel, *MDR* 3 (1949) 373; on the mistake of law solution, also Welzel, *SJZ* 3 (1948) 368 (371 including fn 8).

interest, although they are certainly worth reading,[816] but the clear position he (now!) takes against NS law, such as the validity of Hitler's secret edict of 1 September 1939 –which in his view (according to the opinion dominant "now" ["jetzt"] [!]) is "neither a law nor an objective legal norm at all"[817]– or the utilitarian reckoning up of life "as mere items on an total account", of whose "ethical and legal inadmissibility" he is "deeply convinced".[818] Welzel claims insofar that he already expressed this clear rejection of the destruction of "unworthy" life "unequivocally" ("unzweideutig") during the Third Reich, referring to the third edition of his textbook (1944, p 165, 169) and the aforementioned article in the *FS Kohlrausch* (1944).[819] However, these references do not absolve Welzel at all. In the textbook, we read that a "special-preventive 'protective killing' only because of...inferiority" would be "ethically unjustifiable" ("spezialpräventive 'Sicherungstötung' nur wegen...Minderwertigkeit...ethisch nicht zu rechtfertigen"), but immediately before this Welzel states that "the inferiority of the perpetrator and the burden upon the *Volksgemeinschaft*" ("die Minderwertigkeit des Täters und die Belastung der Volksgemeinschaft") can

816 See, for example, his considerations —against the view of the OGH (*MDR* 3 [1949] 372)—of the fundamental applicability of extra-statutory necessity in particular in the exceptional situation of an unjust regime (*MDR* 3 [1949] 374); generally critically however Matus, *ZIS* 9 [2014], 627.

817 Welzel, *MDR* 3 (1949) 373 ("weder ein Gesetz noch überhaupt eine objektive Rechtsnorm").

818 Ibid, 375 ("als bloße Rechnungsposten in eine Gesamtrechnung"; "ethischen und rechtlichen Unzulässigkeit", "zutiefst überzeugt"). This notwithstanding, Welzel grounds the fundamental possibility of an unavoidable mistake of law on the lack of "self-evidence in natural law" ("naturrechtlichen Evidenz"), concerning "the question of the admissibility or inadmissibility of the destruction of life unworthy of living" ("der Frage der Zulässigkeit oder Unzulässigkeit der Vernichtung lebensunwertens Lebens"), which is why unavoidable mistakes are possible where this issue is concerned (376). Fundamentally also Welzel (1949), p 5 ff, where he argues, based upon an analysis of the history of philosophy, that there are no "self-evident propositions of natural law" ("evidenten Naturrechtssätze") and therefore an excusable mistake is a possibility, which is only avoidable or inexcusable "in the case of unscrupulous acts, that is, the blind carrying out of recognisably reprehensible demands" ["bei Gewissenlosigkeit, d.h. bei blinder Ausführung erkennbar verwerflicher Anforderung", 26]; critically Frommel, *JZ* 2016, 919. The effects of the recognition of mistake of law in *BGHSt* 2, 194 and Welzel's part in this (theory of guilt) in regard to NS case law are proved thoroughly in Stopp (2018), p 98 ff (165 ff), 170–1 (exclusion of guilt or mitigation, especially in euthanasia cases), although this theory alone—if not fully embraced by the still existing network of NS practitioners—could not have had this exempting impact (Frommel, *JZ* 2019, 197).

819 Welzel, *MDR* 3 (1949) 376.

> also "require" ("erfordern") the death penalty.[820] In the *FS Kohlrausch* (1944), Welzel argues that *private* persons are not allowed to kill "a socially worthless living person" ("einen sozial wertlosen Lebensträger"), but that "the state" certainly has "the right to destroy life" ("dem Staat...das Recht der Lebensvernichtung").[821]

At any rate, *implicit* dissociations, including historicising references,[822] are something that Welzel has in common with many of his colleagues,[823] and they live on in the silence or open apologetics of his students and disciples.[824] That Zaffaroni still adopts this apologetic stance today is astonish-

---

820 *Cf* Welzel (1944), p 169 with p 168. Welzel's reference to p 165 (in *MDR* 3 (1949) 376) is irrelevant in this respect).

821 Welzel, *FS Kohlrausch* (1944), p 108–9. Thus, a too positive interpretation is given by Kubiciel, in: Frisch et al (2015), p 150 ("scarcely any 'problematic' passages, on the contrary" ["kaum 'problematische' Passagen, im Gegenteil"]).

822 *Cf* Welzel, *FS Engisch* (1969), p 91, 100 ("constructions of meaning" ["Sinnentwürfe"], "in which we seek to comprehend the obligatory tasks of our life under the requirements and changing conditions of the *historical situation*" ["in denen wir die verpflichtenden Aufgaben unseres Lebens unter den Voraussetzungen und den wechselnden Bedingungen der *geschichtlichen Situation* zu erfassen suchen"], which also include "the norms of a *historical law*" ["die Normen eines *geschichtlichen Rechts*", italics K.A.], which Politoff, *NFP* 45 (1989), 320, relates to the historical situation of the NS period).

823 The way the textbook develops over the course of its various editions is also interesting: Welzel (1940), p 2 (offence as "breaking out or falling away from the real moral communal ordering of the people" ["Ausbrechen oder Abfallen von den wirklichen sittlichen Gemeinschaftsordnungen des Volkes"]) and third ed 1944, p 1 (criminal law's roots "in the specific basic moral values of a people" ["in den spezifisch sittlichen Grundwerten eines Volkes"] that arise from the right "attitude" ["Gesinnung"]: "loyalty towards the people, Reich, leadership, the obedience to state authority, the readiness to defend, the purity of oaths" ["Treue gegenüber Volk, Reich, Führung, der Gehorsam gegenüber der Staatsgewalt, die Wehrbereitschaft, die Reinheit des Eides"]; against this background, the summary account of the legislation of the Third Reich on p 11 appears to go beyond mere description); in the subsequent version of 1947 (the first part is simultaneously the fourth edition of the General Part), Welzel then describes the NS reforms as "apolitical" ("unpolitisch", p 10), which is surprising as this contradicts his mention of the political task of legal science (ch I 2. including fn 35 above).

824 Of Welzel's direct students, Fritz Loos was the only one to comment on his mentor's NS involvement, albeit only when engaging with Sticht's book (see fn 812 above) and two years later (Loos, *JZ* 2004, 1118 including fn 48–9 ["irritating statements on the foundations of legal science based upon the National Socialist reshaping of the state" ("irritierende Aussagen zu den Grundlagen der Rechtswissenschaft aufgrund der nationalsozialistischen Neugestaltung des Staates")]) and not before (particularly not in Loos, in: Loos [1987], p 486). Loos's evaluation of the so-called "Persilscheine" (attestations of "cleanliness" or innocence, a reference to Persil, a brand of washing powder) produced for Welzel by Rudolf Smend and Eb. Schmidt is probably too positive (*ZStW* 114 [2002], 675 including fn 24; critically also Sticht (2000), p 25 ff (28–9); Matus, *ZIS* 9 (2014) 524 including fn 22). Welzel's disciples Jakobs and Schreiber at least unearthed Welzel's article on Hegel's political philosophy (fn 809), which is not mentioned in Welzel's list of publications in the *FS Welzel* (1974) edited by Stratenwerth et al (Kubiciel, in: Frisch et al [2015], p 149 including fn 110); however, Jakobs sees Welzel's con-

ing and difficult to understand for at least two reasons. For one, Zaffaroni's teacher Jiménez de Asúa—in his abovementioned remarkable study of 1947 on NS criminal law—already criticised Welzel's theory of crime as "authoritarian".[825] Furthermore, within Spanish-language and particularly Latin American[826] criminal law science a critical reception of Welzel's works set in during the 1980s at the latest, confirming and enlarging upon Jiménez de Asúa, so to speak. This movement was started by the Chilean Sergio Politoff,[827] continued by the Colombian Fernando Velásquez[828] and

---

tribution thereto as "minimal", attributing the "discovery" ("Entdeckung") mainly to Loos and Schreiber (in an email to the author of 12 March 2018). By contrast, Hirsch always defended Welzel, whether by characterising Welzel's theory as irrelevant for the NS period or as a "kind of revolutionary act" against the prevailing opinion (Hirsch, *ZStW* 116 [2004], 1, 3, 7) or orally in conversations with colleagues (thus Jakobs in an email to the author of 7 March 2018). More recent criticism has only been voiced by Kubiciel, a late (indirect) disciple of Welzel (via his direct disciple Jakobs who was in turn the supervisor of Pawlik, Kubiciel's supervisor), in: Frisch et al (2015), p 137 ff (against Hirsch among others, but also showing a tendency to defend Welzel where his NS involvement is concerned); earlier critical texts include Amelung (1972), p 223, 225 (who is not one of Welzel's students, however); also Ziemann (2009), p 133 ("criticism of Neo-Kantian formalism and...turn towards ontologically predetermined material" ["Kritik am neukantianischen Formalismus und...Hinwendung zu einem ontologisch vorgegebenen Material"]).

825 Jiménez de Asúa (1947), p 100.

826 In this regard, criminal law science from Latin America has proven to be more critical than that from Spain, also *cf* Llobet (2018), p 24. One exception is Tomás Vives Antón, who discusses Welzel's closeness to National Socialism in his textbook, criticising both finalism and value philosophy as authoritarian (Vives Antón [2011], p 40–1, 452) and in his foreword to Llobet's book states that Welzel's commitment to National Socialism is "indisputable" (in Llobet [2018], p 14: "compromiso de Welzel con el nacionalsocialismo...indiscutible"). Critically also Muñoz-Conde, in Zaffaroni (2017), p 20–1 (Welzel "tuvo ningún problema...en asumir algunos de los postulados de moda entre los penalistas nazis").

827 Politoff, *DPC* VII, no 22 (1984), 71 (critical analysis of Welzel's writings since 1933, 73–4, albeit—counter to what the title suggests—no examination of the theory of social adequacy); Politoff, *NFP* no 45 (September 1989), 313, 318 ff (criticising in particular the understanding of the state and focus on attitude that draw upon Schmitt and find expression in the *FS Kohlrausch*, following Frommel in the main); Politoff (2001), p 64 ff (identically Politoff/Matus/Ramirez [2004], p 41 ff) (criticism of finalism together with *Willens-/Gesinnungsstrafrecht* instead of protected legal interests as authoritarian theory); Politoff, *LH Rivacoba y Rivacoba* (2004), p 529, 537–8, 543 (criticising among other things the hypothesis put forward by Welzel, *FS Kohlrausch*, 1944, that killings and other acts committed during war do not constitute criminal offences but are "purposive measures" ["Zweckmassnahmen", 537–8] and his defence of the Führer principle [543]).

828 Velásquez, in: Moreno et al (2005), p 69, 79 ff (including a critical reception of Welzel's Habilitation thesis and some of the texts quoted here, including the article in the *FS Kohlrausch*, and recognising his links to the NS regime, but ultimately against over-emphasising the NS period when evaluating Welzel overall [87–8]); Velásquez (2009), p

Politoff's student Jean Pierre Matus,[829] and recently perfected, as it were, by Javier Llobet in a comprehensive monograph on NS criminal law.[830] Zaffaroni ignores all of these authors (with the exception of Matus[831]), giving rise to the impression that his aim is less to provide a comprehensive, unprejudiced review of NS criminal law than to continue the conflict between causalism and finalism—a conflict that Zaffaroni himself criticises —by other means.

Even though Welzel—like other criminal law scholars of this period—should not be cast as a "criminal law ideologist of Hitler's dictatorship",[832] nor his writings classed as National Socialist "polemic"[833]—characteristics that apply above all to the Kiel School[834]—the National Socialist content of the texts he wrote during this time cannot be denied. Thus, Welzel can be included among those authors who engaged "in a rivalry of sorts to cre-

---

383 (stating especially in reference to the essay in the *FS Kohlrausch* that Welzel in some "paragraphs...placed his entire construction in the service of the [NS] terror regime prevalent in Germany at the time" ["párrafos en los cuales el autor ponía toda su construcción al servicio del régimen de terror que entonces imperaba en Alemania", translated K.A.]).

829 Matus, *ZIS* 9 (2014), 622 ff (who emphasises the continuity between NS criminal law and the finalist theory of action [623] and furthermore criticises both Welzel's personal conduct [624 including fn 22] and his work [625 ff], using detailed references).

830 Llobet (2018), p 247 ff (thorough investigation of Welzel's biography, writings and reception; here, Llobet himself criticises the NS ideology in Welzel's texts—which the present study has proven, too—and locates his turn towards the rule of law and emphasis on human dignity in the post-war period, but does not see Welzel himself as a fanatic, activist Nazi like the representatives of the Kiel School, for example; *cf* ibid, p 334 ff [339, 352], 440–1). From a Portuguese perspective Sousa Mendes (2007), p 371 ff, who distinguishes between two phases in Welzel's oeuvre and emphasises his affinity to Schmitt's order-based thinking and the Kiel School during the first phase (lasting until around 1945) (ibid, p 371–2 with further references to Portuguese and Spanish literature).

831 Zaffaroni (2017), p 287; see fn 789 and main text above.

832 Müller (1989), p 223 ("Strafrechtsideologen der Hitlerdiktatur"); critically Sticht (2000), p 21–2 ("doubtful" ["fraglich"]); Kubiciel, in: Frisch et al (2015), p 146; Stopp (2018), p 65 (who writes that Müller's appraisal "goes too far in terms of content" ["inhaltlich zu weit"]); also against Zaffaroni, Velásquez, in: Moreno et al (2005), p 87.

833 Thus Frommel, in: Reifner/Sonnen (1984), p 90 ("Kampfliteratur") ("despite his more moderate tone" ["trotz der moderateren Töne"]); also Frommel, *JZ* 2016, 919 ("terrible jurist" ["furchtbarer Jurist"]).

834 However, on the equation of Welzel with Dahm and Schaffstein, *cf* the statement made by Riechelmann, leader of the Göttingen body of students, in 1936: "In scientific terms, W. takes the same line represented by the two Kiel criminal law scholars Dr Dahm and Dr Schaffstein" ("Wissenschaftlich steht W. in derselben Richtung, wie sie von den beiden Kieler Strafrechtlern Dr. Dahm und Dr. Schaffstein vertreten wird", quoted from Sticht [2000], p 22).

ate a basic ideological structure as acceptable as possible to the new ruling powers",[835] opportunistically placing themselves in the regime's service.[836]

3. *A continuity of National Socialist criminal law thought in Latin America?*

In the conclusion to his book, Zaffaroni draws attention to the continuity of National Socialist thought in today's criminal law—especially in Latin America.[837] According to Zaffaroni, the core of this thinking lies in the romanticising, never completely realised concept of the Volksgemeinschaft,[838] which has been integrated into criminal law in a threefold manner.[839] The aim was to establish the abovementioned "ant society" as described by Nider,[840] the main task of criminal law in this process being to destroy the insubordinate ants, that is, dissidents and traitors. In this regard, Zaffaroni once again criticises the focus on the perpetrator's attitude as the foundation of criminal liability,[841] and the involutionary NS racism that served as the ideological foundation for the destruction of the "unhealthy elements" of the body of the people.[842] He repeats his assertion that this represents a continuation of neo-colonial European racism, and again distinguishes between Spencer's evolutionary racism and involutionary racism.[843] NS criminal law, including and indeed particularly that of the Kiel School, ultimately is based upon an imaginary ethics of the Volksgemeinschaft and the Führer, meaning it is able to evade any kind of empirical review or control.[844] Zaffaroni writes that the political content of romantic NS irrationalism was incorporated into criminal law science in order to punish all those who opposed National Socialism's programme and model of society as harshly as possible.[845]

---

835 Hilgendorf, in: Hilgendorf/Joerden (2017), p 160 (165) ("einer Art Konkurrenzkampf um die Schaffung eines den neuen Machthabern möglichst genehmen ideologischen Grundgerüsts").

836 Also *cf* Frommel, *JZ* 2016, 919 ("terrible" ["furchtbar"]… "the silence with which Hans Welzel could be opportunistic" ["die Lautlosigkeit, mit der Hans Welzel opportunistisch sein konnte"]).

837 Zaffaroni (2017), p 299 ff.

838 Zaffaroni (2017), p 289 ff.

839 Zaffaroni (2017), p 297 ff (referring to the theory of *Willensstrafrecht*, the NS-inspired Neo-Kantians [!] and the Kiel School).

840 Ch II 1. including fn 131 and main text above.

841 Zaffaroni (2017), p 294.

842 Zaffaroni (2017), p 295.

843 Zaffaroni (2017), p 297.

844 Zaffaroni (2017), p 299.

845 Zaffaroni (2017), p 299.

Zaffaroni also recognises the continuity of this thought in the present day (in Latin America), including in the form of a moralisation of criminal law, media terrorism and the stigmatising of dissidents,[846] including and indeed particularly in case law.[847] He sees the noblest function of criminal law doctrine, namely the setting of rational boundaries to the state's penal authority, as threatened by the populist or even *völkisch* nationalism of Latin American leaders, supported by the populist media.[848] Those familiar with the (often media-driven) practice of Latin American criminal justice—the public naming and shaming of individuals merely suspected of an act is just one example—will hardly be able to contradict Zaffaroni's verdict, although specialist studies—particularly with regard to the authoritarian tendencies of police practice[849] and case law towards a "criminal law of the enemy"—would be needed to provide the necessary—concrete and precise—evidence to back up Zaffaroni's propositions. In this sense, we—along with Zaffaroni[850]—can only hope that his book will increase the scepticism towards authoritarian, inhumane criminal law, including and indeed particularly in Latin America, and that further studies will take up this line of thinking.

846 Zaffaroni (2017), p 299 ff.

847 Zaffaroni (2017), p 301 ("signos áun más marcados"); similarly Batista, in Zaffaroni (2017), p 111–2.

848 Zaffaroni (2017), p 301, 303.

849 Batista, in Zaffaroni (2017), p 109–10, draws an accurate parallel with the so-called "Pacification Police" ("Policia Pacificadora") in the slums of Rio de Janeiro ("palavra 'paz'...desmoralizada pelo programa das Unidades de Polícia Pacificadora, que compartilha algumas caracerísticas com o modelo do 'campo', que tanto deve ao nazismo").

850 Zaffaroni (2017), p 303.

Bibliography

I. *Literature before 1945*

Binding, Karl (1885): Handbuch des Strafrechts. In: Binding, Karl, Systematisches Handbuch der deutschen Rechtswissenschaft, Abtheilung 7, Theil 1, Leipzig 1885.

Binding, Karl (1905): Lehrbuch des gemeinen deutschen Strafrechts, Besonderer Teil, Band II, Abteilung 2, Leipzig 1905.

Binding, Karl (1913): Grundriß des deutschen Strafrechts: Allgemeiner Teil, Leipzig 1913.

Binding, Karl/Hoche, Alfred (1920): Die Freigabe der Vernichtung lebensunwerten Lebens. Ihr Maß und Ihre Form, Leipzig 1920 [Spanish translation by B. Serigós in Zaffaroni, ed (2009b), 47–97].

Blasco y Fernández de Moreda, Francisco (1943): Las escuelas de Kiel y de Marburgo y la doctrina penal nacional-socialista. In: *Criminalia* (Mexico), IX, 4 (1943), 235–251; republished in Zaffaroni, ed (2011), p 109–132.

Bruns, Hans-Jürgen (1938): Die Befreiung des Strafrechts vom zivilistischen Denken, Berlin 1938.

Cavaleiro de Ferreira, Manuel (1938): A Reforma do Direito Penal Alemão. In: Cavaleiro de Ferreira, Manuel, Obra Dispersa, vol I, Lisbon 1996 (reprint), p 69–81.

Dahm, Georg (1931): Die Zunahme der Richtermacht im modernen Strafrecht, Tübingen 1931 [Heidelberg inaugural lecture].

Dahm, Georg (1933): Autoritäres Strafrecht. In: *MSchrKrimPsych* 24 (1933), 162–180.

Dahm, Georg (1934): Das Ermessen des Richters im nationalsozialistischen Strafrecht. In: *DStR* 80 [new numbering 1] (1934), 87–96.

Dahm, Georg (1934): Die Ehre im Strafrecht. In: *DR* 4 (1934), 417–419.

Dahm, Georg (1934): Die Erneuerung der Ehrenstrafe. In: *DJZ* 39 (1934), 821–832.

Dahm, Georg (1935a): Gemeinschaft und Strafrecht, Hamburg 1935.

Dahm, Georg (1935b): Nationalsozialistisches und faschistisches Strafrecht, Berlin 1935.

Dahm, Georg (1935): Verbrechen und Tatbestand. In: Dahm, Georg et al, Grundfragen der neuen Rechtswissenschaft, Berlin 1935, p 62–107.

Dahm, Georg (1938): Der Methodenstreit in der heutigen Strafrechtswissenschaft, *ZStW* 57 (1938) 225–294. (also printed in: Dahm/Schaffstein, Methode und System des neuen Strafrechts, Berlin 1938, p 1 ff).

Dahm, Georg (1938): Staatsanwaltschaft und Kriminalpolizei. In: *DRWis* 3 (1938), 148–169.

Dahm, Georg (1940): Der Tätertyp im Strafrecht, Leipzig 1940.

Dahm, Georg/Schaffstein, Friedrich (1933): Liberales oder autoritäres Strafrecht?, Hamburg 1933 [Spanish translation by L.G. Brond in Zaffaroni, ed (2011), 57–107].

Dahm, Georg/Eckhardt, Karl August/Höhn, Reinhard/Ritterbusch, Paul/Siebert, Wolfgang: Leitsätze über Stellung und Aufgaben des Richters, *DRWis* 1 (1936), 123–124.

Donnedieu de Vabres, Henri (1938): La Politique criminelle des États autoritaires, Paris 1938.

Exner, Franz (1934): Das System der sichernden und bessernden Maßregeln nach dem Gesetz v. 24. November 1933 [Habitual Offenders Act]. In: *ZStW* 53 (1934), 629–655.

Exner, Franz (1939): Kriminalbiologie, Hamburg 1939.

Forsthoff, Ernst (1933): Der totale Staat, Hamburg 1933.

Fraenkel, Ernst (1941): The Dual State, Oxford 1941.

Frank, Hans, ed. (1934): Denkschrift des Zentralausschusses der Strafrechtsabteilung der Akademie für Deutsches Recht über die Grundzüge eines Allgemeinen Deutschen Strafrechts, Berlin 1934.

Frank, Hans, ed. (1935): Nationalsozialistische Leitsätze für ein neues deutsches Strafrecht, Part 1 (General Part), 2nd ed 1935.

Frank, Hans, ed. (1936): Nationalsozialistische Leitsätze für ein neues deutsches Strafrecht, Part 2 (Special Part), 1936.

Frank, Reinhard (1907): Über den Aufbau des Schuldbegriffs, Giessen 1907.

Freisler, Roland (1933): Gedanken zur Strafrechtserneuerung. In: Preußischer Justizminister, Denkschrift des preußischen Justizministers, Nationalsozialistisches Strafrecht, Berlin 1933, p 6–9.

Freisler, Roland (1934): Des Führers Tat und unsere Pflicht. In: *DJ* 96 (1934), 850–851.

Freisler, Roland (1934): Willensstrafrecht; Versuch und Vollendung. In Gürtner (1934), p 9–36. [Spanish translation by E.R. Zaffaroni, F.J.Arnedo, A. Bartos and G. Otano in Zaffaroni (2017), p 113–157].

Freisler, Roland (1934): Ergebnisse der Beratungen des Zentralausschusses der Strafrechtsabteilung der Akademie für deutsches Recht. In: Frank, Hans, Denkschrift des Zentralausschusses der Strafrechtsabteilung der Akademie für deutsches Recht über die Grundzüge eines Allgemeinen Deutschen Strafrechts, Berlin 1934, p 7–24.

Freisler, Roland (1935): Aufbau des Besonderen Teils und seine Stellung im Gesetz. In Gürtner (1935), p 9–66.

Freisler, Roland (1935): Schutz des Volkes oder des Rechtsbrechers, Fesselung des Verbrechers oder des Richters. In: *DStR* 2 (1935), 1–32.

FREISLER, Roland (1935): Der Wandel der politischen Grundanschauungen. In: *DJ* 97 (1935), 1247–1254.

FREISLER, Roland (1936): Staatssekretär Staatsrat Dr. Freisler über "Recht und Gesetzgeber" [speech given to mark the installation of the Breslau OLG president]. in: *DJ* 98 (1936), 153–156.

FREISLER, Roland (1936): Der Rechtswahrer im Kampfe des Vierjahresplans. In: *DJ* 98 (1936), 1630.

FREISLER, Roland (1941): Gedanken über das Gesetz zur Änderung des Reichsstrafgesetzbuchs. In: *DJ* 103 (1941), 929–938.

GALLAS, Wilhelm (1936): Zur Kritik der Lehre vom Verbrechen als Rechtsgutsverletzung. In: Dahm, Georg et al, Festschrift zum 60. Geburtstag von Graf W. Gleispach, Berlin, Leipzig 1936, p 50–69.

GEMMINGEN, Hans Dieter von (1933): Strafrecht im Geiste Adolf Hitlers, Heidelberg 1933.

GEMMINGEN, Hans Dieter von (1933): Willensstrafrecht oder Gefährdungsstrafrecht? In: *JW* 62 (1933), 2371–2373.

GERLAND, Heinrich (1933), Neues Strafrecht. In: *DJZ* 38 (1933), 857–861.

GOBINEAU, Arthur de (1853–1855), Essai sur l'inegalité des races humaines, Paris 1967 (first published 1853).

GÖRING, Hermann (1935): Die Rechtssicherheit als Grundlage der Volksgemeinschaft, Hamburg 1935.

GRISPIGNI, Filippo (1940), Expiación y defensa en el nuevo código penal alemán. In: Zaffaroni (2009a), p 29–42.

GRISPIGNI, Filippo (1941a), Los principios fundamentales del nuevo derecho penal alemán. In: Zaffaroni (2009a), p 51–70.

GRISPIGNI, Filippo (1941b), El significado de las nuevas disposiciones sobre el derecho penal de la juventud en Alemania. In: Zaffaroni (2009a), p 71–92.

GROSSMANN, Hans (1926): Die Grenze von Vorsatz und Fahrlässigkeit, Hamburg 1926.

GÜRTNER, Franz, ed (1934), Das kommende deutsche Strafrecht. Allgemeiner Teil, Bericht über die Arbeit der amtlichen Strafrechtskommission, Berlin 1934.

GÜRTNER, Franz, ed (1935), Das kommende deutsche Strafrecht. Besonderer Teil, Bericht über die Arbeit der amtlichen Strafrechtskommission, Berlin 1935.

GÜRTNER, Franz (1936): Eröffnungsansprache Internationaler Strafrechts- und Gefängniskongress, 1935. In: Actes du Congrès pénal et pénitentiaire international de Berlin Aout 1935, Procès-verbaux des séances, Volume I a, Berne 1936, p 4–23.

HARTMANN, Nicolai (1926): Ethik, Berlin 1926.

HEGLER, August (1915): Merkmale des Verbrechens. In: *ZStW* 35 (1915), 19–44.

HENKEL, Heinrich (1933): Der Begriff der Wissenschaft in Forschung und Lehre. In Krieck, Ernst/Staufing, Friedrich, Die deutsche Hochschule, Marburg 1933, p 8–29.

Henkel, Heinrich (1934a): Strafrichter und Gesetz im neuen Staat. Die geistigen Grundlagen, Hamburg 1934.

Henkel, Heinrich (1934b): Die Unabhängigkeit des Richters in ihrem neuen Sinngehalt, Hamburg 1934.

Hentig, Hans v. (1933): Nationalsozialistisches Strafrecht. In: *MSchrKrimPsych* 24 (1933), 633–634.

Heuber, Wilhelm (1937?): Die Paragraphen-Sklaverei und Ihr Ende, Berlin 1937(?).

Hoefer, Frederick (1945): The Nazi Penal System – I. In: *JCL&Crim* 35 (1945), 385–393.

Honig, Richard (1919): Die Einwilligung des Verletzten. Die Geschichte des Einwilligungsproblems und die Methodenfrage, vol 1, Mannheim 1919.

Jiménez de Asúa, Luis (1920): El estado peligroso del delincuente y sus consecuencias ante el Derecho penal moderno. In: Publicaciones de la Real Academia de Jurisprudencia y Legislación de Madrid, 27 de febrero de 1920, 6–34.

Jiménez de Asúa, Luis (1922): El estado peligroso. Nueva fórmula para el tratamiento penal y preventivo, Madrid 1922.

Jiménez de Asúa, Luis (1933): Manual de Derecho Penal, Volumen Primero, Madrid 1933.

Kerrl, Hanns (1933): Nationalsozialistische Staatskunst und Strafrechtserneuerung. In: Preußischer Justizminister, Denkschrift des preußischen Justizministers, Nationalsozialistisches Strafrecht, Berlin 1933, p 3–5.

Kirchheimer, Otto (1939/40): Criminal Law in National Socialist Germany. In: *Studies in Philosophy and Social Science* VIII (1939/40), 444–463.

Kohlrausch, Eduard (1936): Das kommende deutsche Strafrecht. In: *ZStW* 55 (1936), 384–398.

Lange, Friedrich Albert (1915): Geschichte des Materialismus und Kritik seiner Bedeutung in der Gegenwart, Zweites Buch: Geschichte des Materialismus seit Kant, Leipzig 1915.

Lange, Heinrich (1933): Liberalismus, Nationalsozialismus und Bürgerliches Recht: Ein Vortrag, Tübingen 1933.

Lange, Heinrich (1934): Vom alten zum neuen Schuldrecht, Hamburg 1934.

Larenz, Karl (1933): Über Gegenstand und Methode des völkischen Rechtsdenkens, Berlin 1933.

Larenz, Karl (1934): Deutsche Rechtserneuerung und Rechtsphilosophie, Tübingen 1934.

Larenz, Karl (1935): Rechtsperson und subjektives Recht. Zur Wandlung der Rechtsgrundbegriffe. In: Dahm, Georg/Huber, Ernst Rudolf/Larenz, Karl/Michaelis, Karl/Schaffstein, Friedrich/Siebert, Wolfgang, Grundfragen der neuen Rechtswissenschaft, Berlin 1935, p 225–258.

Larenz, Karl (1935): Volksgeist und Recht. Zur Revision der Rechtsanschauung der Historischen Schule. In: *ZKph* 1 (1935), 40–60.

Liszt, Franz von (1883): Der Zweckgedanke im Strafrecht. In: *ZStW* 3 (1883), 1–47.

Liszt, Franz von (1907), Das "richtige Recht" in der Strafgesetzgebung. II., *ZStW* 27 (1907), 91–96.

Luetgebrune, Walter (1934): "Nullum crimen sine lege, nulla poena sine lege". In: Frank (1934), p 42–45.

Maunz, Theodor (1943): Gestalt und Recht der Polizei. In: Huber, Ernst Rudolf, Idee und Ordnung des Reiches. Vol 2, Hamburg 1943, p 1–104.

Mayer, Max Ernst (1901): Die schuldhafte Handlung und ihre Arten im Strafrecht, Leipzig 1901.

Mayer, Max Ernst (1915): Der Allgemeine Teil des deutschen Strafrechts, Heidelberg 1915.

Merkel, Adolf (1899): Vergeltungsidee und Zweckgedanke im Strafrecht. In: Gesammelte Abhandlungen aus dem Gebiet der allgemeinen Rechtslehre und des Strafrechts, Zweite Hälfte, Strasbourg 1899.

Mezger, Edmund (1924): Die subjektiven Unrechtselemente. In: *GerS* 89 (1924), 207–314.

Mezger, Edmund (1928): Konstitutionelle und dynamische Verbrechensauffassung. In: *MSchKrimPsych* 19 (1928), 385–400.

Mezger, Edmund (1934): Kriminalpolitik auf kriminologischer Grundlage, Stuttgart 1934.

Mezger, Edmund (1934): Willensstrafrecht, Gefährdungsstrafrecht und Erfolgsstrafrecht. In: *DJZ* 39 (1934), col 97–104.

Mezger, Edmund (1936): Deutsches Strafrecht. Ein Leitfaden, Berlin 1936.

Mezger, Edmund (1936): Das neue Strafrecht und die Strafrechtswissenschaft. In: *DJZ* 41 (1936), 601–607.

Mezger, Edmund (1936): Die materielle Rechtswidrigkeit im kommenden Strafrecht, *ZStW* 55 (1936), 1–17.

Mezger, Edmund (1938): Deutsches Strafrecht. Ein Grundriss, Berlin 1938.

Mezger, Edmund (1940): Vergeltung und Schutz im neuen Deutschen Strafrecht, *MSchKrimBio* 31 (1940), 105–110; Spanish translation in: Zaffaroni (2009a), 43–50.

Mezger, Edmund (1942): Kriminalpolitik auf kriminologischer Grundlage, Stuttgart 2nd ed 1942.

Mezger, Edmund (1944): Rechtsirrtum und Rechtsblindheit. In: Boeckelmann, Paul et al, Probleme der Strafrechtserneuerung, Festschrift für Eduard Kohlrausch zum 70. Geburtstage, Berlin 1944, p 180–198.

Mittasch, Helmut (1939): Die Auswirkungen des wertbeziehenden Denkens in der Strafrechtssystematik, Berlin 1939.

Mittermaier, Wolfgang (1924): Über den Begriff "Verbrechen", *ZStW* 44 (1924), 2–15.

Mittermaier, Wolfgang (1938): Die Krise in der deutschen Strafrechtswissenschaft. In: *SchwZStR* 52 (1938), 209–226.

NAUCKE, Alfred (1920): Einführung. In Binding, Karl/Hoche, Alfred, Die Freigabe der Vernichtung lebensunwerten Lebens, Berlin: BWV, 2006 [reprint], p VI–LXXI.

NEUMANN, Franz (1942): Behemoth: The Structure and Practice of National Socialism, Toronto/New York/London 1942.

NEUMANN, Franz (1944): Behemoth: The Structure and Practice of National Socialism, 2nd ed with new appendix, Toronto/New York/London 1944 (reprint Octagon Books 1963).

NICOLAI, Helmut (1932): Die rassengesetzliche Rechtslehre: Grundzüge einer nationalsozialistischen Rechtsphilosophie, Munich 1932.

NIDER, Johannes (1473): Formicarius, Cologne 1473 (year unclear).

OETKER, Friedrich (1934): Die Teilnahme am Verbrechen. In: Frank (1934), p 116–134.

ÖSTERREICH, Traugott Konstantin (1951): Friedrich Ueberwegs Grundriss der Geschichte der Philosophie, Vierter Teil, Tübingen 1951.

PREUSSISCHER JUSTIZMINISTER (1933): Denkschrift des preußischen Justizministers, Nationalsozialistisches Strafrecht, Berlin 1933 (frequently cited as: Denkschrift).

RADBRUCH, Gustav (1932): Rechtsphilosophie, Leipzig 1932 (cited according to the student's edition, edited by Dreier, Ralf/Paulson, Stanley, Heidelberg 1999).

RADBRUCH, Gustav (1933/1957): Autoritäres oder soziales Strafrecht? In: *Die Gesellschaft* X (1933); cited according to the republished version in: Radbruch, Gustav, Der Mensch im Recht, Göttingen 1957, p 63–79.

RADBRUCH, Gustav (1936/1990): Rezension zu 'Welzel, Naturalismus und Wertphilosophie im Strafrecht, 1933', *Zentralblatt für die Juristische Praxis* 54 (1936), 43–45. In: Radbruch, Gustav, Gesamtausgabe vol 3, Heidelberg 1990, p 29–31.

RADBRUCH, Gustav (1939): Rezension zu Erich Schwinge, Irrationalismus und Ganzheitsbetrachtungen in der deutschen Rechtswissenschaft, Bonn 1938. In: *SchwZStR* 53 (1939) 109–110.

RADBRUCH, Gustav (1945): Fünf Minuten Rechtsphilosophie, reprinted in: Dreier/Paulson (1999), p 209–10 (Appendix 2).

RAUCH, Herbert (1936): Die klassische Strafrechtslehre in ihrer politischen Bedeutung, Leipzig 1936.

RIECKE, Heinz (1935): Der Rassegedanke und die neuere Philosophie, Leipzig 1935.

RIEMER, Svend (1933): Autorität – Wofür? In: *MSchrKrimPsych* 24 (1933), 222–226.

RAUCH, Herbert (1936): Die klassische Strafrechtslehre in ihrer politischen Bedeutung, Leipzig 1936.

SAUER, Wilhelm (1936): Lebendes Recht und lebende Wissenschaft, Tübingen 1936.

SCHÄFER, Ernst (1934): Die Schuldlehre. In: Gürtner (1934), p 37–55.

SCHAFFSTEIN, Friedrich (1933): Die Nichtzumutbarkeit als allgemeiner übergesetzlicher Schuldausschließungsgrund, Leipzig 1933.

SCHAFFSTEIN, Friedrich (1934): Ehrenstrafe und Freiheitsstrafe in ihrer Bedeutung für das neue Strafrecht. In: *DStR* 80 [new numbering 1] (1934), 273–281.

SCHAFFSTEIN, Friedrich (1934): Formalismus im Strafrecht. In: *DR* 4 (1934), 349–352.

SCHAFFSTEIN, Friedrich (1934): Nationalsozialistisches Strafrecht. In: *ZStW* 53 (1934), 603–628.

SCHAFFSTEIN, Friedrich (1934): Der Begriff "Strafanspruch" und sein rechtspolitischer Gehalt. In: *DJZ* 39 (1934), col 1174–1180.

SCHAFFSTEIN, Friedrich (1934): Politische Strafrechtswissenschaft, Hamburg 1934 (inaugural lecture Leipzig).

SCHAFFSTEIN, Friedrich (1935): Das Verbrechen als Pflichtverletzung. In: Dahm, Georg/ Huber, Ernst Rudolf/Larenz, Karl/Michaelis, Karl/Schaffstein, Friedrich/ Siebert, Wolfgang, Grundfragen der neuen Rechtswissenschaft, Berlin 1935, p 108–142.

SCHAFFSTEIN, Friedrich (1935): Das Verbrechen eine Rechtsgutsverletzung? In: *DStR* 81 (1935), 97–105.

SCHAFFSTEIN, Friedrich (1936): Das subjektive Recht im Strafrecht. In: *DRWis* 1 (1936), 39–49.

SCHAFFSTEIN, Friedrich (1936): Die Bedeutung des Erziehungsgedankens im neuen deutschen Strafvollzug. In: *ZStW* 55 (1936), 276–290.

SCHAFFSTEIN, Friedrich (1936): Die unechten Unterlassungsdelikte im System des neuen Strafrechts. In: Dahm, Georg et al, Gegenwartsfragen der Strafrechtswissenschaft, Festschrift zum 60. Geburtstag von Graf W. Gleispach, Berlin, Leipzig 1936, p 70–114.

SCHAFFSTEIN, Friedrich (1936): Strafrechtsreform und unechte Unterlassungsdelikte, *DJ* 98 (1936), 767–770.

SCHAFFSTEIN, Friedrich (1936): Zur Problematik der teleologischen Begriffsbildung im Strafrecht. In: Leipziger Juristenfakultät, Festschrift der Leipziger Juristenfakultät für Dr. Richard Schmidt, Leipzig 1936, p 47–77. (Reprinted in Ellscheid, Günter/Hassemer, Winfried, Interessenjurisprudenz, Darmstadt 1974, p 380–417).

SCHAFFSTEIN, Friedrich (1937): Literaturbericht Strafrecht. Allgemeiner Teil. In: *ZStW* 56 (1937), 104–175.

SCHAFFSTEIN, Friedrich (1937): Rechtswidrigkeit und Schuld im Aufbau des neuen Strafrechtsystems, *ZStW* 57 (1937), 295–336 (also printed in Dahm, Georg/ Schaffstein, Friedrich, Methode und System des neuen Strafrechts, Berlin 1938).

SCHELER, Max (1915/1919): Vom Umsturz der Werte, 2 vols, Leipzig 1915, 1919.

SCHELER, Max (1916): Der Formalismus in der Ethik und die materiale Wertethik, Paderborn 1916.

SCHMIDT, Eberhard (1933): Inaugural speech "Juristisches Denken und Politik". In: Hamburgerische Universität, Reden gehalten bei der Feier des Rektorswechsels am 7. Nov. 1933, Hamburg 1933, p 27–49.

Schmidt, Eberhard (1942): Anselm von Feuerbach und Franz von Liszt. In: *MschrKrim* 33 (1942), 205–223.

Schmidt-Leichner, without first name (1942): Der Durchbruch der materiellen Gerechtigkeit im Strafrecht. In: *DStR* 9 (1942), 2–18.

Schmitt, Carl (1934): Der Führer schützt das Recht. Zur Reichstagsrede Adolf Hitlers vom 13. Juli 1934. In: *DJZ* 39 (1934), 945–960.

Schmitt, Carl (1934): Der Weg des deutschen Juristen. In: *DJZ* 39 (1934), 691–698.

Schmitt, Carl (1934): Nationalsozialismus und Rechtsstaat. In: *JW* 63 (1934), 713–718.

Schmitt, Carl (1934): Über die drei Arten des rechtswissenschaftlichen Denkens, Hamburg 1934.

Schumacher, Oskar (1927): Um das Wesen der Strafrechtsschuld, Mannheim 1927.

Schwinge, Erich (1930): Teleologische Begriffsbildung im Strafrecht: ein Beitrag zur strafrechtlichen Methodenlehre, Bonn 1930.

Schwinge, Erich (1938): Irrationalismus und Ganzheitsbetrachtung in der deutschen Rechtswissenschaft, Bonn 1938.

Schwinge, Erich/Zimmerl, Leopold (1937): Wesensschau und konkretes Ordnungsdenken im Strafrecht, Bonn 1937.

Seidenstücker, Herbert (1938): Strafzweck und Norm bei Binding und im nationalsozialistischen Recht, Quakenbrück 1938.

Siegert, Karl (1934): Der Treuegedanke im Strafrecht. In: *DR* 4 (1934), 528–531.

Siegert, Karl (1934): Grundzüge des Strafrechts im neuen Staate, Tübingen 1934.

Spencer, Herbert (1851): Social Statistics: Or, the Conditions Essential to Human Happiness Specified and the first of them developed, London 1851.

Spencer, Herbert (1860): The Social Organism. In: *The Westminster Review* 17 (1860), 90-121.

Spencer, Herbert (1864): Principles of Biology, London 1864.

Strauss, Friedrich (1934): Die Erweiterung des Rechtsgüterschutzes im nationalsozialistischen Strafrecht. In: Frank (1934), p 31–41.

Thierack, Georg (1934): Sinn und Bedeutung der Richtlinien für die Strafrechtsreform. In Frank (1934), p 25–30.

Torino y Roldan, Fernando (1945): Lineas fundamentales del nuevo derecho penal juvenil de Alemania – una crítica a las ideas de Erik Wolf. In: *RDP* (Buenos Aires) 1 (1945), 507–514.

Welzel, Hans (1931): Kausalität und Handlung. In: *ZStW* 51 (1931), 703–720.

Welzel, Hans (1935): Naturalismus und Wertphilosophie im Strafrecht, Münster 1935.

Welzel, Hans (1938): Tradition und Neubau in der Strafrechtswissenschaft. In: *DRWis* 3 (1938), 113–121.

Welzel, Hans (1938): Über die Ehre von Gemeinschaften. In: *ZStW* 57 (1938) 28–52.

Welzel, Hans (1938): Über die Grundlage der Staatsphilosophie Hegels. In: Schürmann, Artur, Volk und Hochschule im Umbruch, Oldenburg 1937, p 87–104.

Welzel, Hans (1939): Studien zum System des Strafrechts. In: *ZStW* 58 (1939), 491–566.

Welzel, Hans (1940): Der Allgemeine Teil des deutschen Strafrechts in seinen Grundzügen, Berlin 1940.

Welzel, Hans (1941): Persönlichkeit und Schuld. In: *ZStW* 60 (1941), 428–474.

Welzel, Hans (1944): Über den substantiellen Begriff des Strafgesetzes. In: Boeckelmann, Paul et al, Probleme der Strafrechtserneuerung, Festschrift für Eduard Kohlrausch zum 70. Geburtstage, Berlin 1944, p 101–119.

Welzel, Hans (1944): Der Allgemeine Teil des deutschen Strafrechts in seinen Grundzügen, Berlin 3rd ed 1944.

Wolf, Erik (1932): Vom Wesen des Täters, Tübingen 1932.

Wolf, Erik (1933): Krisis und Neubau der Strafrechtsreform, Tübingen 1933 (lectures held in Heidelberg on 23 May 1933 and in Freiburg on 16 June 1933).

Wolf, Erik (1934): Das Rechtsideal des nationalsozialistischen Staates. In: *ARSP* 28 (1934), 348–363.

Wolf, Erik (1934): Literaturbericht "Rechts- und Staatsphilosophie". In: *ZStW* 53 (1934), 544–574.

Wolf, Erik (1934): Richtiges Recht im nationalsozialistischen Staat, Freiburg 1934 (lecture held in Freiburg on 7 December 1933).

Wolf, Erik (1935): Das künftige Strafensystem und die Zumessungsgrundsätze. In: *ZStW* 54 (1935), 544–574.

Wolf, Erik (1936): Tattypus und Tätertypus. In: *ZAkdR* 3 (1936), 358–363.

Wolf, Erik (1939): Der Methodenstreit in der Strafrechtslehre und seine Überwindung In: *DRWis* 4 (1939), 168–181.

Wolf, Erik (1944/45): Lineas fundamentales del nuevo derecho penal juvenil de Alemania, REP (Universidad de Valladolid, Facultad de Derecho) vol II (1944/45), 7–27.

Zimmerl, Leopold (1935): Täterschaft, Teilnahme, Mitwirkung. In: *ZStW* 54 (1935), 575–590.

Zimmerl, Leopold (1936): Zur Auslegung des § 2 StGB. In: Dahm, Georg et al, Gegenwartsfragen der Strafrechtswissenschaft, Festschrift zum 60. Geburtstag von Graf W. Gleispach, Berlin et al 1936, p 173–187.

II. Literature after 1945

ALEXY, Robert (1992): Fortwirkungen nationalsozialistischer Denkweisen in Rechtslehre und Rechtsprechung nach 1945? In: Säcker, Franz Jürgen, Recht und Rechtslehre im Nationalsozialismus, Baden-Baden 1992, p 219–226.

ALLER, Germán (2009): Dogmática de la acción y praxis penal, Montevideo/Buenos Aires 2009.

AMBOS, Kai (2007): Toward a universal system of crime: comments on George Fletcher's Grammar of Criminal Law. *Cardozo Law Review* 28 (2007), 2647–2673.

AMBOS, Kai (2013): Rechtsgutsprinzip und harm principle: theoretische Ausgangspunkte zur Bestimmung der Funktion des Völkerstrafrechts. Ein zweiter Beitrag zu einer grundlegenden Theorie des Völkerstrafrechts. In: Zöller, Mark et al, eds, Gesamte Strafrechtswissenschaft in internationaler Dimension. Festschrift für Jürgen Wolter zum 70. Geburtstag, Berlin 2013, p 1285–1310.

AMBOS, Kai (2015): The Overall Function of International Criminal Law: Striking the Right Balance between the Rechtsgut and the Harm Principles. In: *Criminal Law and Philosophy* 9 (2015), 301–329.

AMBOS, Kai (2017): Stand und Zukunft der Rechtsvergleichung. In: *RW* 8 (2017), 247–276. English version in: 24 *UCLA J. Int'l L & For. Aff.* (forthcoming 2020).

AMBOS, Kai (2018): Book Review, Kim Christian Priemel, The Betrayal, The Nuremberg Trials and German Divergence, Oxford 2016. In: *CLF* 29 (2018) 157–164.

AMBOS, Kai (2019): NS-Kriminologie. In: Dessecker, Axel/Harrendorf, Stefan/Höffler, Katrin, Angewandte Kriminologie – justizbezogene Forschung, Göttingen, 2019, xx–xx.

AMELUNG, Knut (1972): Rechtsgüterschutz und Schutz der Gesellschaft, Frankfurt am Main 1972.

AMELUNG, Knut (2002): Der Einfluss des südwestdeutschen Neukantianismus auf die Lehre vom Rechtsgüterschutz im deutschen Strafrecht. In: Alexy, Robert et al, Neukantianismus und Rechtsphilosophie, Baden-Baden 2002, p 363–373.

AMOS, Maximilian (2019): Juristische Fachverlage im 3. Reich. Die Verleger des Unrechts. In: *LTO*, 7.8.2019 <https://www.lto.de/recht/hintergruende/h/juristische-verlage-nationalsozialismus-ideologie-erbe-verantwortung/>.

ARNEDO, Fernando J., Roland Freisler: "El soldado político de Hitler". In Zaffaroni, ed (2017), p 9–84.

AYASS, Wolfgang (1998): "Gemeinschaftsfremde". Quellen zur Verfolgung von "Asozialen" 1933–1945, Koblenz 1998.

BACIGALUPO, Enrique (2005): Die Diskussion über die finale Handlungslehre im Strafrecht. In: Arnold, Jörg et al, Menschengerechtes Strafrecht. Festschrift für Albin Eser zum 70. Geburtstag, Munich 2005, p 61–75.

BATISTA, Nilo, Atualidade de Roland Freisler. In Zaffaroni, ed (2017), p 103–112.

BEULKE, Werner (2002): In memoriam Friedrich Schaffstein. In: *MSchrKrim* 85 (2002), 81–83.

BEYER, Wilhem (1947): Rechtsphilosophische Besinnung, Karlsruhe 1947.

BOCKENFÖRDE, Ernst-Wolfgang (1990): Zur Kritik der Wertbegründung des Rechts. In: Dreier, Ralf, Rechtspositivismus und Wertbezug des Rechts (*ARSP* supplement 37), Stuttgart 1990, p 33–46.

BÖCKENFÖRDE, Ernst-Wolfgang (1991): Recht, Staat, Freiheit, Studien zur Rechtsphilosophie, Frankfurt am Main 1991.

BRAUN, Johann (2001): Rechtsphilosophie im 20. Jahrhundert, Munich 2001.

BRAUN, Jens-Daniel/FALK, Georg D. (2015): Die deutschen Richter im Jahre 1933. In: Wolfgang Form, Theo Schiller and Lothar Seitz, NS-Justiz in Hessen. Verfolgung, Kontinuitäten, Erbe, Marburg 2015, p 21–44.

CAROLI, Paolo (2019), Die Strafbarkeit des Römischen Grußes in Italien. In: Vormbaum, Thomas, JJZ 19 (2018), Berlin 2019, p 48–64.

CATTANEO, Mario A. (2001): Strafrechtstotalitarismus, Baden-Baden 2001.

CODINO, Rodrigo, Algunas consideraciones sobre Filippo Grispigni, in Zaffaroni (2009a), p 115–132.

COHN, Ernst J. (1973): Gelehrter in Zeiten der Wirrnis. In: Evers, Hans Ulrich et al, Persönlichkeit in der Demokratie. Festschrift für Erich Schwinge zum 70. Geburtstag, Cologne/Bonn 1973, p 1–6.

CZOLLEK, Max (2018): Desintegriert Euch! 3rd ed Munich 2018.

DAHM, Georg (1956): Zur Problematik des Völkerstrafrechts, Göttingen 1956.

DAHM, Georg (1963): Deutsches Recht. Die geschichtlichen und dogmatischen Grundlagen des geltenden Rechts. Eine Einführung, 2nd ed Stuttgart 1963.

DETERING, Heinrich (2019): Was heißt hier »wir«? Zur Rethorik der parlamentarischen Rechten, Stuttgart 2019.

DIERLAMM, Alfred (2014): § 266 StGB. In: Joecks, Wolfgang et al, Münchener Kommentar zum Strafgesetzbuch, Munich 2014, p 547–652.

DONNA, Edgardo Alberto (2005): El pensamiento de Hans Welzel, entre el positivismo y el nacionalsocialismo. In: Moreno, Hernández et al, Problemas Capitales del Moderno Derecho Penal, Mexico D.F 2005, p 45–67.

DÖLLING, Dieter (1989): Kriminologie im "Dritten Reich". In: Dreier, Ralf/Sellert,Wolfgang, Reich und Justiz im "Dritten Reich", Frankfurt am Main 1989, p 194–225.

DREIER, Ralf/PAULSON, Stanley, eds (1999): Gustav Radbruch – Rechtsphilosophie. Student's edition, Heidelberg 1999.

DREIER, Ralf/PAULSON, Stanley (1999): "Vorwort" and "Einführung in die Rechtsphilosophie Radbruchs", in Dreier/Paulson (1999), p V–VIII und p 235–250.

ECKERT, Jörn (1992): Was war die Kieler Schule. In: Säcker, Franz Jürgen, Recht und Rechtslehre im Nationalsozialismus, Baden-Baden 1992, p 37–70.

ESER, Albin (2001): "Sozialadäquanz": eine überflüssige oder unverzichtbare Rechtsfigur? – Überlegungen anhand sozialüblicher Vorteilsgewährungen. In: Schünemann, Bernd, Festschrift für Claus Roxin zum 70. Geburtstag, Berlin 2001, p 199–212.

ESER, Albin (2010): Über Grenzen – Streben nach Mitte. In: Hilgendorf, Eric, Die deutschsprachige Strafrechtswissenschaft in Selbstdarstellungen, Berlin 2010, p 75–122.

ESER, Albin and STERNBERG-LIEBEN, Detlev (2019), Vorbemerkungen zu den §§ 211 ff. In: Eser, Albin, Schönke/Schröder, *Strafgesetzbuch*, Munich 30th ed 2019, p 2055–2096.

ETZEL, Matthias (1992): Die Aufhebung von nationalsozialistischen Gesetzen durch den Allierten Kontrollrat (1945–1948), Tübingen 1992.

EXNER, Frank (1949): Kriminologie, Berlin/Heidelberg 1949.

FALK, Georg D. (2017): Entnazifizierung und Kontinuität. Der Wiederaufbau der hessischen Justiz am Beispiel des Oberlandesgerichts Frankfurt am Main, Marburg 2017.

FELDMÜLLER–Bäuerle, Berit (2010): Die strafrechtliche Kieler Schule, Hamburg 2010.

FERRAJOLI, Luigi (2005): Derecho y razón. Teoría del garantismo penal, Madrid 7th ed 2005.

FOLJANTY, Lena (2013): Recht oder Gesetz, Tübingen 2013.

FORSTHOFF, Ernst (1968): Zur heutigen Situation einer Verfassungslehre. In: Barion, Hans, Epirrhosis, Festgabe für Carl Schmitt, subvolume 1, 1968, p 185–212.

FRAENKEL, Ernst (1974): Der Doppelstaat, Frankfurt am Main 1974.

FREI, Norbert (1996): Vergangenheitspolitik: die Anfänge der Bundesrepublik und die NS–Vergangenheit, Munich 1996.

FREI, Norbert/MAUBACH, Frank/MORINA, Christina/TÄNDLER, Maik (2019): Zur Rechten Zeit. Wieder die Rückkehr des Nationalismus, Berlin 2019 (e-book, quoted with position).

FROMMEL, Monika (1984): Welzels finale Handlungslehre. Eine konservative Antwort auf das nationalsozialistische Willensstrafrecht—oder die Legende von der "Überwindung des Wertneutralismus" im Strafrecht. In: Reifner, Udo/ Sonnen, Bernd-Rüdeger, Strafjustiz und Polizei im Dritten Reich, Frankfurt am Main/New York 1984, p 86–96.

FROMMEL, Monika (1987): Präventionsmodelle in der deutschen Strafzweckdiskussion, Berlin 1987.

FROMMEL, Monika (2016): Rechtsphilosophie in den Trümmern der Nachkriegszeit. In: *JZ* 2016, 913–920.

FROMMEL, Monika (2019): (review) Heike Stopp, 2018. In: *JZ* 2019, 196–197.

GARBE, Detlef (1989): In jedem Einzelfall—bis zur Todesstrafe: der Militärstrafrechtler Erich Schwinge: ein deutsches Juristenleben. Hamburg 1989.

GARCÍA AMADO, Juan Antonio (2019): Neokantismo y Derecho Penal. Sobre el papel y el sentido de la dogmática penal y sobre el papel de los penalistas en los regímenes autoritarios. In: Almacén Derecho, 7 February 2019, https://almacenderecho.org/neokantismo-y-derecho-penal/

GEYER, Christian (2018), Gibt es Germanen?, *FAZ*, 7 June 2018.

GOLTSCHE, Friederike (2010): Der Entwurf eines Allgemeinen Deutschen Strafgesetzbuches von 1922 (Entwurf Radbruch), Berlin 2010.

GÖRTEMAKER, Manfred/SAFFERLING, Christoph (2016): Die Akte Rosenburg, Munich 2016.

GRAVER, Hans Petter (2018): Why Adolf Hitler spared the Judges: Judicial Opposition against the Nazi State. In: *GLJ* 19 (2018), 845–877.

GRILL, Bartholomäus (2019): Wir Herrenmenschen. Unser rassistisches Erbe: Eine Reise in die deutsche Kolonialgeschichte, Munich 2019.

GROSS, Raphael (2010): Anständig geblieben: Nationalsozialistische Moral (Die Zeit des Nationalsozialismus), Frankfurt am Main 2010 (e-book, quoted with position).

GROSSE-VEHNE, Vera (2005): Tötung auf Verlangen (§ 216 StGB), "Euthanasie" und Sterbehilfe: Reformdiskussion und Gesetzgebung seit 1870, Berlin 2005.

GUEZ, Oliver (2018): Das Verschwinden des Josef Mengele, Berlin 2018 (e-book).

GÜNTHER, Klaus (1995): Von der Rechts- zur Pflichtverletzung. Ein "Paradigmawechsel" im Strafrecht? In: Institut für Kriminalwissenschaften der Johann Wolfgang Goethe-Universität, Vom unmöglichen Zustand des Strafrechts, Frankfurt am Main/Berne 1995, p 445–460.

GUSY, Christoph (2019): Aus der Geschichte lernen: NS-Unrecht im Jurastudium—Einige Vorüberlegungen und 10 Thesen. In: *ZDRW* 1 (2019), 1–15.

GUZMÁN DALBORA, José Luis (2017), Contexto histórico-ideológico del Derecho penal de la voluntad. In Zaffaroni (2017), p 85–102.

GUZMÁN DALBORA, José Luis (2017), Doctrina penal nazi etc. [book review], *RDPC* VII, no 10 (November 2017), 229–232.

HAMMON, Kathrin (2011): Karl Binding/Alfred E. Hoche, "Die Freigabe der Vernichtung lebensunwerten Lebens. Ihr Maß und Ihre Form", Göttingen 2011.

HARTL, Benedikt (2000): Das nationalsozialistische Willensstrafrecht, Berlin 2000.

HARTUNG, Fritz (1971): Jurist unter vier Reichen, Cologne et al 1971.

HARZER, Regina (1999): Die tatbestandsmäßige Situation der unterlassenen Hilfeleistung, Frankfurt am Main 1999.

HATTENHAUER, Hans (2005): Eine Türkenschrift im "langen Krieg" aus dem Jahre 1606. In: *JJZG* 7 (2005), 173–202.

HENKEL, Heinrich (1955): "Kollektivschuld". In: Nottarp, Hermann et al, Monumentum Bambergense. Festgabe für Benedikt Kraft, Munich 1955, p 106–128.

HENKEL, Heinrich (1977): Einführung in die Rechtsphilosophie, Munich 1977.

HILLIGER, Fedja Alexander (2018): Das Rechtsdenken Karl Bindings und die "Freigabe der Vernichtung lebensunwerten Lebens", Berlin 2018.

HILGENDORF, Eric (2017): Rechtsphilosophie zwischen 1860 und 1960. In: Hilgendorf, Eric/Joerden, Jan, Handbuch Rechtsphilosophie, Stuttgart 2017, p 160–169.

HIRSCH, Hans Joachim (2002): Die verfehlte deutsche Gesetzesfigur der "besonders schweren Fälle". In: Dölling, Dieter/Erb, Volker, Festschrift für Karl-Heinz Gössel zum 70. Geburtstag, Heidelberg 2002, p 287–302.

Hirsch, Hans Joachim (2004): Zum 100. Geburtstag von Hans Welzel. In: *ZStW* 116 (2004), 1–14.

Höffler, Katrin (2018): Vom juvenilen Rechtsbrecher und dessen "schädlichen Neigungen" – Zeit, mit einem überkommenen Menschenbild aufzuräumen. In: Bartsch, Tillmann/Görgen, Thomas/Hoffmann-Holland, Klaus/Kemme, Stefanie/Stock, Jürgen: Festschrift für Artur Kreuzer zum 80. Geburtstag, Frankfurt am Main, p 239–249.

Hollerbach, Alexander (2009): Zum Verhältnis von Erik Wolf und Martin Heidegger: Ein nicht abgeschickter Brief Erik Wolfs an Karl Barth. In: Heidegger-Jahrbuch 4, Freiburg/Munich 2009, p 284–347.

Hollerbach, Alexander (2017): Rechtsphilosophische Irrlehre: Monika Frommel über Erik Wolf. Zu Monika Frommel. In: *JZ* 2017, 455–457.

Holzhey, Helmut (1984): Neukantianismus. In: Ritter, Joachim/Gründer, Karlfried, Historisches Wörterbuch der Philosophie, vol 6, Darmstadt 1984, 747–754.

Honig, Richard (1962): Das amerikanische Strafrecht. In: Mezger, Edmund/Schönke, Adolf/Jescheck, Hans-Heinrich, Das ausländische Strafrecht der Gegenwart: Amerika – Norwegen – Türkei, vol IV, Berlin 1962, p 7–262.

Höffler, Katrin (2017): Tätertypen im Jugendstrafrecht. In: Schumann, Eva/Wapler, Friederike, Erziehen und Strafen, Bessern und Bewahren. Entwicklungen und Diskussionen im Jugendrecht im 20. Jahrhundert, Göttingen 2017, p 61–71.

Hoyer, Andreas (1997): Strafrechtsdogmatik nach Armin Kaufmann. Lebendiges und Totes in Armin Kaufmanns Normentheorie, Berlin 1997.

Hoyer, Andreas (2008), Strafrechtswissenschaft und Nationalsozialismus. In: Hoyer, Andreas/Hattenhauer, Hans/Meyer-Pritzl, Rudolf/Schubert, Werner, Gedächtnisschrift für Jörn Eckert, Baden-Baden 2008, p 351–368; in Spanish: Ciencia del derecho penal y nacionalsocialismo, *RP* 23 (January 2009), 41–51.

Jäger, Herbert (1967): Verbrechen unter totalitärer Herrschaft. Studien zur nationalsozialistischen Gewaltkriminalität, Frankfurt am Main 1967.

Jäger, Herbert (2006): [interview] In: Horstmann, Thomas/Litzinger, Heike, An den Grenzen des Rechts. Gespräche mit Juristen über die Verfolgung von NS–Verbrechen, Frankfurt am Main/New York, 2006, p 35–67.

Jakobs, Günther (1993): Strafrecht – Allgemeiner Teil, Berlin 1993.

Jessberger, Florian (2019): Heinrich Henkel (1903–1981): Ideologie und Recht. In: Jeßberger, Florian/Kotzur, Markus/Repgen, Tilman, Festschrift 100 Jahre Fakultät für Rechtswissenschaft der Universität Hamburg, Tübingen 2019, p. 235–254.

Jiménez de Asúa, Luis (1946–1952): *El Criminalista*, volumes 1–10, Buenos Aires 1946–1952.

Jiménez de Asúa, Luis (1947): El derecho penal totalitario en Alemania y el derecho voluntarista. In: *El Criminalist*a, vol VII, Buenos Aires 1947, p 63–186.

Jiménez de Asúa, Luis (1957–1970): Tratado de Derecho penal, volumes 1–7, Buenos Aires 1957–1970.

KALE, Steven (2010): Gobineau, Racism, and Legitimism: A royalist heretic in nineteenth-century France. In: *MIH* 7 (2010), 33–61.

KAUFMANN, Arthur/VON DER PFORDTEN, Dietmar (2016): Problemgeschichte der Rechtsphilosophie. In: Hassemer, Winfried et al, Einführung in die Rechtsphilosophie und Rechtstheorie, Heidelberg 2016, p 80–101.

KAZIM, Hasnain (2018): Auf rechts gedreht (Gespräch mit Sommerfeld), Spiegel Online, 10 April 2018, available at: http://www.spiegel.de/politik/deutschland/caroline-sommerfeld-ikone-der-neuen-rechten-und-identitaeren-a-1201899.html (last accessed 26 June 2019).

KINDHÄUSER, Urs (2017): § 266 StGB. In: Kindhäuser, Urs et al, Nomos Kommentar Strafgesetzbuch, Baden-Baden 2017, p 1142–1169.

KINDHÄUSER, Urs (2019): Günther Jakobs und Hans Welzel. In: Kindhäuser, Urs et al, Strafrecht und Gesellschaft, Tübingen 2019, p 155–193.

KIRCHHEIMER, Otto (1976): Das Strafrecht im nationalsozialistischen Deutschland. In: id, Von der Weimarer Republik zum Faschismus: Die Auflösung der demokratischen Rechtsordnung, Frankfurt am Main 1976, p 186–212.

KIRCHHEIMER, Otto (1976): Staatsgefüge und Recht im Dritten Reich. In: KJ 9 (1976), 39–59; reprinted in id, Von der Weimarer Republik zum Faschismus: Die Auflösung der demokratischen Rechtsordnung, Frankfurt am Main 1976, p 152–185.

KLIPPEL, Diethelm (1995): Subjektives Recht und gemanisch-deutscher Rechtsgedanke in der Zeit des Nationalsozialismus. In: Rückert, Joachim/Willoweit, Dietmar, Die Deutsche Rechtsgeschichte in der NS-Zeit, Tübingen 1995, p 31–54.

KROESCHELL, Karl (1992): Rechtsgeschichte Deutschlands im 20. Jahrhundert, Göttingen 1992.

KROESCHELL, Karl (1995): Führer, Gefolgschaft und Treue. In: Rückert, Joachim/Willoweit, Dietmar, Die Deutsche Rechtsgeschichte in der NS-Zeit, Tübingen 1995, p 55–76.

KROESCHELL, Karl (1995): Studien zum frühen und mittelalterlichen Recht, Berlin 1995.

KRÜPER, Julian (2018): Auf der Suche nach neuer Identität. Die Verfassung der Berliner Republik verlässt den Schonraum der Nachkriegszeit. In: Duve, Thomas/Ruppert, Stefan, Rechtswissenschaft in der Berliner Republik, Frankfurt am Main 2018, p 238–269.

KUBICIEL, Michael (2015): "Welzel und die anderen". Positionen und Positionierungen Welzels vor 1945. In: Frisch, Wolfgang et al, Lebendiges und Totes in der Verbrechenslehre Hans Welzels, Tübingen 2015, p 135–156.

KUBINK, Michael (2002): Strafen und ihre Alternativen im zeitlichen Wandel, Berlin 2002.

LEPSIUS, Oliver (1994): Die gegensatzaufhebende Begriffsbildung, Munich 1994.

LEPSIUS, Susanne (2003): Die mittelalterliche italienische Stadt als Utopie. In: Cordes, Stadt–Gemeinde–Genossenschaft: Festschrift für Gerhard Dilcher, Berlin 2003, p 389–455.

LINDNER, Josef Franz (2017): Rechtswissenschaft als Metaphysik, Tübingen 2017.

LLOBET R., Javier (2018): Nacionalsocialismo y antigarantismo penal (1933–1945), Valencia 2018.

Loos, Fritz (1970): Zur Wert- und Rechtslehre Max Webers, Tübingen 1970.

Loos, Fritz (1987): Hans Welzel (1904–1977). Die Suche nach dem Überpositiven im Recht. In: Loos, Fritz, Rechtswissenschaft in Göttingen, Göttinger Juristen aus 250 Jahren, Göttingen, 1987, p 486–509.

Loos, Fritz (2002): Literaturbericht Rechtsphilosophie. In: *ZStW* 114 (2002), 657–680.

Loos, Fritz (2004): Hans Welzel (1904–1977). In: *JZ* 2004, 1115–1119.

LÜBBE, Hermann (2007), Vom Parteigenossen zum Bundesbürger. Über beschwiegene und historisierte Vergangenheiten, Munich 2007.

LUIG, Klaus (1995): "Römische und germanische Rechtsanschauung, individualistische und soziale Ordnung". In: Rückert, Joachim/Willoweit, Dietmar, Die Deutsche Rechtsgeschichte in der NS-Zeit, Tübingen 1995, p 95–137.

MAHLMANN, Matthias (2017): Rechtsphilosophie und Rechtstheorie, Baden-Baden 2017.

MAIWALD, Manfred (2002): Friedrich Schaffstein. In: *NJW* 2002, 1250–1251.

MARXEN, Klaus (1975): Der Kampf gegen das liberale Strafrecht, Berlin 1975.

MARXEN, Klaus (1983): Die rechtsphilosophische Begründung der Straftatlehre im Nationalsozialismus. In: Rottleuthner, Hubert, Recht, Rechtsphilosophie und Nationalsozialismus (*ARSP* supplement 18), Wiesbaden 1983, p 55–64.

MARXEN, Klaus (1984): Zum Verhältnis von Strafrechtsdogmatik und Strafrechtspraxis im Nationalsozialismus. In: Reifner, Udo/Sonnen, Bernd–Rüdeger, Strafjustiz und Polizei im Dritten Reich, Frankfurt am Main/New York 1984, p 77–85.

MARXEN, Klaus (1990): Das Problem der Kontinuität in der neueren deutschen Strafrechtsgeschichte. In: *KritV* 73 (1990), 287–289.

MATUS, Jean Pierre (2014): Nacionalsocialismo y derecho penal. Apuntes sobre el caso de H. Welzel. In: *ZIS* 9 (2014), 622–628.

MAUS, Ingeborg (1989): "Gesetzesbindung" der Justiz und die Struktur der nationalsozialistischen Rechtsnormen. In: Dreier, Ralf/Sellert, Wolfgang, Reich und Justiz im "Dritten Reich", Frankfurt am Main 1989, p 81–104.

MAYER, Hellmuth (1947): Das Analogieverbot im deutschen Strafrecht. In: *SJZ* 2 (1947), 12–19.

MEISTER, Hans-Georg (1949): Wandlungen und Entwicklungen des Strafrechts seit der Kapitulation, Bleckede an der Elbe 1949.

MERCURIO, Ezequiel (2013), El estado peligroso del delincuente: 90 años después. Psiquiatría y prognosis criminal en el ámbito de ejecución de la pena, January 2013 <https://www.researchgate.net/publication/305850976>.

MEZGER, Edmund (1949): Strafrecht. Ein Lehrbuch, Berlin 1949 (reprint 2014).

MEZGER, Edmund (1950): Moderne Wege der Strafrechtsdogmatik, Berlin 1950.

Muñoz Conde, Francisco (2003): Edmund Mezger y el Derecho Penal de su tiempo. Estudios sobre el Derecho Penal en el Nacionalsocialismo, Valencia 2003.

Muñoz Conde, Francisco (2003): Comentario a "La Riforma Penale Nazionalsocialista", de Filippo Grispigni y Edmund Mezger, *NDP* 2003A, 303–315.

Muñoz-Conde, Francisco (2017): Prólogo. In: Zaffaroni, Eugenio Raúl, Derecho penal humano. La doctrina de los juristas y el poder en el siglo XXI, Buenos Aires 2017, p 15–23.

Murmann, Uwe (2005): Die Selbstverantwortung des Opfers im Strafrecht, Heidelberg 2005.

Müller, Claudius (1994): Die Rechtsphilosophie des Marburger Neukantianismus, Tübingen 1994.

Müller, Ingo (1989): Furchtbare Juristen. Die unbewältigte Vergangenheit der Justiz, Munich 1989.

Naucke, Wolfgang (1953): Naturrecht und Rechtspositvismus. In:Universität Göttingen. Rechts- und Staatswissenschaftliche Fakultät, Festschrift für Hans Nidermayer zum 70. Geburtstag, Göttingen 1953, p 279–294.

Naucke, Wolfgang (1981): Die Aufhebung des strafrechtlichen Analogieverbots 1935. In: Institut für Zeitgeschichte, NS-Recht in historischer Perspektive, Berlin 1981, p 71–108.

Naucke, Wolfgang (2010): "Schulenstreit"? In: Herzog, Felix et al, Festschrift für Winfried Hassemer, Heidelberg 2010, p 559–572.

Neumann, Franz (1984): Behemoth. Struktur und Praxis des Nationalsozialismus 1933–1944, Frankfurt am Main 1984.

Nolte, Ernst (1963): Der Faschismus in seiner Epoche, Munich 1963.

Oneca, José Antón (1970): La obra penalista de Jiménez de Asúa. In: Anuario de Derecho Penal y Ciencias Penales 23 (1970), 547–535.

Ott, Walter (2016): Die Vielfalt des Rechtspositivismus, Baden-Baden 2016.

Paulson, Stanley (2002): Einleitung. In: Alexy, Robert et al, Neukantianismus und Rechtsphilosophie, 2002, p 11–22.

Paulson, Stanley L., Die spätere Allgemeine Rechtslehre von Hermann Kantorowicz. In: *JZ* 2018, 1061–1068.

Pfordten, Dietmar von der (1996): Die gegensatzaufhebende Begriffsbildung. Methodenentwicklungen in der Weimarer Republik und ihr Verhältnis zur Ideologisierung der Rechtswissenschaft unter dem Nationalsozialismus (Münchener Universitätsschriften. Reihe der Juristischen Fakultät, vol 100) by Oliver Lepsius. In: *ARSP* 82 (1996), 591–593.

Pfordten, Dietmar von der (2004): Die Rechtsidee bei Kant, Hegel, Stammler, Radbruch und Kaufmann. In: Shing-I-Liu, ed, Value, Pluralism, Tolerance and Law, Taipeh 2004, p 333–379.

Pfordten, Dietmar von der (2010): Gustav Radbruch – Über den Charakter und das Bewahrenswerte seiner Rechtsphilosophie. In: *JZ* 2010, 1021–1027.

Politoff, Sergio (1984): Adecuación social y terror en América Latina, el papel de la Justicia. In: *Derecho Penal y Criminologia* VII, no 22 (1984), 71–81.

Politoff, Sergio (1989): Sistema jurídico-penal y legitimación política en el Estado democrático de derecho. In: *NFP* no 45 (1989), 313–327.

Politoff, Sergio (2001): Derecho Penal. Tomo I, Santiago de Chile 2001.

Politoff, Sergio (2004): Obediencia y delito en contextos cambiantes. In: Guzmán Dalbora, José Luis, El penalista liberal. Libro Homenaje a Manuel de Rivacoba y Rivacoba (FS Rivacoba), Buenos Aires 2004, p 529–562.

Politoff, Sergio/Matus, Jean Pierre/Ramírez, Cecilia (2004): Lecciones de Derecho Penal Chileno. Parte General. Santiago de Chile 2004.

Priemel, Kim Christian (2016): The Betrayal, Oxford 2016.

Radbruch, Gustav (1946): Gesetzliches Unrecht und Übergesetzliches Recht. In: *SJZ* 1 (1946), 105–108.

Regge, Jürgen and Schubert, Werner (1989): Quellen zur Reform des Straf- und Strafprozessrechts. Abt. II NS-Zeit (1933–1939) Strafgesetzbuch. Band 2 Protokolle der Strafrechtskommission des Reichtsjustizministeriums. Teil 2: 1. Lesung: Allgemeiner Teil (Strafrahmen, Unternehmen einer Straftat). Besonderer Teil (Fortsetzung und Abschluss der Beratungen), Berlin 1989.

Robbers, Gerhard (1990): Zur Verteidigung einer Wertorientierung in der Rechtsdogmatik. In: Dreier, Ralf, Rechtspositivismus und Wertbezug des Rechts (*ARSP* supplement 37), Stuttgart 1990, p 162–172.

Roxin, Claus (1963): Straftaten im Rahmen organisatorischer Machtapparate, *GA* 1963, 193–207.

Roxin, Claus (2006): Strafrecht, Allgemeiner Teil I, Munich 2006.

Rückert, Joachim (1986): Das "gesunde Volksempfinden"—eine Erbschaft Savignys? In: *ZRG-GA* 103 (1986), 199–247 (reprinted in Rückert, Unrecht durch Recht, 2018, p 40–79).

Rückert, Joachim (1995): Einführung. In: Rückert, Joachim/Willoweit, Dietmar, Die Deutsche Rechtsgeschichte in der NS-Zeit, Tübingen 1995, p 1–5.

Rückert, Joachim (1995): Der Rechtsbegriff der deutschen Rechtsgeschichte in der NS-Zeit: Der Sieg des "Lebens" und des konkreten Ordnungsdenkens, seine Vorgeschichte und seine Nachwirkungen. In: Rückert, Joachim/Willoweit, Dietmar, Die Deutsche Rechtsgeschichte in der NS-Zeit, Tübingen 1995, p 177–240.

Rückert, Joachim (2001): Strafrechtliche Zeitgeschichten – Vermutungen und Widerlegungen. In: *KritV* 94 (2001), 223–264 (reprinted in Rückert, Unrecht durch Recht, 2018, p 163–208).

Rückert, Joachim (2004): Die erste und die zweite Schuld. In: Hartmut Lehmann/ Otto Gerhard Oexle, Nationalsozialismus in den Kulturwissenschaften. Band 1: Fächer-Milieus-Karrieren, Göttingen 2004, p 657–367.

Rückert, Joachim (2011): Zwölf Jahre "Dienst am Recht?" In: Heiner Lück/Armin Holand, Die Rechts- und Staatswissenschaftliche Fakultät der Martin-Luther-Universität Halle-Wittenberg im Nationalsozialismus, Halle-Wittenberg, 2011, p 111–137 (reprinted in Rückert, Unrecht durch Recht, 2018, p 335–360).

Rückert, Joachim (2015): Unrecht durch Recht—zum Profil der Rechtsgeschichte in der NS-Zeit. In: *JZ* 2015, 793–804 (reprinted in Rückert, Unrecht durch Recht, 2018, p 3–32).

Rückert, Joachim (2018): Rezension Whitman (2017). In: ZRG-GA,135 (2018), 669–671.

Rückert, Joachim (2018a): Die NS-Jurisprudenz und ihre methodischen Kontinuitäten. In: id, Unrecht durch Recht, Tübingen 2018, p 271–286.

Rückert, Joachim (2018b): Nachwort. In: id, Unrecht durch Recht, Tübingen 2018, p 361–367.

Rückert, Joachim (2019): Lernen aus der NS-Zeit? Perversion der Verwaltung und Verwaltung der Perversion. In: *ZDRW* 2019, 30–61.

Rüping, Hinrich (1989): Zur Praxis der Strafjustiz im "Dritten Reich". In: Dreier, Ralf/Sellert, Wolfgang, Reich und Justiz im "Dritten Reich", Frankfurt am Main 1989, p 180–193.

Rüping, Hinrich / Jerouschek, Günter (2011), Grundriß der Strafrechtsgeschichte, Munich 6th ed 2011.

Rüthers, Bernd (1968/2017): Die unbegrenzte Auslegung: zum Wandel der Privatrechtsordnung im Nationalsozialismus, Tübingen 1968/8th ed 2017.

Rüthers, Bernd (1989): Entartetes Recht. Rechtslehren und Kronjuristen im Dritten Reich, Munich 1989.

Rüthers, Bernd (2017): "Rechtsphilosophie in den Trümmern der Nachkriegszeit". In: *JZ* 2017, 457–460.

Rüthers, Bernd (2017): Deutsche Funktionseliten als Wende-Experten? Erinnerungskulturen im Wandel der Systeme und Ideologien 1933, 1945/49 und 1989. Konstanz and Munich 2017.

Rüthers, Bernd / Schmitt, Martin (1988): Die juristische Fachpresse nach der Machtergreifung der Nationalsozialisten. In: *JZ* 1988, 369-377.

Safferling, Christoph (2011): Bestimmt oder nicht bestimmt: Der Untreuetatbestand vor den verfassungsrechtlichen Schranken. In: *NStZ* 2011, 376–379.

Safferling, Christoph (2017): Verfolgung der Täter durch Täter? Vom Versagen der Politik und der Justiz bei der Strafverfolgung von NS-Tätern im Nachkriegsdeutschland. In: Lüttig, Frank/Lehmann, Jens, Die letzten NS-Verfahren, Baden-Baden 2017, p 19–40.

Schaffstein, Friedrich (1965): Die Jugendkriminalität in der industriellen Wohlstandsgesellschaft. In: *MschrKrim* 48 (1965), 53–67.

Schaffstein, Friedrich (1974): Nachwort 1974 [on "Problematik der teleologischen Begriffsbildung", originally Schaffstein, FS R. Schmidt (1936)]. In: Ellscheid, Günter/Hassemer, Winfried, eds, Interessenjurisprudenz, Darmstadt 1974, p 417.

Schaffstein, Friedrich (2000): Robert von Hippel und Curt Bondy: Die beiden Persönlichkeiten, die vor anderen bestimmend für meinen strafrechtswissenschaftlichen Weg wurden. In: *RJ* 19 (2000), 647–654.

Schaffstein, Friedrich (2005): Erinnerungen an Georg Dahm. In: *JJZG* 7 (2005), 173–202.

Schmidt, Eberhard (1947): Einführung in die Geschichte der deutschen Strafrechtspflege, Göttingen 1947.

Schmidt, Eberhard (1947a): Unabhängigkeit der Rechtspflege. In: Zentral-Justizamt für die Britische Zone, Reden und Vorträge der Tagung deutscher Juristen in Bad Godesberg, Hamburg 1947, p 223–251.

Schmidt, Eberhard (1951): Einführung in die Geschichte der deutschen Strafrechtspflege, 2nd ed, Göttingen 1951.

Schmidt, Eberhard (1965): Einführung in die Geschichte der deutschen Strafrechtspflege, 3rd ed, Göttingen 1965 (2nd unaltered reprint 1995).

Schmitt, Carl (1967): Die Tyrannei der Werte. In: Forsthoff, Ernst et al, Säkularisation und Utopie, Ebracher Studien, Ernst Forsthoff zum 65. Geburtstag, Stuttgart 1967, p 37–62.

Schreiber, Hans-Ludwig (1989): Die Strafgesetzgebung im "Dritten Reich". In: Dreier, Ralf/Sellert, Wolfgang, Reich und Justiz im "Dritten Reich", Frankfurt am Main 1989, p 151–179.

Schröder, Jan (2016): Rechtswissenschaft in Diktaturen. Die juristische Methodenlehre im NS-Staat und in der DDR, Munich 2018.

Schumann, Eva (2006): Dignitas – Voluntas – Vita. Überlegungen zur Sterbehilfe aus rechtshistorischer, interdisziplinärer und rechtsvergleichender Sicht, Göttingen 2006.

Schumann, Eva (2008): Die Göttinger Rechts- und Staatswissenschaftliche Fakultät 1933–1955. In: Schumann, Eva, Kontinuitäten und Zäsuren. Rechtswissenschaft und Justiz im "Dritten Reich" und in der Nachkriegszeit, Göttingen 2008, p 65–121.

Schumann, Eva (2013): Fortwirken von NS-Juristen in der Bundesrepublik. In: BMJ (ed), Die Rosenburg. 2. Symposium. Die Verantwortung von Juristen im Aufarbeitungsprozess, Berlin 2013, p 70–123.

Schumann, Eva (2017): Die DVJJ und die NS-Zeit. In: *ZJJ* 28 (2017), 313–332.

Schumann, Eva (2017): Der Ausschuss für Jugendrecht der Akademie für deutsches Recht 1934–1941, in Schumann, Eva/Wapler, Friederike, Erziehen und Strafen, Bessern und Bewahren, Göttingen 2017, p 73–138.

Schumann, Eva/Wapler, Friederike (2017): Erziehen und Strafen, Bessern und Bewahren, Göttingen 2017.

Schünemann, Bernd (1984): Einführung in das strafrechtliche Systemdenken. In: Schünemann, Bernd, Grundfragen des modernen Strafrechtssystems, Berlin 1984, p 1–68.

Sontheimer, K. (1962): Antidemokratisches Denken in der Weimarer Republik, Munich 1962.

Spendel, Günter (1994): Nachruf: Zum Tod von Erich Schwinge. In: JZ 1994, 720.

Starck, Christian (1990): Zur Notwendigkeit einer Wertbegründung des Rechts. In: Dreier, Ralf, Rechtspositivismus und Wertbezug des Rechts (*ARSP* supplement 37), Stuttgart 1990, p 47–74.

Stefanopolou, Georgia (2010), Friedrich Schaffstein und die Lehre vom Verbrechen als Pflichtverletzung. In: *JoJZG* 2010, 111–118.

Sticht, Oliver (2000): Sachlogik als Naturrecht? Zur Rechtsphilosophie Hans Welzels (1904–1977), Paderborn 2000.

Stolleis, Michael (2016): Recht im Unrecht. Studien zur Rechtsgeschichte des Nationalsozialismus, Frankfurt am Main 2016.

Stratenwerth, Günter et al (1974): Festschrift für Hans Welzel zum 70. Geburtstag, Berlin 1974.

Stuckenberg, Carl-Friedrich (2019): Neukantianismus. In: Kindhäuser, Urs/Kreß, Claus/Pawlik, Michael/Stuckenberg, Carl-Friedrich, Strafrecht und Gesellschaft. Ein kritischer Kommentar zum Werk von Günther Jakobs, Tübingen 2019, p 125–154.

Sousa Mendes, Paulo de (2007): O torto intrinsecamente culposo como condição necessária da imputação da pena, Coimbra 2007.

Sousa Mendes, Paulo de (2013): Lições de Direito Processual Penal. Lisbon 2013.

Sousa Mendes, Paulo de (2018): O ensino de Cavaleiro de Ferreira. In: Sousa Mendes, Paulo de, Novos Elementos de Estudo de Direito Processual Penal, Lisbon 2018, p 21–29.

Telp, Jan (1992): Ausmerzung und Verrat. Zur Diskussion um Strafzwecke und Verbrechensbegriffe im Dritten Reich, Frankfurt am Main 1992.

Thulfaut, Gerit (2000) Kriminalpolitik und Strafrechtslehre bei Edmund Mezger (1883–1962): eine wissenschaftsgeschichtliche und biographische Untersuchung, Baden-Baden 2000.

Velásquez, Fernando (2005): Hans Welzel: Una aproximación a su vida y a su obra. In: Moreno, Hernández et al, Problemas Capitales del Moderno Derecho Penal, Mexico D.F. 2005, p 69–92.

Velásquez, Fernando (2009): Derecho Penal: Parte General, Bogota 2009.

Vives Antón, Tomás p (2011): Fundamentos del Sistema Penal, Valencia 2011.

Vives Antón, Tomás p (2018): Prólogo, in: Llobet (2018), p 13–18.

Vogel, Joachim (2004): Einflüsse des Nationalsozialismus auf das Strafrecht, Berlin 2004.

Vormbaum, Moritz (2019): Eberhard, Schmidt: Strafrecht im Rechtsstaat und im Führerstaat. In: Jeßberger, Florian/Kotzur, Markus/Repgen, Tilman, Festschrift 100 Jahre Fakultät für Rechtswissenschaft der Universität Hamburg, Tübingen 2019, 399–413.

Vormbaum, Thomas (1995): Review of Godau-Schüttke, Ich habe nur dem Recht gedient. Die 'Renazifizierung' der Schleswig-Holsteinischen Justiz nach 1945, Baden-Baden 1993. In: *GA* 1995, 146–148.

Vormbaum, Thomas (2010): Eduard Kohlrausch (1874–1948). Opportunismus oder Kontinuität? In: Grundmann, Stefan et al, Festschrift 200 Jahre Juristische Fakultät der Humboldt-Universität zu Berlin, Berlin 2010, p 523–544.

Vormbaum, Thomas (2011): Die Strafrechtsangleichungsverordnung vom 29. Mai 1943, Münster 2011.

Vormbaum, Thomas (2014): A Modern History of German Criminal Law, ed Bohlander, Michael, transl Hiley, Margaret, Berlin 2014.

VORMBAUM, Thomas (2015): Einführung in die moderne Strafrechtsgeschichte, Berlin/Heidelberg 3rd ed 2015.

WAIBEL, Dieter (1996): Von der wohlwollen Despotie zur Herrschaft des Rechts. Entwicklungsstufen der amerikanischen Besatzung Deutschlands 1944–1949, Tübingen 1996.

WAPLER, Friederike (2008): Werte und das Recht. Individualistische und kollektivistische Deutungen des Wertbegriffs im Neukantianismus, Baden-Baden: Nomos, 2008.

WALTHER, Manfred (1989): Hat der juristische Positivismus die deutschen Juristen im "Dritten Reich" wehrlos gemacht? In: Dreier, Ralf/Sellert,Wolfgang, Reich und Justiz im "Dritten Reich", Frankfurt am Main 1989, p 323–354.

WEIL, Heinz (1986): Am Rande des Strudels. Erinnerungen 1913–1983, Stuttgart 1986.

WERLE, Gerhard (1989): Justiz-Strafrecht und polizeiliche Verbrechensbekämpfung im Dritten Reich, Berlin 1989.

WELZEL, Hans (1947): Das deutsche Strafrecht in seinen Grundzügen, Berlin 1947.

WELZEL, Hans (1948): Der Irrtum über die Rechtswidrigkeit des Handelns. In: *SJZ* 3 (1948), 368–372.

WELZEL, Hans (1949): Anmerkung zu einer Entscheidung des OGH vom 5.3.1949. In: *MDR* 3 (1949), 373–376.

WELZEL, Hans (1949): Vom irrenden Gewissen: eine rechtsphilosophische Studie, Tübingen 1949.

WELZEL, Hans (1953): Naturrecht und Rechtspositivismus, Festschrift für Hans Niedermeyer zum 70. Geburtstag, Göttingen 1953, p 279 [reprinted in Maihofer, Werner, Naturrecht oder Rechtspositivismus?, Bad Homburg 1962, p 322 ff].

WELZEL, Hans (1961): Das neue Bild des Strafrechtssystems – eine Einführung in die finale Handlungslehre, Göttingen 1961.

WELZEL, Hans (1962), Naturrecht und materiale Gerechtigkeit, Göttingen 1962.

WELZEL, Hans (1969): Gedanken zur "Willensfreiheit". In: Bockelmann, Paul et al, Festschrift Karl Engisch zum 70. Geburtstag, Frankfurt am Main 1969, p 91–102.

WETZELL, Richard F. (2000): Inventing the criminal. A history of German criminology 1850–1945, Chapel Hill and London 2000.

WHITMAN, James Q (2017): Hitler's American Model: The United States and the Making of Nazi Race Law, Princeton and Oxford 2017 (I quote the paperback edition of 2018] (in German: Hitlers amerikanisches Vorbild, 2018).

WIEGAND, Marc Andre (2014): Unrichtiges Recht, Tübingen 2014.

WOLF, Erik (2009): Brief an Karl Barth v. 15.10.1945 u. 11.11.1968. Published by Hollerbach, Alexander. In: *Heidegger-Jahrbuch* 4 (2009), 284–347.

WOLF, Gerhard (1996): Befreiung des Strafrechts vom nationalsozialistischen Denken? In: *JuS* 1996, 189–195.

WOLTERS, Gereon (2001): Das Unternehmensdelikt, Baden-Baden, 2001.

Zaffaroni, Eugenio Raúl, ed (2009a): Filippo Grispigni/Edmund Mezger, La reforma penal nacional-socialista, Buenos Aires, 2009.

Zaffaroni, Eugenio Raúl, ed (2009b): Karl Binding/Alfred Hoch, La licencia para la aniquilación de la vida sin valor de vida, Buenos Aires, 2009.

Zaffaroni, Eugenio Raúl, ed (2011): Georg Dahm/Friedrich Schaffstein, Derecho penal liberal o derecho penal autoritario?, Buenos Aires, 2011.

Zaffaroni, Eugenio Raúl, ed (2016): Willem Pompe/Anton, Peters, La Escuela Penal de Utrecht, Buenos Aires, 2016.

Zaffaroni, Eugenio Raúl, ed (2017): Roland Freisler, Derecho penal de voluntad, Buenos Aires, 2017.

Zaffaroni, Eugenio Raúl (2009a): Introducción. In: Zaffaroni, (2009a), p 9–26.

Zaffaroni, Eugenio Raúl (2009b): Introducción. In: Zaffaroni, (2009b), p 7–46.

Zaffaroni, Eugenio Raúl (2011): Estudio preliminar. In: Gómez, Eusebio, La mala vida en Buenos Aires, Buenos Aires 2011, p 9–28.

Zaffaroni, Eugenio Raúl (2011): Prólogo. In: Zaffaroni, ed (2011), p 7–54.

Zaffaroni, Eugenio Raúl (2017): Derecho penal humano. La doctrina de los juristas y el poder en el siglo XXI, Buenos Aires 2017.

Ziemann, Sascha (2009): Neukantianisches Strafrechtsdenken, Baden-Baden 2009.

Zimmer, Erhard (1990): Reichsgericht. In: Adalbert Erler/Ekkehard Kaufmann, HRG IV, Berlin 1990, 576–580.

Zippelius, Reinhold (2012): Juristische Methodenlehre, Munich 2012.

Index of Persons (selected)

Arabic numerals refer to page(s)

Subject Index

Arabic numerals refer to page(s)